THE HISTORY OF FRANKLIN COUNTY
KENTUCKY

L. F. Johnson, B.A., M.A.

HERITAGE BOOKS
2013

HERITAGE BOOKS
AN IMPRINT OF HERITAGE BOOKS, INC.

Books, CDs, and more—Worldwide

For our listing of thousands of titles see our website
at
www.HeritageBooks.com

A Facsimile Reprint
Published 2013 by
HERITAGE BOOKS, INC.
Publishing Division
5810 Ruatan Street
Berwyn Heights, Md. 20740

Copyright © 1912 L. F. Johnson, B.A., M.A.

— Publisher's Notice —
In reprints such as this, it is often not possible to remove blemishes from the original. We feel the contents of this book warrant its reissue despite these blemishes and hope you will agree and read it with pleasure.

International Standard Book Numbers
Paperbound: 978-0-7884-0883-0
Clothbound: 978-0-7884-6872-8

CONTENTS

CHAPTER I.
Formation, Location, Organization, Government, etc. 5

CHAPTER II.
Indian Incursions and Other Incidents Prior to 1800 14

CHAPTER III.
Geological Formation, Minerals, Soil, Timber, etc. 21

CHAPTER IV.
Settlements and Other Incidents Prior to 1800 28

CHAPTER V.
Events From 1800 to 1810 40

CHAPTER VI.
Events From 1810 to 1820 53

CHAPTER VII.
Events From 1820 to 1830 71

CHAPTER VIII.
Events From 1830 to 1840 91

CHAPTER IX.
Events From 1840 to 1850 111

CHAPTER X.
Events From 1850 to 1860 132

CHAPTER XI.
Events From 1860 to 1870 148

CHAPTER XII.
Events From 1870 to 1880 175

CHAPTER XIII.
Events From 1880 to 1890 195

CHAPTER XIV.
Events From 1890 to 1900 214

CHAPTER XV.
Events From 1900 to 1910 229

CHAPTER XVI.
The Churches of Franklin County 243

CHAPTER XVII.
Present Time (1912) 265

DEDICATION

To the men and women whose lives and achievements have done so much to enrich the history of Franklin County, this work is dedicated.

L. F. JOHNSON.

PREFACE.

Carlyle said: History is the essence of innumerable biographies.

Longfellow said: They who live in history only seemed to walk the earth again.

Voltaire said: History is little else than a picture of human crimes and misfortunes.

Lord Bolingbroke said: I think that history is philosophy, teaching by example.

The Author does not claim that the following pages measure up to the standard given by any of the above Authors, but if this work can create or increase interest in the biography, history and traditions of the Kentucky pioneers it will not have been done in vain.

The Author.

The History of Franklin County, Ky.

CHAPTER I.

Formation of Franklin County, Location, Organization of County Government, History of the County for seven years as shown by the early records of the County.

On December the 31, 1776, the Virginia Legislature passed an act establishing Kentucky County, which included the territory now known as the State of Kentucky. In May, 1780, Kentucky was divided into three counties, to-wit: Jefferson, Fayette and Lincoln; these three counties cornered at Frankfort. What is now known as North Frankfort and that part of Franklin county north or east of the Kentucky river was in Fayette. Where South Frankfort now is, and the part of the county south or west of the Kentucky river and south of Benson Creek, was in Lincoln, and the territory now known as West Frankfort or Bell Point, and that part of the county west of the river and north of Benson Creek was in Jefferson. Nelson county was formed from a part of Jefferson in 1784, Bourbon from a part of Fayette in 1785; Mercer and Madison were formed from portions of Lincoln, in the same year, Mason was formed out of Bourbon, and Woodford out of Fayette in the year 1788. These were the nine counties of the State when it was admitted into the Union on June the 1st, 1792. Franklin county was formed by the Kentucky Legislature in the year 1794 out of portions of Woodford, Mercer and Shelby, and on the 10th day of May of that year the act establishing the county went into effect. At that time its boundary was as follows, to-wit: "Beginning at the Scott line where it leaves the South fork of Elkhorn, thence a straight line to strike the Kentucky river, and crossing the same one mile above the mouth of Glenn's Creek; thence up the Kentucky river to the mouth of Cove Spring branch on the south side thereof; thence up the said branch to the Cove Spring; thence west to the Washington line; thence with same down Salt river to the mouth of Crooked Creek; thence up the main fork of Crooked Creek to the head thereof; thence with the dividing ridge at the junction of the forks of Benson; thence down Benson to where the old wagon road from Boone's old station to Harrodsburg crosses at the mouth of the most northerly fork of Benson; thence a direct line to the mouth of Elkhorn; thence down the Kentucky river to the mouth thereof; thence up the Ohio to the Scott line; thence with the said line to the beginning."

Portions of Franklin were taken to from the county of Gallatin in 1798, Owen in 1819, and Anderson in 1827, and a portion of Gallatin was taken to form Carroll in 1838. One hundred years after its formation, its boundary included only about two hundred and twelve square miles, which is a very small part of its original territory; the county is now about twenty miles long at its greatest length, and about eighteen miles wide at its greatest width. Franklin is bounded on the south by Anderson and Woodford, on the east by Scott, on the north by Henry and Owen and on the west by Shelby; it is located in the north central part of the State, about thirty-eight and one-fourth degrees latitude and about eighty-five longitude; its mean annual temperature is 56 degrees. The Kentucky river runs through it from south to north the entire length of the county, dividing it into two nearly equal parts. The other streams of importance in the county are Benson, Glenn's Creek and Elkhorn.

On the 10th day of May, 1795, which day had been designated by the Kentucky Legislature for the act establishing the county of Franklin to go into effect, Governor Isaac Shelby made the following proclamation and appointments, to-wit: "The State of Kentucky: To all who shall see these presents, greeting. Know ye that reposing special trust and confidence in the knowledge, integrity and abilities of John Logan, Bennett Pemberton, Anthony Crockett, Baker Ewing, Richard Apperson, William Ware, Thomas Lillard and John Arnold,

Esquires, I have nominated and by and with the advice and consent of the Senate do appoint the said John Logan, Bennett Pemberton, Anthony Crockett, Baker Ewing, Richard Apperson, William Ware, Thomas Lillard and John Arnold, Justices of the Peace in and for the County of Franklin, of whom the three first herein named or any two of them are authorized to hold the Court of Quarter Session in said county and to discharge all the duties of Justices of said county; and the remaining Justices of the peace above named, or any three of them, are authorized to hold the County Court for said county, and to discharge all the duties of a Justice for said County Court in manner prescribed by law. In testimony whereof I have caused these letters to be made patent and the seal for the Commonwealth to be hereto affixed.

"Given under my hand as Governor for said State at Lexington, this the 10th day of May, One thousand seven hundred and ninety-five.

"ISAAC SHELBY,
"By the Governor,
"James Brown."

This board of magistrates when organized into a Court, appointed Willis Lee, who by virtue of said appointment was the first County Clerk of Franklin county; and the Governor appointed and commissioned John Smith as the first Sheriff of the county; and the Governor also appointed Turner Richardson, Coroner. January 19, 1796, the Governor appointed and commissioned Stephen Arnold a Justice of the Peace, or Judge of Quarter Session. This completed the official organization of the county. These brave pioneers in whom the Governor of this Commonwealth reposed "special trust and confidence in their knowledge, integrity and abilities," commenced the government and control of this large territory, then more than six times its present area. One of the first orders was "that the county levy be fixed at three shillings each tithable, for the present year."

The sheriff was ordered "to confine such persons as he may, directed by law, take into his custody, in one of the upper rooms of the public jail until a prison be built by order of the Court for this county." James Arnold, who was a brother-in-law of Anthony Crockett, and the father of John and Stephen Arnold, all three of whom were magistrates then in office, was ordered by the County Court to lay off a county road from the mouth of Glenn's creek to Frankfort; the public road entered Frankfort over the present right of way owned by the L. &. N. R. R. Co., but it was west of and below the present tunnel. Thomas Hickman was allowed thirty-five pounds for erecting a stray pen on the square allotted for the court house.

At the April term, 1796, it was "ordered that the gallows be erected at the intersection of the road leading from Saunders' mill with the Lexington old road, three-quarters of a mile from Frankfort." This is now the Feeble Minded Institute property near the intersection of the Georgetown and Millville turnpike roads.

At the August term, 1797, it was "ordered that William Trigg, Thos. Montague and Daniel Weiseger be appointed commissioners to have erected stocks, pillory and whipping-post on the public grounds near the jail, to be paid for out of the county levy."

Charles M. Bird, the first County Attorney, and who acted as both State and County Attorney, was allowed the sum of twenty pounds for his services for one year. During the first several years of this new county, the two most important questions before the Court were the destruction of wolves and the construction of public roads; a bounty was offered for the scalp of each wolf that was over six months old; the county record shows that hundreds of wolves were killed and their scalps were paid for by the County Court.

Public roads were laid off and built in every direction from the city and a great many cross roads were also constructed; nearly all of the public roads leading from Frankfort were established prior to 1800.

Two bridges were built by Nat Saunders and Chas. Patterson across Elkhorn near the Forks in 1798; the contractors agreed to keep these bridges in repair for seven years; but before the expiration of that time they had gotten so much out of repair that the County ordered suit to be brought on the contract.

In 1798, Stephen Arnold and William Payne were appointed a committee of the Court to locate and superintend the erection of a large store-room for the reception of tobacco, flour and hemp. They located the house on the lots number 227 and a part of 226; these are the lots on which the city school now stands. The warehouse was large enough to store four hundred hogsheads of tobacco, five hundred barrels of flour and a large quantity of hemp.

In 1797, after two years of service, Willis Lee was succeeded by Wm. Trigg as County Clerk, and John Smith was succeeded by Nat Richardson as Sheriff of the county. James Roberts was the first Jailer and James Blair succeeded Chas. M. Bird as County Attorney.

The county levy for the year 1797 was fixed at "three shillings each tithable," being the same as the previous year.

On account of the extensive forests and the large amount of mast, the farmers were enabled to fatten their hogs at small expense, and in order to prevent the loss of their stock, they had their distinguishing ear marks recorded, as shown by the following orders:

"Ordered that William Payne's mark, which is as follows to-wit: A crop and two slits in each ear, be recorded. Also John Satterwhite's mark, which is a crop and overkeel in the right and a slit in the left, be recorded." This plan of having their "ear marks" recorded was followed by the farmers of this county for many years.

On Tuesday, November 25, 1800, the following order was entered: "It is ordered that the sheriff do bring immediately before this Court Nancy Hutton, to answer the contempt offered this Court by leaving a young infant on the Clerk's table." The sheriff returned after a short time, and reported that said Nancy Hutton could not be found, and it was thereupon ordered that Samuel Hutton be summoned to appear before the next Court to show cause, if any he could, why he should not support the infant left by the said Samuel's wife on the Clerk's table.

The first District Court for Franklin county was convened at the State House on Tuesday, the 9th day of February, 1796. Buckner Thurston and James G. Hunter were the Judges, Willis Lee was appointed Clerk during good behavior. The first Grand Jury failed to return any indictments and no cases were tried during the term.

Thomas Todd and James Blair were admitted to practice law, and James Hughes was admitted at the following term.

The *Kentucky Gazette* was published in the year 1787, at Lexington, Ky.

On May 12, 1796, John Breckinridge, James Brown, William Murray, Chas. F. Bird, Samuel Irvine, John Allen, William McDowell, Isham Tolbett and Richard Lage were sworn in as attorneys of the Frankfort bar.

On Tuesday, the 6th day of August, 1799, on motion of Henry Clay and William Warren, they were admitted to practice as attorneys at law in this Court, who thereupon severally took the oath prescribed by law, also the oath to support the Constitution of the United States.

Catherine London, a spinster, was charged with murder; she was tried, and on April 3, 1798, was convicted and sentenced to be hung; and on Thursday, the 10th day of May, 1798, between the hours of ten and two o'clock, she was hung upon the gallows near the public jail in the town of Frankfort. Hugh Johnson was tried and convicted of a felony on August 6th, 1798, and on August the 9th was again brought to the bar in custody of the jailor; and it being demanded of him if he had anything to say why the Court should not proceed to give judgment and award execution thereof according to law, he said he claimed the privilege of the law concerning the benefit of clergy; "Thereupon it is considered by the Court that the said Hugh Johnson be burned in the hand, and the Sheriff of the county do cause execution of this judgment to be done immediately upon the said Hugh Johnson in the presence of and at the bar of this Court, which being accordingly done and proclamation being made as the manner is, whereupon the said Johnson is discharged out of custody." "The benefit of clergy" was an arrest of judgment introduced in England early in its history; it had its origin from the pious regard paid by Christians to the church in its infant state, the persons of clergymen were exempt from criminal process before the secular judge. At first no man could claim this benefit except clergymen, but in the course of time, in order to mitigate the severity of the law, the privilege was extended to a great many who were accused of crime; but the laymen were not put upon the same footing as the clergy, being subjected to a slight punishment and denied the privilege a second time. The punishment was by branding in the hand with a hot iron in order to distinguish them from the clergy, in case of a second application for the benefit.

Prior to the installation of the penitentiary system in the year 1800 all felons were punished with death; minor offenses were punished by branding in the hand, pillory, stocks, whipping post and by ducking stool.

Augustine Adams, a laborer, was charged with horse stealing; he was convicted April 2nd, 1799, and on Monday, the 29th day of April, 1799, he was hung near the public jail in the town of Frankfort.

William Dougherty, a laborer, charged with robbery, was tried, convicted and sentenced to be hung April 2nd, 1799; the verdict was set aside and he was released on bail; he was returned to the custody of the Court, but made his escape August the 5th, 1799.

James Mills was charged with a felony and convicted, and on April the 5th, 1799, he claimed the benefit of clergy, was burnt in the hand "and proclamation being made as the manner is," was discharged from custody. This was the last case where the benefit of clergy was granted in Franklin county. Henry Fields, a farmer from Woodford county, was charged with murdering his wife; he was defended by Henry Clay. After a long trial, which lasted several days, he was found guilty on August 10th, 1799, and on the same day, H. Clay, his attorney, filed a motion in arrest of judgment; at that time there was no appeal in a criminal case. His first ground was "because he was indicted for the murder of Sallie Fields and was tried for the murder of Sarah Fields." 2nd.

"That his late wife, whom he was indicted for having murdered, was called and known by the name of Sallie Fields, and never by the name of Sarah Fields." 3rd. "That the description of the manner of the death of the said Sallie in the said indictment contained, is repugnant and impossible." (On August the 12th the Court held that the grounds for the motion were not sufficient, and he was hung upon the gallows near the public jail on Thursday, the 19th day of September, 1799;) $138.75 was paid by the county for guarding Fields from August 12th to September 19th.

The first public jail was located on the north side of Holmes Street, near the intersection of High, a few doors west of the entrance to the female department of the penitentiary, a small store room is now located there. The State House was used as a court house by the Franklin county officials until 1806.

Prior to 1800 there were only four houses built on the ground now known as South Frankfort; there was a small log house near the large warehouse located on the ground now used for the public school. There was a house on Shelby Street just back of James Heeney's property, where the old brick seminary building was located, and there was another one where Miss Exum's property is located, on what is now Murray street.

On December 14, 1793, there was an act of the Legislature for clearing a wagon road from Frankfort to Cincinnati; it was alleged that such a road would be productive of private convenience and public utility; seven years were given in which to complete the road.

There was also a law enacted on December 7, 1794, which gave free transportation across the ferry at Frankfort for all citizens living on the south side of the river "on each county court day, days of holding court of quarter session, days of public elections and general musters." In December, 1798, a ferry was established across the Kentucky river "at the rope walks," one mile above Frankfort. The "rope walks" was the old-fashioned hand factory for spinning hemp, making rope, etc.

The Frankfort Bridge Company was incorporated December 29, 1799, for the purpose of building a bridge from the end of Ann Street to the south side. Prior to 1800 the Court caused to be located and surveyed six thousand acres of land and the same was vested in "The Trustees of the Kentucky Seminary" for educational purposes. This was the first step in the direction of free public schools in the county.

CHAPTER II.

Indian Incursions and other Incidents prior to 1800; Statements from The Palladium; the Pioneer.

Franklin County, within its present boundary, was, to a great extent, protected from the Indian incursions and depredations, committed by them in other sections of the country known as Kentucky, on account of its central location and from the further fact that in the earliest settlement of the county forts were built in nearly every direction from it.

There was McClelland's fort, where Georgetown now stands, which was built in 1776; Harrodstown (Harrodsburg) was built in 1774; Logan's Fort in 1775; Louisville in 1778; Booneborough in 1775; Bryan's Station, in Fayette county in 1779; Houston's (Paris) Station in 1776, Squire Boone's Station (Shelbyville) prior to 1780; Arnold's Station in Anderson County in 1783; Johnson's Station in Scott County in the same year. These Stations practically surrounded Franklin County and though they did not give absolute protection, the presence of Indians in the neighborhood of any of these Stations, as soon as detected, the news was sent to all sections of the country and only a few instances are recorded where death resulted from a conflict between the two races.

In the year 1780, Stephen Frank, Nick Tomlin, Wm. Bryant and others were on their way to Mann's Salt Lick in Jefferson County, and they camped on the present site of Frankfort. In the early morning they were attacked by the Indians and Frank was killed and two other members of the party, Bryan and Tomlin were wounded, but they were able to make their escape. The fact that Frank was killed and the further fact that there was a fairly good ford on the Kentucky River nearly opposite to the entrance of Devil's Hollow gave to Frankfort the name Frank's ford which was contracted to Frankfort.

One of the earliest and most prosperous settlements was in Quinn's Bottom, about four miles from Frankfort on Elkhorn Creek. This settlement was made up of the Cook brothers, Louis Martin, Wm. Dunn and Wm. Bledsoe, with their families and several other families. In April, 1792, about one hundred Indians made a raid on this settlement. The first information the settlers had of their presence, was a volley fired at the two Cooks who were at the time engaged in shearing sheep. Both of the Cooks were killed, one of whom fell on the doorstep. The widows of the two men were all that were left to defend the cabin and their three small children; their courage, however, made them equal to the occasion. They immediately pulled the dead body of the murdered man into the room and barred the door. The Indians made a rush for the door and tried to beat it down; one of the women secured a gun, but having no bullets, she split a piece of lead and rounded it to fit the rifle, and quickly loaded it; the Indians were still persisting in their efforts to break the door; she placed the muzzle of the gun through a small opening between the logs and took deliberate aim and fired at a very large Indian and shot him dead. They then abandoned the idea of breaking in the door and some of them climbed to the roof and set fire to it. One of the women went up to the loft, while the other handed to her some water with which to put out flames as often as the torch was applied; the water failing, she took a lot of eggs and put out the fire; and as a last resort they used the blood soaked vest of the dead husband and smothered the fire with it. The brave defense made by these women prolonged the contest until the Indians became afraid that the rest of the settlement would be warned of their presence, they abandoned the assault; they sunk the body of the dead Indian in Elkhorn Creek and the whole force moved on to attack the other settlers in that neighborhood. During the raid they killed, in addition to the two Cooks, Louis Martin, two sons of William Dunn and a negro man; and they captured and carried away with them two negro men. A company of about one hundred men were quickly collected from the forks of Elkhorn and other sections of the County who went in pursuit of the Indians and followed them to the Ohio River, across from Cincinnati and there abandoned further pursuit.

The camping ground of Hon. Jas. A. Scott, known as "Indian Rock" is located near the scene of the above described contest, the Indian who was killed by the Cook woman, floated down the creek and lodged against a large rock very close to where the camp is located. There are several families, of prominence, now living in Franklin County, (1907) who are direct descendants of the Cooks.

About the year 1788, Stephen Arnold and a companion were hunting wild turkeys. They had reached a point near the present Frankfort and Lawrenceburg road, a few hundred yards north of where the Blakemore Distillery now stands. While passing around the top of a fallen tree, they came within twenty paces of five Indians; as soon as they saw the Indians, Arnold directed his companion to fire and at the same time fired his own gun at the closest Indian; two of them being in line the same bullet killed both of them. Arnold's friend stood as though paralyzed with fear and was captured without firing a shot, one of the Indians remained with the captive and the other two pursued Arnold; his enemies were between him and the fort, which was about three miles away; he made a wide circuit, with them in hot pursuit. He attempted to reload his rifle as he ran but in attempting to shove the bullet down, his ram rod caught on a bush and was knocked out of his hand and his enemies were so close to him that he did not have time to recover it,—then, indeed, there was a race for life; there had been some recent rains, the ground was soft, his mocassins were wet and heavy with mud. He could see that his enemies were gaining on him. He had lost his gun. He took his hunting knife from his belt and cut the strings of his mocassins as he ran and continued his flight barefooted; the race continued until they got in sight of Arnold's Station, when the Indians gave up the pursuit and returned to their captive, whom they took north with them and afterwards sold him to some white man who returned him to his Kentucky home.

"The Palladium" a literary weekly paper, published in Frankfort in the year 1798 and for several years thereafter, published the fact that a white man was killed by the Indians on the waters of Benson Creek, near the falls, at Conway's mill, about four miles from Frankfort, in August, 1794, but the name of the man is not given.

In the year 1793 a party of hunters was pursued within five miles of Frankfort, but none of the party was killed. In 1794 a party of seven Indians came across from what is now Owen County. Crossing into the county at Indian Gap (from which fact the place took its name), two of these Indians made an attack on a man by the name of Stafford at the mouth of Pond's branch. After a desperate fight, Stafford killed one of the Indians and the other one made his escape and joined his other companions, who undertook to return the way they came, but they were followed by a body of white men who succeeded in killing all of them before they could recross the Ohio river.

Marshall's History of Kentucky states that Leestown was named for Willis Lee who was killed by the Indians while camping there, but other authorities say that it was named for Handcock Lee, (a cousin of Handcock Taylor) who owned a large tract of land on a part of which the town was located. The records of the county show that Handcock Lee owned the land on which the town was established.

The Palladium gives the following items, to-wit: Frankfort, June 20, 1799: "Last Saturday week a little girl, daughter of Mr. William Bourn on Benson, was lost from the Plantation and was found on Monday following on Beech Creek, having traveled about fifteen miles,—when found, was still stout and able to travel."

Frankfort, Kentucky, Aug. 7, 1800.—"Yesterday a man by the name of Brown residing in the neighborhood of this place, to decide a wager of one hundred dollars, walked from the Capital to Lexington and returned in eleven hours; he was allowed sun rise to sun set, but performed the journey with apparent ease, two hours under the time."

About the year 1798 a man by the name of Mack Sutton, challenged James Arnold to fight a duel, Arnold accepted and named the conditions, which were: that the weapons should be rifles, the time, on a day named between sun rise and sun set; the place, a heavy woodland of some ten or twelve acres, located nearly opposite the mouth of Glenn's Creek; both of the parties were familiar with these woods; there was a large hollow tree, which stood near the center of the woods, and as Arnold expected, Sutton went out very early in the morning and concealed himself in this hollow tree; Arnold came upon the reverse side and held him there until after sun set and then gave him permission to come out. Ever after that the two men were good friends.

On Oct. 31, 1798, the mercury at Frankfort stood at 22 degrees below zero at sunrise.

The anniversary of American Independence was celebrated on Thursday, July 4, 1799, by the citizens of Frankfort; after dinner a number of suitable patriotic toasts were drunk and the utmost good humor prevailed on that occasion.

The following notice shows how the news of that day was received: "Frankfort, Ky., Aug. 8, 1799. Just as this day's paper was going to press we were favored with Brown's Philadelphia Gazette of the 19th of July, containing some interesting intelligence from Europe."

The Palladium gives a detailed account of the resolutions of 1798, which were passed by the Kentucky Legislature, the discussions by Mr. Breckenridge, Mr. Johnson, Mr. Murray and others, but as this belongs to state history it has no part in the history of Franklin County.   *   *   *

The Pioneer of Franklin County was unique in many respects; he was of necessity a man of courage and endurance. No man would select a home such as this county furnished from 1780 to 1800, who was not brave enough to meet any danger or who did not have force of character and determination sufficient to overcome any difficulty; many of their deeds denoting a noble manhood, have been left unrecorded and succeeding generations only know of them by tradition. In a general way the main evidence, the present generation has of the bravery, the endurance, the self-sacrifice, the determination to maintain the liberties of himself and his people, is shown more in the results upon the succeeding generations than in any other way. A history of the world, is to a great extent a detailed account of the individual actions of men, but in most cases, more credit has been given to him who is termed the leader, than is his just proportion; a good soldier is as essential to a successful campaign as a good general, yet the general has the laurel wreath, while the ready hands and brave hearts which made his success possible find obscure graves. "Peace hath her victories no less renowned than those of war," but the renown is generally given to the official who by circumstances has been elected to some executive, legislative or judicial office, and the hero, whose life has been sacrificed for loved ones, or for the liberty of his countrymen rests in an unmarked grave. The pioneers of this county did a noble work, but their grand children and their great grand children have not shown a proper appreciation for the labor performed, the dangers incurred, the hardships endured and the lives which were sacrificed by these brave men and women, guaranteeing to succeeding generations the peace, prosperity and happiness of this:

"The land of the noble free
Sweet land of liberty."

The following are the names of a few men who were prominent in Franklin County, prior to 1800.

John Smith, Nathaniel Richardson, James, John and Stephen Arnold, Thomas and Pascal Hickman, Turner Richardson, Wm. Trigg, Thos. Montague, Daniel Weisinger, Chas. M. Bird, Harry Bartlett, William, John and John R. Cardwell, William Payne, Thos. Todd, Willis Lee, James Hayden, Robt. Johnson, William Johnson, William Brown, James Blair, John Price, William Quarles, John Bacon, James Roberts, Anthony Crockett, Thos. Hardy, Lewis Overton, Scott Brown, John Lindsey, John Brown, John Patty, Wm. Samuels, Wm. Hall, James Gayle, Walter Ayers, Edward Vaughn, Mathew Clark, Hugh Innis, Ambrose Quarles, Roddy Hawkins, James Miles, Wm. Murray, Lewis R. Major, Daniel James, Samuel McKee and Christopher Greenup.

Some of the attorneys who were prominent practitioners at the Frankfort bar were Isham Talbot, William Murray, William Blackburn, Samuel Irvin, Felix Grundy, Thos. Todd,

James Blair, James Crawford, Mathew Lodge, William McIlhenney, James Hughes, William Hunter, James Brown, John Allen and Wm. McDowell. There were some prominent attorneys from other sections of the state who practiced in all the courts at Frankfort, among whom were Henry Clay, Richard M. Johnson, Robert Breckinridge and Humphrey Marshall.

Chapter III.

Geological Formation, Minerals, Soil, Cereals, etc., Horticulture, Fruits, Timber, Lead, Mineral Waters, Gas, Clay, Drainage, etc., Fertile Valleys, Blue Grass.

Franklin County is of the lower Silurian Age or formation; it is the age of invertebrates; it is called Silurian from Silures in Wales where the same kind of rocks are found. This age has two sub-divisions called the upper and lower Silurian. The lower Silurian age is divided into three periods; the primordial or Cambrian; the Canadian and Trenton. Franklin County is of the Trenton period, this period takes its name from Trenton falls in New York: The life of this period was, as far as evidence shows wholly marine, no trace of a terrestial or fresh water species of plant or animal has ever been found. The only plants were sea weeds; the only animal life was of the lowest order, known as invertebrates, it consisted of invertebrates, mollusks and articulates. The principal fossils found are *Petraia Corniculum, Orthis Testudinaria* and other Occidentals.

The "Birdseye" limestone, which is generally known in Kentucky, as the Kentucky river marble is found in large quantities, it is a most excellent building stone, the Capitol Hotel, the Farmer's Bank, the walls of the State Penitentiary at Frankfort and the old State Capitol, erected in 1829, are built of this marble. It is susceptible of a fine polish but the fact that it is so extremely hard and flint like, it will never become popular as a building material, where a polished surface is required. It is called "Birdseye" because of the small specks which look like glass or bird eyes and which are found all through this stone, these bird eyes can be more readily seen when the stone is freshly broken.

This marble is destined to become very popular for building residence property; it makes a beautiful structure without being polished and it will last, practically, for all time. In the year 1906 United States Senator, Thos. H. Paynter built a residence of this marble on the corner of Shelby and Third Streets in South Frankfort, which is one of the most beautiful homes in the city, and in the following year Mr. Chas. Strausner built a residence of the same material on the corner of Shelby and Todd Streets, which is also an ornament to the city. This character of marble abounds in endless quantity along the banks of the Kentucky river, several quarries have been opened in different parts of the County and within the next few years it will likely become the County's chief commodity of export; but a thousand years will not exhaust the almost limitless supply.

The soil of the county is very fertile, the small particles of stone broken from the limestone rock, in cultivating the land forms a fertilizer which renews the productive power of the soil almost as rapidly as the continual cultivation of it in crops, exhaust it.

For more than a hundred years the farmers of the county have been growing tobacco and other crops from this soil, the recuperative powers of which are so great, that after it has seemingly become exhausted, if permitted to remain idle for a few years and briars and locust bushes are permitted to grow on it, the soil becomes as fertile and productive as virgin soil.

Cereals of almost all kinds are raised in abundance and of fine quality. Corn, wheat, rye, oats, hemp, barley, and tobacco are the chief products of the farm. The soil is especially well adapted for raising white burley tobacco.

During the years of 1904 to 1907 inclusive, alfalfa has been raised with marked success. Clover and timothy hay reach a high state of perfection and sorghum for molasses and as a winter food for cattle is a crop of growing importance to the farmer. Horticulture has received but slight attention, but the rapidly increasing population of the county is directing the attention of the farmers to that branch of industry. Dairy farming is also fast becoming a paying industry.

Fruits of various kinds were raised as early as 1790. Several vineyards were planted prior to 1800. Before the enactment of the present stringent revenue laws which are now in force, wine, apple brandy, peach brandy, and other drinks of that character were made in small quantities by the farmers of the county. The soil of the county is well adapted to raising small fruits and some sections of it seem to be especially well adapted to the growth of peaches; this is so with the hilly sections bordering both sides of the Kentucky river where the broken surface of the land is not susceptible of any other kind of cultivation.

In the early history of the county vast areas of it were covered with cane which were called "cane breaks," other portions of it were covered with dense forests of different kinds of wood. The chief of which were beech, locust, cedar, sycamore, hackberry, poplar, elm, walnut, oaks of several kinds, linn, sugar tree, and many other smaller varieties of wood.

The pine is not a native of the county but it grows as well as it does in its native soil. During the latter part of the last century the demand for beech and walnut timber became so great that nearly all of those two varieties were disposed of prior to 1900. Some species of oak have, to some extent, taken the place of walnut in the manufacture of fine furniture. At the commencement of the present century the best qualities of oak were selling from $40.00 to $80.00 per thousand feet.

To a large extent the original forests trees of the county have been cleared away and the extensive cane brakes have entirely disappeared.

Walnut and ash logs were commonly used by the pioneers in the construction of the log houses built in that day, some of which stood for more than a century. The last log structure torn down in the city of Frankfort was the old Page house on Ewing street. The logs were found to be walnut and ash, but they were so worm-eaten that they were worthless. Mr. T. L. Edelen's home now stands where this log building formerly stood. The James Arnold residence opposite the mouth of Glenn's Creek was built of walnut logs with puncheon ash floors. The chimney was built of the birds-eye limestone. It stood more than a hundred years and it was in good condition when it was torn away about the year 1890. Saltpeter has been found in some sections of the county and lead is found in paying quantities in several sections.

About the year 1886 a large smelting establishment was built at Kissinger near the Scott county line and it has been in constant use since that time. Several mines have been worked in the Switzer and Peak's Mill sections of the county and the lead industry has caused the log cabins of those precincts to give way to neat cottages, and all of that part of the county has the appearance of thrift and prosperity which was unknown prior to 1890.

Lead has been found near Jetts Station and in other parts of the county; a considerable quantity of ore was obtained prior to 1857. Mineral waters are found in nearly all parts of the county. Several small streams of chalybeate water show themselves.

Faught's old sulphur spring on Benson Creek, not far from the Louisville and Nashville railroad, was in the early history of the county much resorted to.

A good sized stream of black sulphur water is found on Flat creek.

Magnesia water was found at Steadman's mill on main Elkhorn Creek. The Scanlan springs which were also called Franklin springs, located about six miles from Frankfort on the Lawrenceburg road, at what was formerly known as the Kentucky Military Institute, and which is now known as The Stewart Home, was for many years prior to 1845 a place of summer resort for invalids. Valuable medical salts have been made from the water. The water from these springs resembles in its medical qualities that of the celebrated Cheltenham Springs in England and the experience of more than a century proves its value in the cure of various forms of chronic diseases. Prior to 1845 these springs belonged to T. N. Lindsey & Co. and hundreds of people spent their summers there. In the year 1845 Col. R. T. P. Allen purchased this property and established there the famous Kentucky Military Institute. At the close of the last century Dr. J. Q. A. Stewart purchased the property and established the Stewart home for the treatment of various kinds of nervous and mental troubles and for the training of children of backward mental development. There is also a fine sulphur well within two hundred feet of this spring. The largest sulphur well in the county is only a few hundred feet below the city limits, located on the land of James Murray near the river and north of Frankfort. Mr. Murray was boring for gas about the year 1884 when he struck a very large stream of black sulphur water, following which he built a large bath house on the corner of Washington and Broadway streets and had the water piped to this bath house which for several years was very popular with the Frankfort people. Many residents of the city have continued to use the water for drinking purposes almost exclusively.

Near Steadmantown, located about four miles east of Frankfort and about one mile from the Georgetown road, a well was bored one hundred and ten feet deep, the bore being four and one-half inches. Nearly the whole depth was through solid limestone, the last three feet being probably sandstone. Considerable gas escaped from the well at first. The water stands 25 feet from the top. It has the odor of petroleum, some little of which is found. The other ingredients are sodium chloride (common salt), carbonate of iron, lime, magnesia and sulphur. Natural gas has been found in several sections of the county but in small quantities, the largest flows being at Steadman's mill on main Elkhorn creek about one mile below the Forks and at Frankfort.

About the year 1880 there was a well bored near the intersection of High and Montgomery streets in the city of Frankfort. A strong flow of natural gas was found and when it was ignited the blaze ran as high as twelve or fifteen feet and it continued to burn for several days. It was finally extinguished by the abutting property owners in order to prevent the cancellation of their fire insurance policies. Though the flow was in sufficient quantity for practical use, the well was plugged, and for some unaccountable reason it has never been reopened.

A superior quality of potters clay is found on Holmes street near the city limit. This clay was used for pottery purposes for many years. A pottery was built near where the Mangan residence now stands which was in use as late as 1849. Several vases made of this clay are in the geological department of the State College at Lexington showing its excellent quality for that purpose.

A good fire clay is also found in that section of the city, but no attempt to make practical use of it has been made.

The Kentucky river is a beautiful stream. Its average width within the county and above lock number four is about four hundred feet, while below the lock it is not so wide. Its bed is some two or three hundred feet below the general surface of the country. It is walled in by immense cliffs of limestone rock, which in some places are as much as four hundred feet high. The topographical situation of Frankfort is higher than any other town of importance located on a river in the state. It is twenty feet higher than Catlettsburg and one hundred and twenty-eight feet higher than Louisville. Elkhorn creek is one of the most beautiful streams in the world and it runs through a valley as fertile as the Nile. It is well supplied with game fish, no finer bass stream can be found. In addition to the drainage by the Kentucky river and Elkhorn creek, the county is further drained by Glenns creek and on the west side of the river by Flat creek, Benson and Little Benson. Along the course of each of these streams is found some very fine farming land. This is especially so along the bottom land of the Kentucky river, a large part of this land is overflowed every winter or spring and these annual deposits make it impossible for the land to ever become impoverished by continued use. The same kind of a crop may be raised on this land year after year for all time.

The surface of the county is generally broken, but it is not so rough or hilly as to prevent much of it from being cultivated. The southern and eastern portions of the county are nearer level than other parts of it.

The soil is limestone, underlaid with a stratum of red clay which is well calculated to hold the moisture.

Franklin county is in what is called the "blue grass region of Kentucky," the soil being about the same as Woodford, Scott and Bourbon, the main difference being that the surface of Franklin is more broken.

Blue grass, which grows only in limestone countries, is a native of Franklin county and it claims every foot of the county as its home. If the sod is taken up and carried away it will retake its former home in a short time. A field which has been cultivated for years, if left undisturbed for a few years, will again be covered with it. Blue grass has formed the muscle and bone of many fine horses, cattle and sheep. It is one of God's most beneficient gifts to man. There is no vegetation more beautiful and at the same time more useful to him than blue grass. It is true the "Roses of Sharon" were more regal in appearance, the lillies of the valley may be more beautifully clad, the *crassula lactea* of Africa, which is the only typical flower, is more regular, more symmetrical and more complete, but nothing in the vegetable world is or could be more unassuming in appearance or better adapted to fill the Divine mission of sustaining life and giving verdue and beauty to nature.

He who spake worlds into existence and "hung them upon nothing" has also changed blue grass into horn, hoof and hair, into body, muscle and bone of the ox, and then changed the meat of the ox into bone, muscle and brain of man, and thereby enabled him to reach a high state of physical and mental perfection and thus demonstrating that it is a divine agent sent upon a divine mission.

CHAPTER IV.

Early Settlements on the South Side of the Kentucky River, Leestown, Frankfort and Other Points of Interest Prior to 1800.

In the year 1775, the Cherokee Indians sold to the Transylvania Company all of that part of Franklin County which lies south or west of the Kentucky river; the purchase was made by the company through Daniel Boone as agent. There were no settlements made on that side of the river until about 1784, the first being by James Arnold who built a double log house opposite the mouth of Glenn's Creek. His land extended from the mouth of Little Benson, down the river to the mouth of Cedar Run. About the year 1790, John Cardwell settled on a tract of land located near where Blakemore's distillery now stands, and about the same time Basil Carlisle and Roddy Hawkins located in the same neighborhood and L. R. Major located near South Benson church and James Payne located in that section about the same time, and James Roberts in the following year. Prior to 1800, James Brewer, William Harrod, William Lewis, Thomas Brewer and several other parties located in the lower part of the county near Flat Creek.

In the year 1773, James, George and Robert McAfee, Samuel Adams, Hancock Taylor and Mathew Bracken came up the Kentucky river and crossed the river at Buffalo Crossing, at Leestown, and on the 16th day of July, they surveyed the present site of Frankfort, their survey including six hundred acres.

These parties described Buffalo Trace as being a hundred feet wide and the dust as being several inches deep; in some places the hoofs of the buffalos had worn the ground down several feet; this "Trace" was made by vast herds of buffaloes in traveling to and from the blue grass fields of Scott, Woodford and other parts of the blue grass country and Drennon Lick (Springs) in Henry County. This road crossed the river at Leestown, and it was so well marked and worn that it can be followed to this day; in that early day it bore evidence of having been traveled for hundreds of years by thousands of buffaloes in their search for salt. The trestle which the Frankfort and Cincinnati Railroad Company built across this trace is 156 feet high and 800 feet long; it is located a short distance east of Frankfort. Leestown, which was located about one mile below Frankfort, was begun with a cabin improvement a year or two prior to 1775 and it became a noted stopping place and camping ground for explorers.

In 1775 it was better established and other cabin improvements were added; these were not in the form of a stockade defense, but rather for the transient use and convenience of emigrants and explorers who came in from Fort Pitt (Pittsburg) by way of the Ohio and Kentucky rivers; it was also a resting place between Lexington and Louisville. The first maps of Kentucky, which are on file in the State Library, show that Leestown was of sufficient importance to be located, while Frankfort was not placed on them.

Leestown is now only about one-half a mile below the present city limits of Frankfort. In 1776, several new houses were built and the town had prospects of becoming of considerable importance, but in the year 1777, on account of its exposed situation and the more menacing attitude of the Indians, it was abandoned for nearly ten years.

In March, 1789, Rev. Jeddiah Morse, D. D. described Leestown as "west of Lexington on the eastern bank of the Kentucky river; it is regularly laid out and is flourishing. The banks of the Kentucky river are remarkably high, in some places 300 or 400 feet, composed generally of stupendous perpendicular rock. The consequence is there are few crossing places; the best is at Leestown which is a considerable circumstance that must contribute much to its importance." The expectations of this early day have never been realized; at present there are two fine distilleries located there with several warehouses and cattle pens; there is also a hemp mill or twine factory which employs a large force of hands. It is run by one of the largest turbine wheels in this country; this wheel is operated by the water from the dam, made in the construction of lock number four. This factory is known as the Kentucky River Mills; the large manufacturing interests which have centered there, have necessarily built many residences and tenement houses in that locality.

From the formation of the ground, to the east and north of Frankfort, extending out the Owenton road and along this valley to Leestown there are many evidences that the Kentucky river, at some early period in its history, ran around to the east and north of Fort Hill in the place of being on the west side as it now runs. In the year 1883 the back-water from the Kentucky river extended up the Leestown branch to the back-water which ran up back of the Penitentiary, thus making an island of Fort Hill and its contiguous territory of several hundred acres. The time is not distant, when all of that section including Leestown, Thorn Hill, Fort Hill and the Noel farm will be included and become a part of Frankfort; many residents of that section are now clamoring to become a part of the city in order that they may enjoy the benefits of the city schools, the water, the gas, sidewalks and other advantages of the city.

The act of the Virginia Legislature establishing the town of Frankfort was entitled, "An act for establishing a town on the lands of James Wilkinson, in Fayette county, and a ferry across Kentucky river." The act was passed in 1786 and it provided, "That one hundred acres of land in the county of Fayette, the property of James Wilkinson, which have been laid off into lots and streets, shall be vested in Caleb Wallace, Thomas Marshall, Joseph Crockett, John Fowler, Jr., John Craig, Robert Johnson and Benjamin Roberts, Gentleman, trustees, and shall be established a town by the name of Frankfort. The said trustees or a majority of them shall within six months after passing of this act, sell at public auction all the lots within the said town which have not been heretofore disposed of by the said James Wilkinson, advertising the time and place of sale at the court house of the said county of Fayette, on two successive court days. The purchaser shall hold the said lots respectively subject to the condition of building on each a dwelling house sixteen feet square with a brick or stone chimney, to be furnished fit for habitation within two years from the date of sale." The same act provides that a public ferry shall be constantly kept across the Kentucky river from the lands of James Wilkinson in the town of Frankfort to the opposite shore, and fixed the rate or toll for men, horses, vehicles, etc.

The sale of lots, evidently did not meet the expectation of General Wilkinson, as he went back before the Legislature and had the above act amended, November 27, 1787, by providing that the further time of three years shall be allowed the said trustees to sell the lots in the said town. The records of the County Court of Fayette county, where the deeds to these lots were recorded, were destroyed by fire in the early part of the last century, and the destruction of these records destroyed all evidence as to whom the sale of these lots were made, but it is evident that nearly all of the lots were sold to the officers and soldiers of the standing army or to those whose time of enlistment had expired, a large majority of whom had served with General Wilkinson in the revolution. Nearly all, and perhaps all of the first trustees whose names were mentioned in the act establishing the town had been in the revolution and had served for several years under General Wilkinson. In the Kentucky Gazette of August 9, 1789, the following advertisement appears: "Whereas, General Wilkinson, in the month of June, gave notice in the Kentucky Gazette that Major Dunn would receive bonds from the purchasers of lots at Frankfort, and that Captain Daniel Gano would, on Major Dunn's certificate, execute the conveyances agreeable to sale; this is therefore, to give notice to the purchasers of said lots that Capt. John Fowler will take the bonds and give the necessary certificates for the conveyance to Capt. Gano who will execute the deeds agreeable to the term of sale.

By Harry Innis,   James Wilkinson.
His Atty. in Fact.

In the year 1791, the following act was passed: "Be it enacted by the General Assembly (of Virginia) that an inspection of tobacco shall be and the same is hereby established on the lands of James Wilkinson, at Frankfort, in the county of Woodford to be called and known by the name of Frankfort Warehouse, the proprietor whereof shall build the same at his own expense."

2. "There shall be allowed and paid annually to each of the inspectors at the said warehouse the sum of twenty-five pounds for their salary."

The streets of Frankfort which were laid off by the first trustees of the town and named by them, were nearly all named for Generals who had taken a prominent part in the Revolutionary war.

Wilkinson street which runs parallel with the river and adjacent thereto, was named for General Wilkinson, who had the town established and who was at that time Commander-in-Chief of the Western Division of the United States army. General James Wilkinson was born in Maryland in 1757; he was thirty years old when Frankfort was established; he had been a revolutionary soldier under Washington; he was with Arnold and Burr, and held the position of Captain, on their expedition to Canada in the latter part of 1775 and the first part of 1776; he was afterwards on the staff of General Gates; in 1796, he became the Commander-in-Chief of the United States army. In 1805, he was made Governor of Louisiana; in 1811, he was court-martialed and charged with treason, in connection with Aaron Burr, but he was acquitted. Evidence was afterwards brought to light which would have convicted him. It has been shown that for several years prior to 1800 he received a pension from the Spanish Government; he was discharged from the United States army. In 1815 he went to Mexico, where he had made large investments and died there in the year 1825. General Wilkinson, not only established Frankfort but he also did a great deal towards reclaiming the lower portions of the town from the swampy condition it was then in. The lower part of the town extending up some distance beyond the penitentiary was very low and swampy and was in such unhealthy condition that it was not habitable. He drained all of this section, with the labor of soldiers then under his command, during the years of 1795 and 1796. In view of what General Wilkinson had done for Frankfort the trustees doubtless thought it was proper to name what was proposed to be the chief resident street, for the man who had established the town.

The next street parallel to Wilkinson, is Washington, which was named for General George Washington with whom General Wilkinson was on very intimate terms and under whom he and several members of the board of trustees had served during the revolutionary war. The next street parallel to Washington, is St. Clair, which was named for General Arthur St. Clair, who was born in Scotland in 1734; he served as Lieutenant under General Wolf, at Quebec, in 1759. On the plains of Abraham he seized the colors which had fallen from the hands of a dying soldier and bore them until victory had been won by the British; he was, again, on the plains of Abraham, but with the American forces, in 1776; he was an intimate friend of General Washington and was one of his most loved and trusted generals during the Revolution. He died in the year 1818.

The next and last street laid off parallel to St. Clair street running from the river to the hill was Ann Street, which was named for Mrs. Ann Wilkinson, the wife of General James Wilkinson, who was not only a very beautiful woman but who was also attractive, "she was more popular with the officers and soldiers, than was her distinguished husband." There is a short street parallel to St. Clair, located on the west of the old State House, which is called Madison, in honor of James Madison, fourth president of the United States.

Wapping street runs east and west, and though it too is parallel with the river, it is at right angles to Wilkinson street, the river makes a bend almost at right angles, nearly opposite the intersection of Wilkinson and Wapping streets.

The name Wapping was suggested by an Englishman who was visiting and prospecting at Lexington and Frankfort at that time and was so named for Wapping street, London, which was then known as the most beautiful residence street in the world.

The next street parallel to Wapping, is Montgomery,

which is now generally known as Main. Montgomery was named for General Richard Montgomery who was born in Ireland in 1736; he was commissioned an officer in the English Army but resigned his commission and came to America in 1773; he was appointed brigadier general by the Continental Congress in 1775, and was in command of the American forces, and fell in the attack on Quebec, December 31, 1775; his last words were "men of New York, you will not fear to follow where your general leads."

The next street parallel to Montgomery or Main, is Broadway or Market; it is the widest street in the town and it was known in the early history of the town as Market street; the first market house was built in the middle of the street near the intersection with Ann, and was directly in front of what is now the Elk or Merriwether hotel.

The next street parallel to Broadway is Clinton, which was named for General George Clinton, who was the first Governor of New York, and was Vice President of the United States; he was a general in the Continental army and was recognized as one of the staunchest of patriots and was one of the greatest men of that age.

The next street was called Mero, properly spelt Miro. This was the last street that was laid off at that time, and was named in honor of the Governor-general of the Spanish territory in America; at that time the gulf states and the Mississippi river were under the control and belonged to the Spanish government; Miro was in charge, and he granted to General Wilkinson some privileges of trade and the free use of the Mississippi river for the transportation of freight. Some twenty-five years later, General Wilkinson and other prominent Frankfort people were accused of entering into a conspiracy to transfer the territory of Kentucky over to Miro and the Spanish control.

The above named are the only streets which were laid off at the time the town was established; since then the city limits have been extended several times and other streets have been opened and named, the chief of which are High, Hill and Holmes streets all of which were named for local reasons. Center street or alley was named by the first trustees of the town, evidently for the reason that it was at that time the center of the residence and business portion of the town running from South to North; this street or alley is also called Long Lane Avenue, Petticoat Alley and Gas-house Alley, all of which names have been applied for local reasons.

Prior to 1800 there were no sidewalks in the town, and the streets were in bad condition. They were not macadamized for several years after that period, and there were but few carriages or other vehicles except log wagons. On November 28, 1799, there was a long article in the Palladium in reference to the improvement of the Kentucky river to its mouth; it was estimated that by an expense of $950,00 the river could be made navigable at all seasons, for boats drawing not more than fifteen inches. Prior to the improvement of the river, there was a large island in the river nearly opposite the mouth of Benson creek, which was known as "Fish Trap" island. It was nine hundred yards long; the descent in this distance was sixty inches. The falls in the river between the mouth of Devil's Hollow and the point where lock number four is located was nearly seven feet. The main channel was on the west side of the island; a grist and saw mill was located on the east side near the lower end of the island. Mr. Zadoc Cramer described this mill as being, "a saw and grist mill one mile below the town of Frankfort, in the river, which in low water, does a good deal of business, but it is not uncommon to see it completely covered by floods of the river, to withstand which it has no roof, is open on all sides, and is heavily loaded down on the corners and in the middle of the frame at top, with piles of stone."

On the 16th of November, 1739, Samuel & Lafon announced in the Gazette the opening of "an elegant livery stable in Frankfort; in addition to feeding horses they also take in horses to cure of almost all the ailments prevalent in the country, nick their tails," etc.

The Palladium, a literary and political paper was published in Frankfort in 1798 by Hunter & Beaumont. There are copies of this paper on file in the State Library commencing October 23, 1798, and continuing down to and including a copy of date Feb. 17, 1803. Humphrey Marshall also published a paper in Frankfort at that time which was known as "The Spirit of 1776." The following are some of the advertisements from the Palladium: "Isaac E. Gano, has just arrived from Philadelphia with a large and general assortment of fresh and genuine medicine which is now opened at his shop in Frankfort, and will be sold cheap for cash; a generous allowance will be made to physicians purchasing a quantity. I continue as usual to practice physic."

Frankfort, September 1st, 1798.
I. E. G.

"Wanted to engage a number of hands to conduct boats to New Orleans. Apply to Daniel Weiseger."

"William Porter, at his tanyard, one mile from Frankfort, pays cash for green and dry hides; he also wants an apprentice. Those to whom it is more convenient can sell hides, intended for the Frankfort tanyard to H. McIlvane, in Lexington."

In 1799, some enterprising citizens of Frankfort had under consideration the question of building a bridge across the Kentucky river as will appear from the following notice of December the 19th, 1799: "The share holders in the Frankfort Bridge Company are hereby notified, that the election for *chusing* seven Directors agreeable to the act of incorporation will be held at the house of Daniel Weiseger in the town of Frankfort on Thursday the 2d day of January next."

C. GREENUP,
D. WEISEGER,
W. TRIGG.

"Whereas, the repose and convenience of many of the citizens of the town of Frankfort, are extremely interrupted by the disorderly behavior of certain immoral persons, who, keeping very late hours walking up and down the town, breaking the windows and doors of moral and orderly citizens thereof; Be it therefore resolved, that if any such person or persons are known or discovered to roam about the town after the hour of ten o'clock at night making a noise or other disturbance, shall pay a fine not exceeding $5.00.

By order of the Board.

MURRAY FORBES, Clerk.
JOHN LOGAN, Chairman."

"The trustees of the Frankfort Academy have the pleasure to inform their fellow citizens that it is now open for the reception of scholars under the direction of able and experienced masters."

THOMAS TODD, President.

"The members of the Frankfort Hiram Lodge are requested to meet at the lodge room on the 24th day of June, 1799, it being the anniversary of St. John the Baptist. By Isaac E. Gano, Sect."

"On February 3, 1800, Haden Edwards advertised for sale one half of his mills on South Elkhorn about one mile below the junction and about four and a half miles from Frankfort, consisting of a water grist mill calculated for four pair of stones, two pair of which are now in motion; the house 58x46, three stories high, all of stone." George Fields offered at public sale, in the town of Frankfort "that valuable, elegant and handsomely situated, new, three story brick house, and the lot of ground on which it is erected now occupied as an Inn by Dr. Gano, together with the improvements consisting of a two story brick kitchen, a small smoke house," etc.

In the year 1799, Harry Innis and John Logan were elected delegates to represent Franklin County in the Constitutional Convention, and Anthony Crockett and John Smith were elected to represent the County in the House of Representatives. "In consequence of the seat of Mr. John Smith being vacated by a resolution of the House of Representatives" another election was held on Tuesday, November 21, 1799, in the town of Frankfort, and Mr. Smith was re-elected by a large majority.

In the early history of this county, when a person could be imprisoned for debt, it meant something to go on the bond of a defendant either in a civil or criminal action as will appear from the bond executed in the Franklin County Court of Quarter session July 18, 1798.

Richard Allen—
Against*** In Covenant
John Arnold.

James Arnold came into the court and undertook for the defendant that in case he shall be cast in this action he shall satisfy and pay the condemnation of the Court to render his body to prison in execution for the same or in failure thereof that he, the said James Arnold will do it for him.

The following is the report of the Franklin County Grand jury made the 17th day of May, 1796. "We present James Gayle for swearing one profane oath, to-wit, by God, on the 16th instant at the house of Simon Hancock, by information of Simon Hancock.

We, of the jury present Theoderick Boler for selling brandy by retail at the race ground at George Blackburn's on the 16th day of September, by information of Anthony Bartlett.

We also present William Hawkins, overseer of the road from South Fork of Elkhorn to the two mile tree, for not having the same in repair on the 12th of October. We present William Porter overseer of the road from the top of the hill above Frankfort to the two mile tree for not having the same in repair the 12th of October; also for not having a sign board at the two mile tree. By the information of Samuel Mosley."

"NATH. RICHARDSON, Foreman."

In Fordham's Personal Narrative, (pp. 160-61) we find the following about Frankfort, 1818, "Jan 31." Started for Frankfort, passed through a fine rolling country; cleared enough to present something like views, though none of them of any extent.

Frankfort is a smart little town on the Kentucky river. It is the seat of Government and the Legislature is now sitting. It was Sunday and a few smartly dressed young men were picking their way through the half frozen mud in the streets. Like others it is hidden in a mud hole with fine commanding sections around it. They have begun to pave the main street—in a way that would make a London Paviour laugh."

Note: Cuming visited (Frankfort) in 1807 and found a town of ninety houses, including a state-house, a jail, a Court house, a State penitentiary, a market-house, a government house, and four Inns which in size, accommodations and business he declares were not surpassed in the United States. (Early Western Travels IV. pp. 191-196.)

CHAPTER V.

Course of Events from 1800 *to* 1810.

The population of Franklin County in the year 1800 was 5,078 of that number 628 lived in the town of Frankfort.

On Tuesday the 26th day of August of that year, James Roberts was appointed jailer of the county; the appointment or selection, was made by the Court of Quarter Session. On the 23rd of September, the following orders were entered: "It is ordered that Stephen Arnold and John Price, Gentlemen, they being the oldest Justices commissioned for said county, as fit persons to fill the office of a sheriff of the County for the next term of two years, be recommended to the Governor." "It is ordered that Stephen Arnold, Robert Blackwell, Anthony Crockett and William Payne or any three of them be appointed to receive the warehouse, for the reception of tobacco in South Frankfort; provided, the same be completed agreeable to law."

Otho Beaty was elected to represent the County in the House of Representatives in the year 1800. In the election for Lieutenant Governor for that year, Franklin County gave Henry Clay only three votes.

Daniel Bradford was postmaster at Frankfort in 1800; John Smith was elected to represent the County in the Lower House in 1801, and Baker Ewing in 1802.

The following news item is copied from the Palladium: "Frankfort, May 29, 1800.—Married in town, on Sunday evening last, Dr. Lewis Marshall of Woodford, to the amiable and accomplished Miss A. Smith of this place."

On Tuesday, November 25, 1800, the following order was entered on the order book in the County Clerk's office: "It is ordered that the sheriff do bring immediately before this Court, Nancy Hutton to answer the contempt offered this Court by leaving a young infant on the clerk's table." The sheriff returned and reported that said Nancy Hutton could not be found," and it was thereupon ordered, "that Samuel

Hutton be summoned to appear before the next Court to show cause, if any he could, why he should not support the infant left by the said Samuel's wife on the clerk's table."

In the year 1798 a ferry was established at the "rope walks" one mile above Frankfort across the Kentucky river, from the lands of Elijah Craig, and an inspection of hemp and flour was established at the said ferry "which shall be called and known by the name of East Frankfort." This ferry crossed the river only a short distance above Cochran's distillery.

The Frankfort Bridge Company was incorporated December 21, 1799, Christopher Greenup, Daniel Weiseger and William Trigg were the incorporators; the right was given to erect the bridge from the south end of Ann street to the south side. In 1805 the act incorporating the Frankfort Bridge Company was repealed and an act passed authorizing John Pope to erect a bridge across the Kentucky river from the end of Annie (Ann) street to South Frankfort and fixed the rate of toll, etc. At the same term of the Legislature there was an act authorizing Thomas Tuntstall to erect a bridge across the Kentucky river from the west end of Montgomery (Main) street to his land on the opposite side of the river, "subject to the same rules, regulations, penalties and emoluments as John Pope." At the same term of the Legislature and on the same conditions, John Brown was authorized to erect a bridge across the Kentucky river "from his land above High street on the North side of the river." There was an act to incorporate the Frankfort Bridge Company, approved January 25, 1810, for the purpose of erecting a bridge across the Kentucky river from the south end of St. Clair street, Thomas V. Loofburrow and William Trigg were authorized to raise by subscription, by stock not to exceed thirty thousand dollars to be composed of shares of one hundred dollars each—"provided said bridge shall not contain more than one pier in the channel of the river, and which pier shall not be less than sixty feet high from its foundation. The act also provided, if the said bridge was not completed within two years, the said company was to forfeit all rights which had been granted by the Legislature.

There was an act approved January 18th, 1812, extending the time of completing the bridge, until 1st day of February, 1816; this was the first permanent bridge which crossed the river at Frankfort. It was built on the plan of Judge Finley's chain bridge and it cost $25,000.00; it was 334½ feet long. It had one pier in the middle 65 feet high; the entire length, with the approaches, was 700 feet and the width was 18 feet. The two chains for the bridge were made at Pittsburg; they were of one and one half inch square bar iron and weighed about six tons each. There was much difficulty in securing a foundation for the south abutment, because of the quicksand found there; the water would rush in at the bottom upon the workmen as fast as they discharged it at the top with pumps and buckets, working day and night. During the time the bridge was under construction, there was a floating bridge across the Kentucky river from the south end of Ann street, similar to a pontoon bridge; it was constructed of anchored flat boats covered with plank for the road way and with railing on each side for protection. Another bridge of the same kind was used at the ferry near the foot of Wilkinson street across to the mouth of Benson Creek; this ferry had been established by act of the Legislature in the year 1801.

On June 23rd, 1801, "Stephen Arnold, Gentleman," presented to the Court of Quarter Session a commission from James Garrard, Governor of Kentucky, appointing him sheriff of the county, whereupon he took the oath required by law and entered into bond with Daniel Weiseger and Christopher Greenup as his securities. At the same time Daniel Weiseger was appointed clerk of the County Court. On the same date an item of news from the Palladium, reads as follows: "We are requested to inform the inhabitants of Frankfort and its vicinity, that on Saturday the 4th of July, several of the students of both sexes under the tuition of Gabriel Nourse will have an entertainment at the State House. In order that the exhibition may not interfere with other commemorations of the day the bell will begin to ring at eight o'clock in the morning and speaking commence in the State House at half past nine." Murray's spring was the usual place for Fourth of July celebrations, picnic, etc. This spring is only a short distance below the north limit of the city.

At the beginning of the last century news traveled very slow. On December 30, 1801, the Palladium made this statement: "Just as this paper was going to press a gentleman informed us that Mr. Charles Lynch, of Shelby County, had arrived about four days ago from South Carolina. The Electors had voted before he left that state, unanimously for Mr. Jefferson; our informant believes the votes for Vice President were divided between Pickney and Burr. Mr. Lynch has been only fifteen days on his journey and was at Camden on the day the Electors met.

The County levy for the year 1802 was fixed at "six shillings per tythable." Zachary, a slave, the property of Lucy Samuels, was accused of trespass, and on January the 31st, tried by a Jury and convicted, the judgment was, "it is therefore considered by this Court that said Zachary receive thirty-nine lashes well laid on his bare back at the public whipping post and that the sheriff of this county do cause execution of this judgment."

At the September term 1802, it was ordered that five magistrates attend at the house of Phill Bush in Frankfort on the first Monday in April, next, to receive proposals for building a court house on the ground given by the Legislature to erect thereon a court house, the walls to be of brick and not less than forty feet square. At the May term 1803, it was ordered that Christopher Greenup, Daniel James and Daniel Weiseger be appointed commissioners "to superintend the building the court house in this county and to lay off the grounds for the court house." At the following June term this order was entered, upon motion; "ordered that Hiram Lodge number four, and its friends be permitted to add a third story to the court house which is now a building, at their own expense and upon their own construction for a mason hall, provided such erection does not impair the contract of the county with the undertaker, either by lessening or enhancing the responsibilities of either except that the undertakers are at the expense of the lodge and its friends to extend each pillar in front of the house one brick in length." At the next term of court leave was given Hiram Lodge "to run up the stairs from the passage below to the landing on the south west or north west room above clerk's room in the court house, in order to ascend to the third story." At August term, 1804, it was ordered that the commissioners for erecting the court house bring suit immediately against the contractor and his bondsmen for the non-compliance of his contract.

Prior to 1806, Franklin county had no court house; the State house was used for holding court and for all other official business of the county. The court house was completed September 15, 1806, and John Rennick was appointed custodian of the house and yard, and he was directed to have as many locust trees planted out as would be necessary to shade the yard. The court house was built on the south east corner of Capitol Square, in front of the present executive building, and across Elk Avenue from Kagin Brothers' restaurant.

Fleming Trigg was authorized to have stone posts set at the corners of the house to prevent wagons and other vehicles from injuring it. Some time after that, Oliver Waggoner was appointed to superintend the inclosure of that part of the public square allotted to the county around the court house, and that he procure the necessary styles or steps to be made leading in and out from the front of the house. A post and rail fence was built around the square, the post on each side of the styles was eight inches square and furnished with a fiddle head; the post had a pin through the top rail of each post. Daniel Weiseger and Daniel James were appointed commissioners to let to the lowest bidder the "securing the arches of the court house," also for erecting stock and whipping post in the court house square; also to let work completing the inside to be done in a plain, neat, workmanlike manner and to be completed by March 1, 1806.

The first term of Circuit Court was held in Frankfort on April 18, 1803, John Logan was the first circuit judge; Willis Lee was appointed clerk during good behavior.

After the conviction and execution of Henry Fields charged with having murdered his wife in 1799, the records of the county do not show another indictment for either murder or manslaughter until July, 1814; however there were numerous indictments for profane swearing during that period of time.

At the June term, 1803, John Price became the fourth sheriff of the county and Daniel Weiseger was re-appointed clerk. At the same term of court Humphrey Marshall was allowed six pounds for defending John Bartlett in the Court of Appeals. Bartlett had been adjudged of unsound mind and was refused a seat as justice of the peace after his appointment. The Court of Appeals adjudged that he was entitled to his seat. The county levy for 1804 was one dollar per "tithe." The first water works ever built in Kentucky were commenced by Richard Thockmorton in 1804. On December 23, 1805, the Frankfort Water Company was incorporated with John Brown, William Trigg and Achilles Sneed as incorporators, for the purpose of completing the works. Wooden pipes were laid from Cedar Cove spring about three miles out on the Owenton road, along Brown's bottom in to the town.

A strong wall about twenty-five or thirty feet high was built across the ravine some distance below the spring, and in that way a reservoir was formed; the pipes used were cedar bored through the center with an inch and a half auger; and they were fastened to each other with wooden pins. These works supplied Frankfort with water until 1886, when the most approved system then known was established instead.

The system of piping the water through cedar, was never a complete success. Harry Bartlett was appointed sheriff in 1805, and on June the 15th of that year he resigned, and Robert Blackwell was appointed in his place and thereby became the sixth sheriff of the county; on November 18th, of the same year Scott Brown was appointed a justice of the peace.

A subscription list with forty-six names attached, forming a fire company for the city of Frankfort was ordered to be recorded in the County Clerk's office on December 15, 1806. On April 21st of this year Daniel Weiseger was granted the right to keep a tavern on Ann street in the town of Frankfort;

this tavern was located where the Capitol Hotel now stands. On the same date there was an order entered removing James Roberts, jailer of Franklin county from office, and John A. Mitchell was appointed in his stead. The charge upon which Roberts was tried, convicted and removed from office was "for malpractice in office by charging the county with his services and the fees attending thereto, and for the same services laying his claim before the Circuit Court to be audited with the Auditor of Public Accounts."

The year 1806 was one of the most exciting epochs in the history of the county. It was during that year that two alleged conspiracies were unearthed, by parties who were living in Frankfort. There was the so-called Spanish conspiracy in which it was alleged that Frankfort citizens were the chief conspirators, and which is said to have been planned about the year 1790; and the other one is known as the Burr conspiracy, with Blenerhassett and others about 1805-6.

An article published in The Western World, October 15, 1806, openly accused Aaron Burr and others of conspiring against the United States. Col. Daviess, who was, at that time, District Attorney, asked for a warrant against Burr which Judge Innis refused; but he convened an extra term of the grand jury. Burr was at Lexington at that time and he immediately came to Frankfort with Henry Clay, his attorney. Burr demanded an immediate investigation of the charges against him; after a bitter fight the grand jury ignored the charge. All the country around Frankfort was crazed with excitement "on the day of the expected trial. Frankfort was crowded and the court house gorged with citizens and strangers." After his release, a ball was given at the Love house in Frankfort, to Col. Burr, which was largely attended, and conspicious in the crowd were many officers of both State and Nation. In a short time after this another ball was given in honor of Col. Daviess, the attorney who prosecuted the case, and this was also numerously attended.

There has been an effort made to prove that some of Frankfort's citizens were connected with the Burr conspiracy; but subsequent facts and circumstances tend to show that the so-called Spanish conspiracy had no connection with the Burr conspiracy, except, perhaps, Col. Burr was trying to take advantage of that independent Kentucky sentiment which was rife at that time, to forward his own nefarious and ambitious designs. The Spanish conspiracy which the editors of the Western World exposed about the same time the charges of conspiracy were made against Col. Burr, deals more particularly with the people of Frankfort and Franklin county. Marshall, in his history of Kentucky, condemns in unmeasured terms the conduct of those who were supposed to be connected with it, and he gives great credit to John Wood and John M. Street, editors of the Western World, who arrived in Frankfort in the early part of 1806. He says in his history: "Then it may be said, there was seen from the front door of Col. Taylor's Inn an elderly looking man of middle size and ordinary dress, with a Godfrey's quadrant strung to his shoulder, a knapsack on his back and a good-looking youth by his side, both on foot, trudging through the muddy streets (then unpaved) and as if travelers who wanted rest. They arrived at the door, entered and are seated; the elder announces himself to be John Wood and his companion Mr. Street, who had traveled with him from Richmond, in Virginia, on a voyage of adventure for enjoyment and support. John Wood was a professed man of letters; the other familiar with newspapers and of good capacity. On July 1, 1806 they commenced publishing a weekly newspaper in Frankfort to be styled 'The Western World.' It was printed by William Hampton, the proprietor of The Palladium. On July 4, 1806, they agitated the people of Frankfort from center to circumference, about the Burr conspiracy; threats were freely made against them. The next edition agitated Frankfort society still more. It was thought that nothing but the death of Street would prevent the exposure of Sebastin, Innis and others; an assassination was attempted by George Adams armed with two pistols, and repelled by Street with a dirk. Street was wounded in the breast by the discharge from the fire-arms. Adams fled but was afterwards arrested. Adams was bailed. Humphrey Marshall went on the bond of Street, with Col. J. H. Daviess.

Street was tried and acquitted, Adams was convicted, but it turned out that the indictment failed to charge "with intent to kill," an omission supposed to have been made on purpose. The guilt of the accused was conclusive. (See Register of State Hist. Society, Sept. 1906, History of Gen. Jos. M. Street.) Benjamin Sebastin was a pensioner of Spain. These exposures brought on a legislative investigation, and to prevent which Sebastin resigned.

Allen B. Magruder stated in his work on the "Cession of Louisiana": "To whatever incomprehensible spirit of delirium the circumstances may have attributed its origin, yet it is a fact that about the year 1789 or 1790 a plan was in agitation to separate Kentucky from the Union and attach it to the Spanish Government of Louisiana. A memorial was drawn up addressed to the executive authority of the colony, expressing the advantage of a union, which was reciprocated in the same terms on the part of the Spanish Government. The chimerical plan proceeded so far in its effects upon the public mind, that a proposition to form the State into an independent government was introduced into a convention held about that time to form articles of separation from the State of Virginia." T. M. Green says in his prefatory to the "Spanish conspiracy," published in the year 1891:

"A few years after this publication was made by Magruder, an exposure of the plan to which he referred was made in 1806 in the columns of 'The Western World,' a newspaper published at Frankfort, Kentucky. As an effect of that exposure, John Brown, one of the principals engaged in the plan, deemed it expedient at the early age of forty eight to retire forever from public life, and, as far as possible, to withdraw himself from public observation, while Sebastin, his friend and one of his coadjutors was driven in merited disgrace from the bench of the Court of Appeals. The Legislative investigation which was forced by that exposure, and the results of the judicial inquiries which he had himself invoked, left the unhappy Innis, another of John Browns' associates in the plan, nothing of which to boast and everything to most bitterly lament. And though a Scotch verdict of acquittal was given to James Wilkinson, the prime mover and leader in the plan by the court-martial which was organized for the purpose, yet his own letters since obtained from the Spanish archives establishes the indisputable truth of the charges made against him, and no one now questions his guilt." He says further:

"In these pages are produced, in their logical connection and relation to each other, the proofs known to the writer, which show that, while Kentucky was yet a district of Virginia, an engagement was entered into by James Wilkinson with Miro, the intendant of Louisiana, to separate Kentucky from the United States, and to subject her people to Spain; that as a result of this intrigue between Wilkinson and Miro, a proposition was, a few months thereafter, made by Gardoqui, the Spanish minister to the United States, to John Brown, then a member of the Old Congress from Virginia, to grant to the people of Kentucky the privilege of navigating the Mississippi, which Spain refused to the people of the United States, on condition that the people of Kentucky would first erect themselves into an independent State and withdraw from the Union; that John Brown, assenting to the proposition made to him by the representative of the government of Torquemada, promised to aid the design; that in accordance with the engagement made by the one and the assurances given by the other, Wilkinson and Brown, on their return to Kentucky, conspired with each other, and with Benjamin Sebastin, Harry Innis, Caleb Wallace, Isaac Dunn and others to accomplish the separation which had been concerted with the Spaniards, did all that they dared do to bring it about, and that their movements in the Danville Convention of July and November, 1788, which were so happily frustrated, were agreed upon and directed to that end."

Mr. Green shows a bitterness and vindictiveness in "The Spanish Conspiracy" which are not fully justified by the facts and circumstances which surround the case.

Steam cars were not thought to be possible at that time. Transportation for farming produce and other freight overland, in wagons, to and from the territory of Kentucky was a gigantic undertaking; so tremendous a proposition was it, and so earnestly did the pioneers desire to have a waterway for the transportation of their freight to the ocean, that a plan was formed to lock and dam the Kentucky river to the three forks, thence up the south fork and Goose Creek to the salt woods, thence by a canal thirty-six miles long with 160 feet of lockage into Cumberland river at Cumberland ford; thence four miles in Cumberland river to the mouth of Yellow creek; thence by canal, in the bed of Yellow Creek to Cumberland Gap; through Cumberland Gap by a tunnel probably 700 or 800 yards long, and by canal from thence to Powells river five miles below; down that river successively into Clinch and Tennessee river and up Hiwassee river by locks and dams; from the Hiwassee continue the improvement by a canal to the navigable waters of the Savannah at the head of steamboat navigation on that river.

The Spanish government had refused to permit the United States to use the waters of the Mississippi for transportation of their freights; a great many Kentuckians doubtless thought that the only thing they could do, in order to reach a market for the produce from the fertile soil of the territory, was to become a part of the government which could do the most for them. Kentucky had been overrun with Indians; their depredations had been frequent and the loss sustained by reason thereof had been severe; the citizens of the territory had made frequent and earnest appeals to the national authorities for help, and each time their appeal had been ignored or refused; these conditions caused many of the leading citizens of the territory to become dissatisfied with the National Government. Then, too, the bond of union between the states and territories of that early date was not considered in the same light as it has been since the termination of the war between the states.

E. Spillsbee Coleman settled in South Frankfort about the years 1806 and established a tan-yard near a spring known then as Brown's Spring, named for Hezekiah Brown who lived adjacent; it was later called Coleman's Spring. In the year 1807, the two bridges across Elkhorn at the Forks were rebuilt; the one across the South Fork was let to Benjamin Head, for which he was allowed the sum of $78.25; the one across North Elkhorn was let to Hezekiah Keeton as contractor and builder.

Jeremiah Myers, an inmate of the Frankfort penitentiary, set fire to that institution on the 22nd day of March, 1807, and a part of it was burnt; on trial it was found that the law was not sufficient to punish him.

In the year 1808 the Legislature passed an act to establish a State Bank; it was fixed at Frankfort, but to follow the seat of government if moved; its capital stock was one million dollars. It was in operation for only a short time.

John Lindsey was appointed constable February 15, 1808, and in the following March John A. Mitchell resigned as jailer of the county, and Paschal Hickman was appointed; Jim, John and Stephen Arnold were his bondsmen. At the same term of court Elisha Herndon was appointed constable on the south side of the river, and Daniel Weiseger was re-appointed clerk of the County Court.

On August 5, 1808, Robert Blackwell became the eighth sheriff of the county, and Christopher Greenup produced a commission from Charles Scott, governor, appointing him a magistrate of the county.

William McBrayer became the 9th sheriff of the county, June 19, 1809; John Arnold was re-appointed magistrate and at the same term of court it was ordered that the fence around the court should be extended around the public square so as to include the Capitol and court house.

Stephen Arnold died December 18, 1809, and his father James Arnold died February 19, 1810. John Milam was appointed his administrator and Scott Brown was appointed to appraise the "slaves and personal estate" left by him. The descendants of all the above named parties have been prominent in Franklin county during the past century.

The total amount of unpaid claims against the county on the 1st day of November, 1809, amounted to $1,466.22.

Steel's ferry was established in 1810, and a bridge was built the same year by the county across the south fork of Benson Creek near Richard Smart's; at the same court James Blair was elected County Attorney; prior to his election the county had no regular attorney. Zadock Cramer, editor of the Navigator published at Pittsburg, Pa., in 1810, said that Frankfort, at that time, contained about one hundred and forty houses, which would give it a population of from 600 to 800 people. He said that Frankfort had three printing offices, one book-store, a circulating library, book bindery, eighteen mercantile stores and one State Bank; he also said in his article that a "steamboat, that is, a large boat to be propelled by the power of steam," was on the stocks a short distance above Frankfort. This boat was probably the "Kentucky," which was the second steam boat built in the State, and which was intended to navigate the Ohio and Mississippi rivers.

The editor was told that Governor Greenup had in contemplation the erection of a glass factory at Frankfort, in order to utilize a bank of fine white sand thrown up by the river, a short distance below the town; there also being agitated the question of establishing a "brew house" at Frankfort.

On motion of Martin D. Hardin on February 19th, 1810, John J. Marshall and himself were admitted to practice law, whereupon they took the oath of office.

A list of the attorneys at the Frankfort bar in the year 1810, included Martin D. Hardin, John J. Marshall, John H. Hannah, William Littel, Adam Beatty, John Rowan, Isham Talbott, William B. Blackburn, Thomas C. Lewis, Robert B. McAfee, John Allen, James Blair, Humphrey Marshall, Jas. Hughes, Matthew Lodge, William Hunter and James Crawford.

Isham Talbott, one of the leading lawyers of Frankfort, was in the habit of walking with his head thrown back. On one occasion a man by the name of Williams was digging a well and had gotten down about ten feet. Talbott came along, with his head up, and fell in the well on top of Williams; and this so enraged him that he called Williams a damn thief because he failed to warn him of his danger. Talbott was very profane. The county records show he was presented and fined several times for using profane language.

CHAPTER VI.

1810 to 1820, Course of Events.

On the motion of Daniel Weiseger, clerk of the County Court of Franklin county, Alexander Rennick was appointed Deputy County Clerk, on Monday the 18th day of February, 1811; at the following April term, Robert McKee was granted a license to build a warehouse at the mouth of Benson Creek, for housing hemp, tobacco and flour; on the same day Christopher Greenup resigned his commission as justice of the peace.

During the year 1811 both of the bridges across Elkhorn creek, at the Forks, were rebuilt by the County Court. On June 17th, 1811, John M. Scott was appointed sheriff of the county; and at the same term of court Martin D. Hardin presented his commission as justice of the peace in, and for the county. On the same day Richard Taylor was granted the right to establish a public warehouse on the Kentucky river at the mouth of Leestown branch, which was known as "Leestown warehouse;" it was used for storing tobacco, flour and hemp.

On December 16, 1811, Daniel Weiseger resigned as County Clerk, and William Trigg was "unanimously" appointed to take that position. Martin D. Hardin and John Morris were appointed a committee to inspect the clerk's office; on the same date a hogshead of tobacco marked "J. F. No. 48 Gross, 1653 tare 166 neat 1448," having been in warehouse over two years was ordered sold, no one claiming same.

The records of the Franklin County Court, show, that during the year 1812 Benjamin Hickman was elected constable by the trustees of Frankfort for said city, and that the sheriff was allowed a credit for two hundred and forty-five "titheables" which he was not able to collect; it also shows that the court allowed the sum of $24.00 per year for keeping a pauper.

Prior to the repeal of the act under which a person could

be imprisoned for debt, a large number of men were confined in the county jail, and in order to prevent too many men from being crowded together there were certain imaginary lines, known as "Prison Bounds," over which the trusty prisoners were not permitted to pass. During the year 1812 it was "ordered that part of the prison bounds that include Captain Taylor's old stable be taken off, and the like quantity be extended up Montgomery street in such manner as to include Samuel's tavern, thence down to the former boundary by Captain Weiseger's."

John M. Scott having died in office (sheriff) William Hall was commissioned sheriff of the county, December 21, 1812. In the early part of 1812, "the Kentuckians, more attentive to the voice of distress, than to the laws of their country volunteered to the number of sixty or seventy men, under the command of Col. Anthony Crockett, and Captain John Arnold, and were marched to Vincennes to see what was the matter, and ten days after, marched home again, to tell they knew not what." (Collins' History.) This company was composed entirely of Franklin County men.

The most dire calamity that ever befell the people of Franklin County happened during this decade (1810 to 1820). The history of the war between the United States and Great Britain; the causes which led up to it and the sequences which followed it are a part of national history. The United States army in the northwest was composed almost exclusively of Kentuckians, a history of which is properly a part of the history of the State. Franklin County, however, did more than her just proportional part; she furnished more men, and more money, and she gave more of her heroic blood for the honor and glory of this great country than could have reasonably been expected from one community.

There were two full companies enlisted from Franklin County; the first under Paschal or Perchal Hickman as captain was mustered into the service August 15, 1912, and was known as Captain Paschal Hickman's company, first rifle regiment, Kentucky militia; it was engaged or enlisted to October 14, 1812. The muster roll shows the following:

Paschal Hickman, Captain.
Peter Dudley, Lieutenant.
Peter G. Voorhies, Ensign.
David Quinn, 1st Sergt.
Benjamin Head, 2d Sergt.
Geo. Nicholls, 3d Sergt.
Jno. Nailor, 4th Sergt.
Alexander Rennick, 1st Corp.
Wm. T. Pemberton, 2d Corp.
Richard Chism, 3d Corp.
Benj. B. Johnson, 4th Corp.

PRIVATES.

Joseph Armstrong.
William Brown.
James Bassett.
William Brattan.
Samuel Blackburn.
Martin Calvert.
Joseph Clark.
John Cox.
Lemuel Davis, Jr.
Nathan Goodrich.
Elisha Herndon.
James B. Humphreys.
John A. Holton.
John Koons.
Gideon King.
John Lane.
Joseph Mosely.
Otho McCracken.
Lapsley McBride.
Timothy Marshall.
Francis Mayhall.
John Noland.
Meriwether Poindexter.
Jno. Richardson.
Benjamin Pannell.
Jesse Poe.
Samuel Reading.
Geo. Robertson.
Jas. Richardson.
Berrisford Arnold.
Isaac Boone.
Overton Brown.
John Brook.
James Biscoe.
Garland Cosby.
Phillip Clark.
Lemuel Davis, Sr.
Lewis Fennick.
John Hays.
Moses Head.
William D. Hensley.
Geo. T. Johnston.
Simon Kenton.
Zachariah B. Lewis.
Jacob Lively.
Timothy T. Moore.
David E. Mathews.
Joshua Moore.
John G. Mullican.
John Mayhall.
Robert Owen.
John Phillips.
James Parker.
Joseph Pitts.
William Pruett.
Jno. Rossen.
Alexander Robinson.
Reuben Sparks.

Wm. Stevens.
John Smith.
Rankin Steel.
Francis Slaughter.
Samuel Throckmorton.
Thomas Tate.
Ben'j Underwood.
James Wilson.
George Yancy.

Samuel Smith.
Jesse Smiley.
Wm. Sanders.
Jno. Sanders.
John Tate.
Wm. Updike.
Van West.
William West.

The eighty-six men composing this company were all killed at the battle of the River Raisin, except thirteen of them, only twelve of whom are known at this date to have returned to their homes in Franklin county, to-wit: Lieut. Peter Dudley, Alexander Renick, Joseph Clark, Lewis Fennick, Elisha Herndon, John A. Holton, Z. B. Lewis, Francis Mayhall, John Mayhall, John Richardson, Alexander Robertson and James Wilson.

The order of battle at the River Rasin was as follows: Lieut. Colonel John Allen, commanding the right wing; Major Graves, the left; and Major Madison, the centre; Captain Ballard (acting Major) was placed in advance of the whole with two companies, one company commanded by Captain Hickman, Subaltern Lieut. Chinn, the other by Captain Graves.

Captain Hickman was severely wounded and was carried from the battlefield, both of his legs were shot off, or were so badly mangled that they were amputated the next morning, January 23, 1813.

The Indians were permitted by General Proctor to slaughter his wounded and defenseless captives, "Captain Hickman was rudely dragged to the door, his brains dashed out with the tomahawk and his body thrown back into the house."

A. B. Woodward, Judge of the Supreme Court of the territory of Michigan, in a letter to General Proctor, dated Detroit, February 2, 1813, stated that some of the prisoners after the capitulation of the 22nd of January had been tomahawked and others had been shot and still others had been burnt at the stake by the savages.

THE HISTORY OF FRANKLIN COUNTY. 57

Captain Paschal Hickman was the Jailor of Franklin county at the time he enlisted for military service. He was a son of the Rev. William Hickman, a noted Baptist preacher and teacher of pioneer days. Paschal Hickman was six feet two inches tall and weighed over two hundred pounds. He was a very handosme man and one of the most popular of that day.

Lapsley McBride, son of Col. William McBride, and great uncle of Judge W. Lapsley Jett, and for whom said Jett was named; and Berrisford Arnold, who was a very handsome man, the son of James Arnold, another great uncle of Judge Jett, were also killed at the River Raisin.

The records in the Adjutant General's office at Frankfort fails to show when any member of this noted company was discharged from service. The discharge of Sergeant Rennick is dated Urbana, Ohio, February 21, 1813.

After the slaughter at River Raisin the few Franklin county men who returned straggled in one at a time, and each time one came home the cannon was fired and the whole surrounding country as far away as it could be heard would hasten to Frankfort to inquire about the lost ones.

Lieutenant Peter Dudley, who made his escape, returned to Frankfort for the purpose of raising another company, though the recent preceding events of the campaign had proven to all that war was in reality a trade of blood, and the badges of mourning were worn by a large part of the population of Franklin county. Notwithstanding so many of her brave sons had been so ruthlessly massacred, and the majority of the large assembly of people, who had met to hear some tidings of loved and lost ones; when the gallant young lieutenant with a drummer and fifer commenced his march through the crowd proclaiming his purpose of raising another company and requesting all who were willing to go with him to fall in to the ranks, in less than thirty minutes one hundred young men were in line.

The Weekly Register published in Baltimore in 1812-13 in a statement dated Frankfort, March 10, 1813, says: "On Thursday, the 4th inst., the regiment of militia of this county

(Franklin) was paraded on the commons in this place for the purpose of furnishing from it seventy-two men, its quota. In less than thirty minutes one hundred men volunteered under Lieut. Peter Dudley, who had but a few days previous returned from the army under General Harrison, yesterday they were mustered and inspected, when the number was increased to one hundred and fifteen. Lieutenant Dudley was appointed Captain, Geo. Baltzell 1st Lieutenant, Samuel Arnold 2nd Lieutenant, and George Gayle Ensign. We understand about thirty-five hundred dollars was subscribed to go towards equipping the volunteers."

"It is reported the Governor has ordered out the two regiments commanded by Cols. Dudley and Boswell as reinforcements to Harrison; they march in a few days."

On Saturday, April 17, 1813, was the following from Georgetown, Kentucky:

"Captain Dudley, of Frankfort, passed through this place on Tuesday night with one hundred and twenty-two as respectable, as brave and as fine volunteers as any county ever produced, destined for the Rapids. We will venture to assert that Captain Dudley and his patriot band will give a good account of themselves and when attacked by the enemy they will leave their mark."

After the cold-blooded murder of the wounded at Frenchtown (River Raisin) an editor in sympathy with the allies said in his paper, "We would advise the recruiting officers of the Government to enlist fat men for the western market that the Indians may not butcher lean unprofitable stock."

In addition to the two companies above named there were several Franklin county men in other companies; Benjamin S. Chambers was Quartermaster, and William Church was a Captain; John Cardwell was in Captain Zachariah Terrell's company, and was at the battle of New Orleans, while his brother George Cardwell was under Captain Simpson, with Richard M. Johnson at the battle of the Thames, and he, like many others claimed the credit of killing Tecumseh. He was known as Tecumseh Cardwell from that time until his death many years after.

Samuel A. Theobald, a lawyer from Frankfort, was Judge Advocate in Richard M. Johnson's regiment, and was one of the immortal "Forlorn Hope" consisting of twenty men who volunteered to advance in front of the army at the Thames, in order to draw the fire from the Indians, who were known to be in hiding, and awaiting the advance of the army. This was the method adopted by Col. Johnson to locate the enemy; of these twenty men only one escaped unhurt, fifteen of them were shot dead. "Their leader (Col. Richard M. Johnson) with a dozen wounds still sat erect, his Judge Advocate (Theobald), close to his side."

The charge of the Light Brigade at Balaklava, led by Lord Cardigan in 1854, was made through the mistake of a superior officer; and the six hundred men rode "Into the jaws of Death" because they were commanded to do so, but the "Forlorn Hope" rode "Into the jaws of Death" a willing sacrifice for their country's honor, and for the protection of their comrades in arms. In the history of the world there has never been recorded a braver act than was performed by Samuel A. Theobald on that 5th day of October, 1813.

Following the battle of the Thames there were a large number of English prisoners brought to Frankfort, Kentucky, and confined for a considerable period in the State penitentiary. The officers vigorously resented this treatment which they designated "ignominious," but little sympathy was aroused on their account. The murders and barbarities at Raisin and Meigs had not put these men of the Forty-first Regiment in a position to ask or expect much from Kentuckians. These prisoners were subsequently exchanged, but not for some months.

After the battle of the Raisin the bodies of the dead soldiers were left unburied, and were devoured by dogs and hogs. Many months after that Governor Shelby directed that the bones of all the brave men who were killed or died, and remained unburied, should be collected and properly interred; sixty-five skeletons were found and buried.

"On July 4, 1818, they were removed and reinterred in the cemetery at Monroe, Michigan; after that a committee was appointed at Detroit to bring them there, where they were again interred. In 1834 the boxes containing these bones were removed to Clinton Street Cemetery in Detroit. In September of the same year they were again exhumed, and placed in boxes marked "Kentucky's gallant dead, January 18, 1913 (should have been January 22-23), River Raisin, Michigan," and brought to Frankfort, where they were again buried, and they will doubtless remain forever in the State Lot in our "Beautiful City of the Dead."

To the shame of Kentucky be it said that no man knows at this day where the bones of these honored dead are buried. The removal to Kentucky was prior to the time the present cemetery was purchased and a part of it dedicated to Kentucky heroes. At that time the cemetery was back of Thorn Hill, and even tradition is silent as to whether or not these bones were removed to the new cemetery.

James Y. Love, the only son of Mrs. Elizabeth Love, joined Captain Dudley's company. She was at first very much grieved, but after thinking over the matter said: "But I would despise him if he did not want to go." She prepared with her own hands the uniform he wore and he went with his mother's prayers, and a mother's love.

Mrs. Elizabeth Love was one of the strong women of pioneer days; she was the wife and afterwards the widow of Major Thomas Love, who was an officer in the army of General Wayne, and served in his western campaigns. The time of enlistment of Major Love having expired he located permanently in Frankfort.

Mrs. Love was noted for her social and Christian virtues. For many years she and her husband were proprietors of a hotel known as the "Love House," where they entertained Aaron Burr, and other noted men of that day. She was remarkable for her personal beauty and grace of manner, and her literary attainments were marvelous considering the age and the section of the country in which she lived. She was a woman of strong character; on one occasion when she was a young lady, the Prince, afterward King of the French, was traveling through the United States, she attended a ball given in honor of the King. He was struck with her graceful movements, and commanding air, and did her the honor to single her out as his partner for the dance; she declined this flattering preference to the mortification of the Prince and to the surprise of all, but her reason for not dancing was that she had only a few moments before refused to dance with one of her neighbor's sons, and if she must give offense she would rather offend the illustrious foreigner than one of her own companions and countrymen; she tried at all times to be just; she sought for the right and when found she fearlessly followed it. She was one of the great women of this country.

It was she who established the first Sabbath schools in this country, and which were also the first established in this State; her influence was always for good. For a period of fifty years she was a resident of Frankfort. "None knew her but to love her, none named her but to praise." She died at Frankfort on the 19th day of January, 1845.

Another strong character those times produced was Col. Anthony Crockett, a native of Virginia. He was born in 1758; he enlisted in the Revolutionary war in 1776, and only left the army when peace was declared; he was at White Plains, Brandywine, Monmouth, Saratoga, Germantown, Princeton and Trenton. At the battle of Brandywine when LaFayette was severely wounded Col. Crockett took him in his arms and carried him to a place of safety. When General LaFayette visited Frankfort in 1825 he expressed great pleasure in meeting him again.

In 1784 he came to Kentucky and purchased from his brother-in-law, James Arnold, a tract of land located on the Lawrenceburg road about three miles south of Frankfort, which tract of land remained in the hands of his descendants for more than a century.

In 1790 he was a member of the Virginia Legislature from Kentucky; in 1796 and 1799 he was a member of the Kentucky House of Representatives from Franklin county. When the war of 1812 came on he was exempt from military service, but he volunteered and rendered valiant service, though he was then an old man. For thirty years he was Sergeant at Arms of the Kentucky Senate. He died in 1838, and was buried in the Benson church yard in Franklin county. He was a man of fine physique, six feet three inches in height; he was gentle by nature, but fearless and valiant in battle.

In the year 1813 William Arnold and John A. McDowell were admitted to practice law in all the courts at Frankfort. On February 15th of that year William Trigg resigned as Clerk of the County Court and Fleming Trigg was appointed in his stead. On the same day Silas M. Noel produced credentials of his ordination and of his being in regular communion with the Baptist Society, and having taken the oath of fidelity, a testimonial was granted him in due form.

On April 19, 1813, William Hall resigned as Sheriff and John A. Mitchell was commissioned Sheriff, with John J. Marshall and others as his sureties. On the same day Anna Arnold was appointed Administratrix of Berrisford Arnold. The order recites the fact that Berrisford Arnold was killed at River Raisin, and the next succeeding order recites that Benjamin Hickman was elected Jailer of the county to take the place of Paschal Hickman, who was murdered in his tent after his surrender at the same battle.

On May 13th Jephtha Dudley, a magistrate of Franklin county, resigned as magistrate and was commissioned an officer in the United States Army. On the same day Theodrick Boulware, a Baptist preacher, was granted a testimonial and empowered to celebrate the rites of matrimony.

On June 21, 1813, William E. Quarles was commissioned Sheriff of the county, and John Parker was granted the right to erect and operate a grist mill on Glenn's Creek; this mill was operated for more than half a century; a part of the old dam still remains to mark the site.

The Order Book of the County Court shows that tavern keepers were allowed to charge not exceeding the following rates, to-wit: for supper and breakfast, 25 cents each; dinner, 37 cents; grain, per gallon, 12½ cents; horse at hay one night or twenty-four hours, 25 cents; Maderia or other imported wines, $2.00 per quart; Jamaica spirits, French brandy or Holland gin, 50 cents per pint; county made gin, 18 cents per half pint; Sangaree, or punch, 75 cents per quart.

George Major was admitted as an attorney at the Frankfort bar September 20, 1813. During this year a new jail was built at a cost of one thousand dollars. This jail was located on Clinton street where the colored Methodist church now stands; the jail had formerly been on Holmes street, nearly opposite the woman's entrance to the State Penitentiary.

There was an act of the Kentucky Legislature, approved January 24, 1812, for the benefit of William and Lapsley McBride. The act recites that their father, Col. William McBride, had been appointed commissioner to open a road from Holstein to Crab Orchard and that he was killed at the battle of Blue Licks, having received no part of the consideration for said work. The act authorizes the issuing of warrants for 2,800 acres of land to his said sons.

Henry Davridge, Circuit Judge, had for his associate Circuit Judges Nathaniel Richardson and Hugh Innis for many years prior to 1813; and for many years subsequent thereto his associate Judges were Nathaniel Richardson and Silas M. Noel.

There was an act of the Kentucky Legislature to incorporate the Frankfort Library Company, approved January 13, 1812.

Fleming Trigg resigned as County Court Clerk, April 18, 1814, and Willis A. Lee was appointed in his place.

John J. Marshall was appointed magistrate April 18, 1814, and during the same year John Green established a ferry across the Kentucky river at the mouth of Glenn's Creek; this ferry was afterwards known as Arnold's ferry for many years, later it was known as Cardwell's ferry. It was the most important crossing on the river outside of Frankfort. Mrs. Mary E. Johnson, daughter of John Cardwell, and granddaughter of James Arnold, still owns the Arnold homestead (1908) located opposite the mouth of Glenn's Creek on the south side of the river, having inherited same from her grandfather; it was a part of ten thousand acres of land granted to him in 1784 for services in the Continental army.

During the same year John Green also established a warehouse for tobacco, flour and hemp at the mouth of Glenn's

Creek; John Green was a Baptist preacher; he was uneducated, but a man of strong character, and did much good in his day and generation. On one occasion while holding divine service, he had his song book up-side-down, and some one called his attention to the fact. He said it made no difference to him, he could read as well that way as if it was right-side-up.

In the year 1814 John D. Cook and Samuel D. Fishback were admitted to practice law in Frankfort. In the same year Benjamin Hickman was elected jailer.

The county levy was fixed at $1.25 each "titheable" for the year 1815.

In the year 1814 James Russell established a mill on the south fork of Benson Creek that has been one of the noted landmarks of the county for nearly a century.

In the year 1815 Richard Taylor and John J. Marshall were appointed commissioners to superintend the reconstruction of the county jail, the cost of which was not to exceed twenty-five hundred dollars ($2,500.00). At the same term of court commissioners were appointed to act with commissioners from Shelby county to build a bridge across Big Benson, at Bohannon's ford, but the cost was not to exceed four hundred dollars ($400.00), for Franklin county's part of the contract.

In June, 1815, William Samuels produced a commission from the Governor appointing him Sheriff of the county. At the same court Charles S. Todd and John H. Todd were admitted to practice law.

John J. Marshall resigned the position of magistrate August 19, 1817. On the same day the Trustees of the town of Frankfort complained of the manner in which Sunday taverns were run, and they asked that the licenses of Leonard Altemus, William Duckham, James W. Pruett, George W. Gayle, James Hampton, William Downing and Lewis Pruett be revoked.

In August, 1817, Lewis R. Major was appointed magistrate, and during that year a grist mill and saw mill was built on Elkhorn, near Jones' station.

Francis P. Blair, Jacob Swigert and Thomas A. Marshall were admitted to practice law. John Bartlett was appointed Sheriff June 16, 1817. On the same day on motion of Reuben

THE HISTORY OF FRANKLIN COUNTY. 65

Medley, a Methodist minister, oath was administered and certificate issued.

On September 15, 1817, the following order was entered, to-wit: "This Court doth certify that Western B. Thomas, who intends making application for license to practice law, is a man of honesty, probity and good demeanor."

"A report of the inspectors of the Frankfort warehouse state that during last season they received 389 hogsheads of tobacco, and have shipped 306, they also report the warehouse in bad condition."

Given under our hands this 17th day of November, 1817.
(Signed) "JAMES & BROWN."

"Also that they received 38 hogsheads at Leestown and shipped 27; they also report this warehouse out of repair."

In the year 1817 there were assessed 2,206 titheables at one dollar per tithe.

In 1818 Joseph M. White and Harry J. Thornton were admitted to practice law. During this year Achilles Sneed built a water grist mill at the Falls of Big Benson, which place is now known as Conway's mill.

During this year Jeremiah Green, a Baptist preacher, and Eli Smith, a Presbyterian preacher were granted certificates by the county court.

The bridge at Hardinsville was rebuilt during this year. On December 22, 1818, Benjamin Hickman resigned as Jailer, and Stanley P. Gower was appointed in his stead.

The income of the county for the year 1819 was three thousand dollars. During the year 1819 Isaac Caldwell, Martin Marshall, Silas M. Noel, Robert Hughes, Nathaniel Sawyer, Horace Warring and George Oakley were admitted to practice law at Frankfort. Philip White was appointed Sheriff of the county June 28, 1819.

At the September term 1819, the following order was entered: "It appearing to the satisfaction of the Court, that the bridge across Big Benson on the lower road to Shelbyville has been completed agreeable to contract, it is therefore ordered that the Sheriff of this county pay to Charles S. Todd the sum of $480.00 for doing the stone work, and to Joseph Russell the sum of $247.00 for doing the wood work of said bridge."

Isaac Caldwell was County Attorney by appointment during the year 1819. John Bartlett, as Sheriff, failed to pay the money which he had collected for the county and there were a great many suits filed against him and his sureties during the year.

Jacob Swigert produced a commission from G. Slaughter, Governor of the Commonwealth, appointing him a magistrate which position he held for many years.

In 1820 a contract for building a jail yard and a jailer's residence was entered into; the wall around the yard was to be twelve feet high, made of brick, with a timber on top, well secured. The residence and yard were to cost three thousand dollars ($3,000), the residence was back of the jail on Lewis street, now Elk Avenue.

In the year 1820 there were 2759 tithes assessed in the county, and there were fifty-seven roads in the county to which hands and overseers were appointed.

The first man charged with murder after the conviction of Henry Fields in 1798, was Benjamin Mayhall in July, 1814; he was tried by a jury and acquitted. There were several indictments for murder during the years 1818 and 1819. Thomas P. Major, James Ransdale, Zepheniah Jackson, Elijah Kendall, Jeremiah Kendall, Jacob Holeman and William P. Greenup were all charged with murder. The indictments against the Ransdales, Jackson and the Kendalls were for the murder of Albert Carter in July, 1818. The charge was for "Striking said Carter with a certain gun of the value of ten dollars, which the said Wharton Randsdale in both his hands, then and there had and held, etc."

The Commentator gave the following account, headed:

"INHUMAN OUTRAGE."

On Friday, the 10th inst. a most savage and atrocious murder was committed on the body of Abraham Carter, a respectable citizen of Franklin county. The scene of this diabolical butchery was at the Forks of Elkhorn, in the porch of a tavern occupied by Mr. Benjamin Luckett. Mr. Carter was stabbed in the groin, his skull was broken to pieces by a gun, and other parts of his body injured; he expired in a few hours. The indictment against Holeman gives not only the historical fact of the crime, but it shows the particularity with which indictments were drawn. The indictment charges that Jacob H. Holeman and William P. Greenup, of Franklin county, "Not having the fear of God before their eyes, but being moved and seduced by the instigation of the Devil, on the 16th day of July, 1819, with force and arms, in the county aforesaid, in and upon Francis G. Waring, in the Peace of God, and of said Commonwealth then and there being feloniously, willfully and of their malice aforethought did make and assault, and that the said Jacob H. Holeman, a certain pistol, then and there loaded and charged with gunpowder, and one leaden bullet, which pistol, he, the said Jacob H. Holeman in his right hand then and there, had and held to, against and upon the said Francis G. Waring, then and there feloniously, willfully and of his malice aforethought, did shoot and discharge giving to the said Francis P. Waring then and there with the leaden bullet aforesaid, by the said Jacob H. Holeman, in and upon the right breast of him, the said Francis P. Waring, a little behind the right pap of him, the said Francis P. Waring one mortal wound of the depth of nine inches, and of the breadth of half an inch, of which said mortal wound the aforesaid Francis P. Waring then and there instantly died."

The indictment further charges that Willson P. Greenup was present, aiding, abetting, etc. After a long trial the jury brought in a verdict of "not guilty."

At the July Court, 1819, the grand jury indicted the County Court "For not keeping a sufficient jail." There was a verdict and judgment against the defendants. The defendants thereupon moved the court to "set aside and arrest the judgment herein for the following reason, viz: The Court erred in giving judgment for money when the penalty is imposed in tobacco."

There was an act to establish an Independent Bank at

Frankfort, approved January 26, 1818. It was denominated the Frankfort Bank with a capital stock of $500,000.00, divided into 5,000 shares of $100.00 each; under the direction of John H. Hannah, Henry Crittenden, Samuel Lewis, William Hunter and George Adams; at the same session the trustees of Frankfort were authorized "to open a street upon the top of the bank of the Kentucky river between Ann and Wapping streets, by extending Ann street down and Wapping street up said river, said street to be 30 feet wide and shall be called and known as "Water street."

This improvement has never been made, but the necessity for it has been urgent for the past century.

There was an act approved January 31, 1818, which authorized a company to "make an artificial road from Lexington, by the way of Versailles, to Frankfort" and the same act provided for the re-incorporation of the Frankfort and Shelbyville turnpike road.

Public roads and water-ways were the only means of transportation known to the people at this early period in their history. Much attention was paid to the construction of roads, and every available means was used in securing water transportation.

There was an act of the Kentucky Legislature, approved February 10, 1819, "To Incorporate a company to improve the navigation of Elkhorn." The purpose for which the corporation was formed is set out as follows: "That a company be incorporated to improve the navigation of Elkhorn, commencing at the mouth thereof on the Kentucky river, thence up Elkhorn to the Forks thereof, thence up the north Fork to the neighborhood of Georgetown and from the Forks up the south Fork to the neighborhood of Lexington."

The capital stock was one hundred thousand dollars. Books were opened to take subscriptions at Georgetown, Versailles and Lexington.

In 1820 the Governor was authorized to make such repairs on the "Governor's house" as he may deem necessary for the preservation of the building and the decent appearance of the house, and for building a brick stable and carriage house on said lot."

A few of Franklin county's public men of this period are mentioned as follows: George Adams, represented the county in the Kentucky Legislature in 1810, 1811 and 1814; Martin D. Hardin in 1812, 1818 and 1819; John Arnold in 1813; John J. Marshall in 1815 and 1816; Philip White also in 1816; George M. Bibb in 1817; Charles S. Todd in 1817 and 1818; Harry Innis was Judge of the United States Circuit Court for the District of Kentucky from 1784 to 1816; John Brown was twice a Representative and three times a Senator in the Congress of the United States.

Thomas Todd was Judge of the Court of Appeals in 1801, Chief Justice in 1806, and was an Associate Justice of the Supreme Court of the United States from 1807 to 1816.

Harry Toulmin was Secretary of State under Governor Garrard from 1796 to 1804.

Isham Talbott was a member of the State Senate from 1812 to 1815, and was United States Senator from 1815 to 1825.

George Madison was State Auditor from 1796 to 1816, and was Governor of Kentucky in 1816.

George M. Bibb was a Judge of the Court of Appeals of Kentucky in 1808, and was Chief Justice in 1827; he was again Chief Justice in 1827; he was United States Senator from 1811 to 1814 and from 1829 to 1835, and was Secretary of the Treasury under President Taylor in 1849.

Humphrey Marshall was United States Senator from 1795 to 1801, and was a member of the Kentucky Legislature from Franklin county in 1808 and 1809. He was the author of Marshall's History of Kentucky.

William Littell was Reporter of the Court of Appeals, and was compiler of the Statute Laws of Kentucky.

Martin D. Hardin was a Major in the war of 1812; Secretary of State during Governor Shelby's second term and was United States Senator in 1816.

John J. Marshall was Representative of Franklin county

in the Kentucky Legislature in 1815, State Senator from 1820 to 1824, and Court of Appeals Reporter from 1829 to 1832.

Charles S. Todd was Colonel on the Staff of General Harrison in the war of 1812; was Secretary of State under Governor Madison; Representative of Franklin County in the Kentucky Legislature in 1817 and was the Agent of the United States to Columbia, and minister to Russia under President Harrison in 1841.

CHAPTER VII.

From 1820 *to* 1830.

The records of the County Court show that during the year 1821, a bridge was built across the Leestown branch near its mouth; this stream has more recently been known as the Cove Spring branch.

William T. Johnson was appointed keeper of the Benson bridge; his especial duty was to take the drift from the bridge, and protect the bridge during high tides.

Stanley P. Gower who had been appointed Jailer to serve out the unexpired term of Benjamin Hickman, was re-appointed for the full term.

Scott Brown being the oldest magistrate from a point of service, was appointed, and commissioned by the Governor as Sheriff of the County June 18th.

The County Court made an agreement with Francis P. Blair who was at that time Clerk of the Franklin Circuit Court, to build a Circuit Clerk's office on his lot, located on the corner of Broadway and Lewis streets. This office was located where Kagin's restaurant now stands; the Court House at that time was on the southeast corner of Capital Square, just across the street from this office.

During the decade from 1820 to 1830 eight men in the County made proof that they had been Revolutionary soldiers, and were placed on the pension list. Their names are as follows: John Saterwhite, John Story, Matthew Cummins, Lieut. Samuel Woods, James Montgomery, Henry Roberts, Mashack Pearson and James Bisco. In addition to these, there was proof introduced to show that Capt. Matthew Jouett died from the effects of a wound received in that war, and that John Jouett was his only son, and heir at law.

At the end of this decade there were forty-three Revolutionary soldiers living in Franklin County; in addition to the eight above named there were on that roll the following, to-wit: Austin Lawler, Captain; Moses Hawkins, Moses Perkins, James

THE HISTORY OF FRANKLIN COUNTY.

Hayden, Thomas McQuiddy, Joseph Vance, John Oliver, Capt. Joseph Mitchell, Capt. Thomas Patterson, Alexander McClure, John Stephens, Thos. C. Scroggins, John Steele, Levi House, James Hayden, Benjamin Penn, John Jacobs, Philip Webber, Ambrose White, Lawrence Gordon, George King, Basil Carlisle, Robert Craig, Philemen Grancy, Dr. John Roberts, Samuel Syeva, Major Thomas Quirk, John Reading, Robert Hedges, Col. Anthony Crockett, Silas Douthett, James Taylor, John Magill and Thomas Keaten. A large number of the Revolutionary soldiers who lived in the county died prior to the year 1820.

In the year 1822 the order abolishing the office of County Attorney was rescinded, and an order entered re-establishing that office, and fixing the salary at one hundred dollars per year; and thereupon Harry J. Thornton was appointed County Attorney.

During the same year the County Court appointed Achillies Sneed, Allen F. Macurdy, Jepthia Dudley, Roger Devine and Amos Kendall, commissioners to let out and superintend the re-building the County Jail, and repairing the Jailer's residence. A full description of the plans is given in the Order book "G," page 291, Franklin County Court Clerk's office. These buildings were located on Clinton and Lewis streets, across from Bowman Gaines' livery stable, and where the colored Methodist church now stands.

In 1820 the Franklin County Court established the town of Lawrenceburg. In 1822 James Parker and James B. Wallace were appointed patrols for that town, and in 1827 the Legislature took that portion of Franklin County to help form the County of Anderson.

In the year 1822 there were 2611 tithes assessed in the county at $1.37 1-7 per tithe. During this year Charles S. Bibb and Patrick H. Darby were admitted to practice law.

In this year there was passed an Act to amend the Act incorporating the Frankfort and Shelbyville Turnpike Road Company. Section two of said Act was as follows: Be it further enacted that the said Company of Frankfort and Shelbyville are authorized and empowered to erect one tollgate at or near Matthew Clark's in Franklin County; provided, that said Company shall not receive more than half the toll heretofore allowed by law, and provided further, that all the citizens southwest of the Kentucky river, residing in Franklin County shall pass toll free on all County Court days, and election days.

In the year 1823 John McIntosh was appointed Jailer, and Daniel James came into court and resigned his office as keeper of the stray pen in the County, and thereupon Simeon Beckham was appointed to fill that office. At the same term of Court the overseers of the roads leading through Lawrenceburg were directed to work and keep in repair the street and alleys of that town.

Porter Clay, a Baptist preacher, and brother of Henry Clay, and John J. T. Mills, a Methodist preacher, were granted testimonials of honesty, probity, etc., and were empowered to perform marriage ceremonies.

On account of the death of Willis A. Lee, Clerk of the Franklin County Court, Alexander H. Rennick was appointed Clerk, and Andrew R. Lindsey was appointed deputy on November 15th, 1824. During that year Jacob Swigert resigned the position of magistrate and accepted that of Clerk of the Court of Appeals.

In 1823 there were assessed 2771 tithes at 75 cents each, and in 1825 there were 2908 tithes assessed at one dollar each.

In the year 1824 the County Court directed John Brawner to build a bridge across main Benson Creek. Scott Brown's term of office having expired, Clement Bell was appointed Sheriff in June, 1823; and the office becoming vacant, John Walker was appointed in 1824.

In 1822 there was an Act of the Legislature establishing a public Library at the seat of Government; this was the beginning of a magnificent Law Library, and also of a good collection of miscellaneous books. The same Legislature added to Franklin County all of that part of Owen County, "Beginning at West's Landing on the Kentucky river, running to Van West's including Saint West's in Franklin County; thence a straight line to the nearest point of the Franklin and Owen County line."

The keeper of the Penitentiary was authorized to build a smoke-house within the Penitentiary; at that time a great deal of pork was packed in and about Frankfort. Pork packing was one of the chief industries of the County for many years.

In the year 1821, it was resolved by the General Assembly of the Commonwealth of Kentucky, that a tombstone be erected to the memory of General Charles Scott, a hero of the Revolution. General Scott died in 1820, at his home in Woodford county, aged eighty years. His remains were interred in the Frankfort Cemetery, November 8th, 1854. (See Sept. Register, 1903.) One to the memory of Col Christopher Greenup, and one to the memory of Major George Madison, late Governors of Kentucky, with suitable inscriptions on each, and that they be furnished by the keeper of the Penitentiary, and that the same be placed over the respective graves, under the direction of the Governor.

In 1825 Thomas Page was allowed the sum of $280.00 for his services in erecting monuments over the graves of the late Governors Madison and Greenup, and the late Thomas Dollerhide, Senator from the Counties of Pulaski and Wayne, and inclosing the same. In 1842 the remains of these distinguished men were removed from the burying ground north of the city, to the Frankfort Cemetery, and new monuments were erected by the State.

In 1821 the Legislature passed an Act abolishing imprisonment for debt, and subjecting equitable interest to execution. This very materially affected the interest of all debtors in the County; the wonder is that such a relic of barbarism should have been permitted to remain so long upon the statute books of the State.

Some time prior to 1816 the State granted certain lottery privileges, and from the proceeds four thousand dollars were raised with which a church was built on the Public Square; it was located on the southwest corner near Broadway and Madison streets; it was non-sectarian, and was used interchangeably by all denominations. This was the first church built in the town, and was for many years the only church. In 1821

"There was an Act to amend an Act concerning a House of Public Worship in the town of Frankfort;" the amendment repealed the power of the Governor to appoint, and empowered the pew-holders, and the qualified voters of the City of Frankfort to elect "The Trustees of the House of Public Worship in the town of Frankfort."

At the same term the Governor was empowered to have a stone wall built in front of the "Governor's House" and have same properly coped. John Bartlett, John Crutcher, and James I. Miles were empowered to build a bridge across Main Elkhorn, where Knight's bridge is now located, and they were granted the right to charge and collect certain tolls, from parties crossing same.

The first Sabbath school in Kentucky was established in March, 1819, in Frankfort, with from thirty to thirty-nine scholars. During the year ending September 30, 1822, those who distinguished themselves by their assiduity were, A. M. B. Crittenden, who memorized 2,851 Bible verses in twelve months; Cornelia Crittenden (six years of age), 2,177; Margaret B. Sproule, 2,022; Emily South, 1,908; Cordelia Price, 1,514; Maria R. Miles, 2,010; Elizabeth S. Todd, 1,373; Ann Price, 1,202; Ann Miles, 1,039; Catherine Baltzell, 1,028; Jane Castleman, 742; Gabriella Lewis, 565; Maria Lewis, 544; Agnes Todd, 471; M. A. Watson, 404; Margaret Smith, 558; Arabella Scott, in six months, 893; Elizabeth Scott, in five months, 719; Nancy McKee, in four months, 601; Louisa Jones, in three months, 630; Mary Lafon, in three months, 364. The number of verses memorized by all the scholars, collectively, is 36,640. One class during two years and a half attendance read the Bible once entirely through, and some books of it several times over, memorized from five to seven thousand verses each—were perfect in Brown's, and the Assembly's Shorter Catechism—had each searched out, transcribed and memorized nearly six hundred verses of Scripture proofs in support of the doctrines which they had been taught, and had drawn, and studied maps of such parts of the world as are connected with Scripture history." (Collin's History, page 244.)

The Sabbath school referred to, was founded by Mrs. John Brown in the Love House.

There was a resolution appointing a committee to inquire into the cause of the destruction of the Capitol, approved November 5, 1824.

John Brown, Daniel Weiseger, John Harvie, John J. Crittenden, Peter Dudley, Evan Evans and James Shannon (all of them were Frankfort men) were appointed a committee to rebuild the State Capitol; they were empowered to employ an architect, and given general power in reference to the re-construction, and directed to build "a suitable Capitol." Fifteen thousand dollars in money was appropriated, and the commissioners were allowed to use certain material at the Penitentiary, not exceeding in amount the sum of five thousand dollars.

The above-named Commissioners, with this small sum, supplemented by private donations from the public-spirited citizens of Frankfort, constructed the old Capitol building, which still stands as a monument to them. When it was built it was considered a model of neatness and beauty; the plan of architecture was the finest ever used on the Western Continent, and it was second only, in point of grandeur to the National Capitol at Washington.

In order to understand the condition of affairs in the county in 1825, it is necessary to consider a few things which led up to the formation of the Relief and the Anti-Relief parties. These parties grew out of the disturbed condition of the financial affairs of the country prior to the year 1818, which resulted in the withdrawal of gold and silver, to a large extent, from circulation and an inflated currency having taken their places.

Kentucky had chartered about forty banks, with an aggregate capital of more than ten million dollars. During the summer of this year, the State was flooded with the paper of these independent banks. Speculation ran rife; the whole country seemed to have gone daft on the subject. Within the next two years nearly all of these banks had failed, and the pressure of debt was greater than was ever known before in the history of the country. The Legislature of 1819-20 passed a twelve months replevy law; and that of 1821 chartered the Bank of the Commonwealth; this bank was not required to redeem its notes in specie, though made receivable for taxes and all debts. Lands owned by the State west of the Tennessee river were pledged for the final redemption of these notes, and if a creditor refused to receive this paper for his debt, the law permitted the debtor to replevy for two years. This new bank issued such an immense quantity of paper money that it sank to less than half of its nominal value, and creditors had to take it at its nominal value in full payment of their debts, or wait two years, and risk the bankruptcy of their sureties on the replevying bonds.

The power of the Legislature to pass such an Act, was held by Judge Clark, of the Circuit Court, to be unconstitutional. The Legislature was convened in extraordinary session which resulted in nothing being done. The case was then passed on by the Court of Appeals, and the opinion of the lower Court was upheld. The opinion of the Court of Appeals created the greatest excitement that was ever known in the State, the financial interests of almost every man in the State were effected in some way, and the storm center was at Frankfort. The Relief party was led by Judge Rowan, Judge Barry, Col. Solomon P. Sharp, T. B. Monroe, and others, while the Anti-Relief side was led by Judge Robertson, John J. Crittenden, Ben Hardin, Robert Wickliffe, and men of that class, the leaders on both sides being men of national reputation.

The campaign for State offices and seats in the Legislature for 1824 was very bitter, and all kinds of charges and counter charges were made against the candidates. The result was favorable to the Relief party, though the majority was not sufficiently large to give that party the two-thirds majority which was necessary in order to remove the incumbent members of the Court of Appeals.

The Relief party not being able to impeach the Court, it passed a bill repealing the Act by which the Court of Appeals had been organized; after which an Act was passed re-organizing the Court. The debate continued for three days, and to a late hour each night, John Rowan for and Robert Wickliffe against the measure. The most intense excitement prevailed; the lobbies were crowded to suffocation. Visitors from every section of the State were present, State officials were on the floor of the House lobbying for the Relief party, "Great disorder prevailed, and the Governor himself was heard to urge the calling of the previous question." The bill was passed by a good majority in both the House and Senate, and was signed by the Governor as soon as presented to him, and in a short time a new Court of Appeals was organized. The old Court claimed that these proceedings were irregular, unconstitutional and void, each claiming to be the Court of last resort; this was the condition of affairs when the race for the Legislature was made in 1825. Never before in the history of the State had the passions of men been raised to such an intense heat; the excitement during this campaign was greater than ever known before. The Relief or New Court party was largely dominant in Franklin County, and in order to overcome the majority, the Old Court party selected as candidate for the State Legislature John J. Crittenden, who had represented the State in the United States Senate, and who had served in various other public places with distinction; a man of international reputation, and the idol of Franklin County people, as a lawyer, statesman and orator. He was the greatest this country possessed in that day.

The New Court party selected a man of national reputation in the person of Col. Solomon P. Sharp; Col. Sharp had served two terms in the Kentucky Legislature, and two terms in the lower House of the United States Congress, and was then holding the position of Attorney General of the State, which position he resigned for the purpose of making the race for Representative. Col. Sharp was also an orator, and a great friend of the common people. It was thought he was the only man in the county who had a chance to defeat Mr. Crittenden. The contest between these two great men soon became of State and almost of National interest; every method known to modern politics seems to have been used in that day. The political contest stirred the county of Franklin from center to circumference; the friends of both sides were accused of buying votes, and of voting ex-convicts, charges being made that the inmates of the Penitentiary were dressed in citizen's clothes and voted for the New Court candidate. Col. Sharp had sixty-nine more votes than Mr. Crittenden, but in the contest between Mr. Crittenden and James Downing another representative of the New Court party, the popularity of Mr. Crittenden easily overcame the majority which Col. Sharp had secured in his race. During these exciting times, there were five newspapers ably edited and published in Frankfort. The Argus and the Patriot were advocates of the New Court. The Spirit of Seventy Six, The Commentator, and The Constitutional Advocate were for the Old Court.

Amos Kendall, the editor of The Patriot, was, perhaps the ablest editor of that period; he was in the very thickest of these political fights, and thereby made for himself a reputation which ultimately placed him in the Cabinet of President Jackson, as Postmaster General. His opponents called "The Patriot" the "mud machine;" on the other hand, John J. Marshall, and Patrick Henry Darby were able representatives of the other side. "The Spirit of '76," edited by John Marshall, was called by "The Patriot," "The Spirit of Seven and Six Pence."

In the year 1826, "The Commentator" and "The Constitutional Advocate" were consolidated; Mr. Kendall in "The Patriot" announced that fact as follows: "Hymeneal." "Married on the —— inst. in this place, by the R—— ——. "Spirit of Seven and Six," the notorious agent and Prime Minister of their Majesties, the ex-Judges of the Old Court, Mr. "Commentator" to the refined and celebrated lecturess, on the moral integrity of the laws, Miss "C. Advocate." We are told that the parties were full cousins before their marriage. The public may expect a hopeful issue from this alliance, especially, as it is understood that Messrs. Darby and Dana are to stand "God Fathers" to the whole progeny. We learn that a few days after the ceremony, the Duke of the Town Fork, (Robert Wickliffe) the common friend and patron, paid them a visit to congratulate them on their happy union; what sum he will settle upon them, has not been made public.

"But from the known munificence of His grace, every confidence is entertained that it will be amply sufficient to maintain them during the reign of their present majesties."

The fight which was made against Col. Sharp in his race to represent the county was extremely bitter. The friends of the old court party used every influence known in political warfare to deaden his influence and defeat him. John U. Waring, the most desperate and dangerous man who ever became prominent in the politics of the state, was an ardent supporter of the old court; he and Patrick H. Darby became the most active and bitter partisans against Col. Sharp. Waring wrote him two letters threatening his life, in which he boasted that he had stabbed to death six men. He also took up the story in reference to Miss Ann Cook, and gave it to the public in flaming hand-bills.

Patrick H. Darby took up these charges against Sharp, and a great many threats both private and public were made against him. Darby was heard to say on several occasions, that if Col. Sharp was elected that he would never take his seat, and that he would be as good as a dead man.

The legislature was to convene on Monday morning, November 6th, 1825. On Sunday evening prior thereto, Col. Sharp in the interest of his candidacy for speaker (and to which office he doubtless would have been elected) went first to the Weiseger House where the Capitol Hotel now stands, and met several members of the legislature, and later came down to the Mansion House, at that time the chief hotel in the city, and stayed there until about twelve o'clock, after which he went to his home on Madison street, (the house in which Mr. Louis Weitzel now lives) and about two hours later was called to his door and assassinated. The assassination created the wildest excitement in Frankfort. The legislature convened that day, and authorized the Governor of Kentucky to offer a reward of three thousand dollars for the apprehension and conviction of the assassin. The trustees of Frankfort were convened in extraordinary session, and they too offered a reward of a thousand dollars for the same purpose. After some days suspicion rested on Jereboam O. Beauchamp, a young attorney located at Glasgow, Kentucky. A warrant was sworn out, and Beauchamp was arrested, and brought to Frankfort, he was tried before an examining court, and released from custody; he at the time asserting his innocence, and volunteering to stay in Frankfort for ten days, in order to give the Commonwealth ample opportunity to investigate the case, and formulate a new charge. The Commonwealth first asked for fifteen days and at the expiration of that time fifteen days longer were granted in which to secure sufficient evidence.

In the meantime John U. Waring and Patrick H. Darby had come under suspicion, Mrs. Sharp having stated that the voice of the assassin had sounded to her like that of Waring, a warrant was issued for him and sent to Woodford County, and from there to Fayette County, but an investigation revealed the fact, that Waring had been shot through both hips, on the Saturday preceding the Sharp tragedy, which precluded further proceedings against him. Patrick Darby having heard that he was suspected of the murder, in order to relieve himself from that suspicion, undertook to investigate the facts in the case, and it was through his efforts that Beauchamp was again arrested, and afterward convicted.

The indictment now on file in the Franklin Circuit Court Clerk's office charges that, "Jereboam O. Beauchamp, Attorney at Law, on the sixth day of November, 1825, in the night of the same day, at Frankfort, Franklin County, Kentucky, with a certain dirk, which he held in his right hand, stabbed upon the front side of the body of said Solomon P. Sharp, and two inches below the breast bone of the said Sharp, a mortal wound, of the breadth of one inch, and of the depth of six inches, from which he instantly died." Patrick H. Darby was one of the chief witnesses against Beauchamp.

In the fall of 1824, Beauchamp had applied to him to bring a suit against Col. Sharp, for certain claims, which are not specified in the record on file in the Franklin Circuit Court Clerk's office. In this conversation Beauchamp stated that he had married Miss Cook, and spoke of Col. Sharp's bad treatment of her, and he swore that if he ever saw him he would kill him, and said if he could not see him in any other way, he would ride to Frankfort, and shoot him down on the street. (From evidence in record.)

Darby went to Simpson County, the home of Beauchamp, to look up the evidence in the case; while there he found a man by the name of Capt. John F. Lowe, who had received a letter from Beauchamp, in which there were some very damaging admissions against himself. (Letter still on file in Clerk's office.)

Lowe also stated that Beauchamp gave him, on Thursday evening, within a few hours after his return from Frankfort, a detailed account of the assassination, and in conclusion said, "Don't speak of this before Ann, you know what a talk has been about Sharp and her, none of the people about here talk to us about him, they all think he was the cause of her leaving society."

There has been a doubt in the minds of some, as to whether or not the alleged confession of Beauchamp was made by him; but it is perfectly evident from the facts disclosed in the damage suit of Darby vs. Jereboam Beauchamp, uncle of the assassin, that Beauchamp did make the confession, which was given to the public at that time. Darby not only sued Col. Beauchamp, but he also brought suits for libel against Dr. Leander Sharp, Mrs. Eliza T. Sharp, and Amos Kendall. The three last named cases were tried in the Woodford Circuit Court on a change of venue.

The depositions of Ben Hardin, General Andrew Jackson, and Governor Desha were taken as witnesses in these cases, all of which are on file in the clerk's office of the Woodford Circuit Court.

Jereboam O. Beauchamp was the second son of a man who owned a small farm and a few slaves, his father gave him a good English education. Young Beauchamp tried merchandising, and afterward school teaching, and at the age of eighteen commenced the study of law at Glasgow, Kentucky, where he became acquainted with Col. Sharp. While Beauchamp was at Glasgow, Miss Ann Cook purchased a small farm in Simpson county, about a mile from the home of Beauchamp's father, after his return to his home, he persisted in calling on her, and in a short time he found himself desperately in love with her; he solicited her hand in marriage, she refused him, but afterward said she would marry him upon the condition that he would kill Sharp; Beauchamp agreed to her proposition, and he came to Frankfort for that purpose in the fall of 1821, but his plans failed and he returned to his home without accomplishing what he came for.

In the year 1824, Beauchamp became of age, and about that time was admitted to the bar, and in a short time thereafter, (June, 1824), he and Miss Cook were married. He came to Frankfort after dark on Sunday night, November 5th, 1825; after considerable effort he secured a room at Joel Scott's, who was at that time warden of the penitentiary; he brought with him a mask, two pairs of yarn socks, and some old clothes; he slipped out of his room early in the night, hid his shoes, coat and hat down on the river near the foot of Mero street, and waited there until about two o'clock in the morning.

In his confession, he describes the circumstances of the murder as follows: "I put on my mask, drew my dagger, and proceeded to the door, I knocked three times loud and quick, Col. Sharp said: "Who's there"—"Covington," I replied, quickly Col. Sharp's foot was heard upon the floor, I saw under the door he approached without a light, I drew my mask from my face, and immediately Col. Sharp opened the door, I advanced into the room, and with my left hand I grasped his right wrist, the violence of the grasp made him spring back, and trying to disengage his wrist, he said, "What Covington is this," I replied John A. Covington, "I don't know you," said Col. Sharp, "I know John W. Covington." Mrs. Sharp appeared at the partition door, and then disappeared, seeing her disappear, I said in a persuasive tone of voice, "Come to the light Colonel, and you will know me," and pulling him by the arm, he came readily to the door, and still holding his wrist with my left hand, I stripped my hat and handkerchief from over my forehead, and looked into Col. Sharp's face. He knew me the more readily I imagine, by my long, bushy, curly suit of hair. He sprang back, and exclaimed in a tone of horror and despair, "Great God it is him," and as he said that he fell on his knees.

I let go his wrist, and grasped him by the throat, dashing him against the facing of the door, and muttered in his face, "die you villain." As I said that I plunged the dagger to his heart.

The next morning Beauchamp left Frankfort, "when the sun was about half an hour high, reached his home on Thursday afternoon, and was arrested the afternoon of the next day. There were a large number of witnesses in the case, who came from all parts of the State. Beauchamp was prosecuted by Charles S. Bibb, (Prosecuting Attorney for this district), Daniel Mays, and Attorney General James W. Denny, he was defended by J. Lacy, Samuel Q. Richardson, and John Pope. Mr. Pope closed the argument for the defense. He became so personal against Darby, that Darby attempted to assault him with his cane, and this little incident caused the wildest excitement, which resulted in a stampede from the court room.

"The Patriot," of May 22nd, 1826, says, "During the whole of this tedious trial, the courthouse has been crowded with citizens and strangers, and the most intense interest is manifested by every person acquainted in the least with the history and progress of the prosecution. The trial has been managed on both sides with considerable ability, which has much increased the public curiosity and interest." Beauchamp was on Friday, after an hour's consultation, found guilty by the jury. His wife on Saturday, was taken before the justices, on a charge of having been accessory to the murder, but was acquitted."

Beauchamp was publicly hanged on Friday, July 7th, 1826. At an early hour the drums were beating, and a large crowd of people from all sections of the country, filled the streets, and thousands surrounded the gallows, which was erected near where the Glenn's Creek road intersects the Versailles road on what is now the F. M. I. property. Mrs. Beauchamp remained with him until just prior to his removal to the scaffold. Some days prior to this she had secured a vial of laudanum, which was divided between them, each of them took a dose, but it failed to have the desired effect, she then secured a case knife, and about ten o'clock in the morning, on the day of the execution, upon the urgent request of Mrs.

Beauchamp, the guard went up the ladder, and turned the trap door, when Beauchamp called to him, he immediately returned, and Beauchamp said, "we have killed ourselves," the guard then says that Mrs. Beauchamp had a knife in her hand which was bloody about half way up. It was found that Mrs. Beauchamp had a stab a little to the right of the centre of the abdomen, which had been laid bare for that purpose; she did not sigh or groan, or show any symptoms of pain. The guard asked Beauchamp if he was stabbed, he said "yes," and raised his shirt which had fallen over the wound, he was stabbed about the centre of the body, just below the pit of the stomach, but his wound was not so wide as that of his wife, Beauchamp said that he had stabbed himself first, and that his wife had taken the knife from him, and plunged it into herself.

Beauchamp was in a dying condition when he was taken to the gallows, he was too weak to stand while the rope was being adjusted around his neck, he was held by two negro men, for that purpose.

The Patroit says: "It was now half past twelve o'clock. The military were drawn up along Lewis street, and the alley in continuation which passes by the Jailer's house, surrounded by an immense crowd, all of whom were listening with intense interest to every rumor from the dying pair. As Beauchamp was too weak to sit on his coffin, in a cart, a covered dearbon had been provided for his convenience to the gallows. He was now brought out in a blanket and laid in it. At his particular request, Mr. McIntosh (the Jailer) took a seat by his side. Some of the ministers of the gospel had taken their leave of him just as they were ready to start, he said in a severe tone, "I want to see Darby." He was asked why he wished to see Darby, he said "I want to acquit him."

"The drums beat, and the military, and crowd moved up Clinton to Ann street, along Ann to Montgomery (Main) street at Weiseger's tavern, and up Montgomery street to the place of execution.

Beauchamp and his wife died about the same hour, and were buried in the same grave at Bloomfield, Kentucky. Each of the three victims of this tragedy, had a wound located at almost the same point in the body.

Beauchamp and his wife, Col. Sharp and his wife, were members of the most prominent families in the State at that time. Col. Jereboam Beauchamp, the uncle of the assassin, had represented Washington County in the Legislature, and was at that time prominent in the political and social circles of the State.

The Cook family was very wealthy and influential, Miss Ann Cook and her sister were noted belles, they traveled in elegant style with their servants and a team of four horses, and out-riders, they were educated, vivacious and fascinating and notwithstanding they were known as great gamblers, they were leaders in the society of the "four hundred." They were frequent visitors at Frankfort, and they never failed to visit the city during each legislative session.

Dr. Leander J. Sharp's description of Miss Ann Cook (in his vindication of his brother) is not very complimentary to her, and does not accord in any way with the traditions concerning the Cooks. He says: "Ann Cook was then (1820), according to the most accurate information I can obtain, thirty-three or thirty-four years old, she was small in stature, probably not exceeding ninety pounds in weight, had dark hair and eyes, dark skin, inclined to be sallow, a large forehead, slender nose, large mouth, large chin, face tapering downward, and lost her fore teeth, was stoopshouldered, and in no way a handsome or desirable woman."

Col. Sharp was thirty-eight years old when he was assassinated, he was raised on a farm, commenced to practice law at Bowling Green when he was nineteen years of age, four years later he was elected to the Kentucky Legislature, and from 1813 to 1817 was a member of Congress. In 1818 and 1819 he was again in the Kentucky Legislature, and was married to Miss Eliza T. Scott during that term, and moved to Frankfort. He was appointed Attorney General in 1821, and resigned in 1825, he was one of the great men which this State has produced, and had scarcely reached the prime of life when the tragic end came. Col. Sharp and his wife are buried in the Frankfort Cemetery, a square marble shaft about ten feet tall, and each side about eighteen inches broad, marks their last resting place, on the west side of the shaft in this inscription: "Eliza T., wife of S. P. Sharp, died January 4th, 1844, in her 46th year," under which the following "Precious in the sight of the Lord, is the death of His saints," on the east side is: "Solomon P. Sharp was assassinated while extending the hand of hospitality on the morning of November 7th, (should be 6th,) 1825, and beneath this is, "What thou knowest not now, thou shalt know hereafter."

General LaFayette visited Frankfort on May 14th, 1825. He came by way of Lexington, seven military companies, and a large number of private citizens in carriages, on horse-back, and afoot, met him on the Lexington road, and escorted him to the city, a grand dinner and public ball were given in his honor.

The portrait of General LaFayette was painted by Matthew H. Jouett, and placed in the Hall of Representatives in 1825, this portrait is still in a good state of preservation, it now hangs near the speaker's chair in the House of Representatives.

Hon. Thomas Todd died February 7th, 1826, at a meeting of the members of the Frankfort Bar, convened at the office of Jacob Swigert, Esq., for the purpose of testifying their respect to the memory of the deceased, John J. Crittenden being called to the chair, and C. S. Bibb being appointed Secretary, the following preamble, and resolutions were unanimously adopted: "The members of the Bar of the Federal Circuit Court, for the district of Kentucky, have learned with feelings of deepest regret, that the Hon. Thomas Todd, Judge of the Supreme Court of the United States, and the Seventh Judicial Circuit, departed this life about three o'clock this morning: Therefore, Resolved, That in consideration of the acknowledged virtues, and distinguished talents, learning and character of the deceased, and the high respect and esteem entertained for him by the Bar, they will attend his funeral on tomorrow, and wear crape on the left arm for the space of thirty days.

C. S. BIBB, Secretary,   JOHN J. CRITTENDEN,
February 7th, 1826.   Chairman.

THE HISTORY OF FRANKLIN COUNTY.

In the year 1826, there were 2,998 tithes assessed in the county.

In 1827 Simeon H. Crane, a Presbyterian preacher located in Frankfort, he presented testimonials to the court, and was granted the right to perform the marriage ceremony.

During the legislative term of 1827, a small part of Henry County was added to Franklin, this addition included "All the inhabitants of Flat Creek, and LeCompte's bottom. During this session (1827) the county of Anderson was formed out of the counties of Franklin, Mercer and Washington, Lawrenceburg had prior to that time been in Franklin County. Several sheriffs of Franklin, and at least one Representative of the county lived in that part which was cut off, to help form Anderson; this was the last section cut from Franklin to help form a new county.

Simon Kenton visited Frankfort, in January, 1827, he was then about seventy years of age, he traveled from Urbana, Ohio, to Frankfort, on horse-back, when he reached the town a large number of people went to see him. His old clothes were soon replaced by good ones, he was taken to the House of Representatives, and introduced to the members of the General Assembly. His land had been sold for taxes. The Legislature passed an Act releasing this land from taxation, and granting him a pension of $240.00 a year. The Act was approved January 24th, 1827.

There was also an Act of this session which granted to Samuel South the right to plead the loss of certain money, as an off set in the case of the Commonwealth against him, this suit was for money, which he claimed was burned, when the Capitol buildings were burned, in 1824, Samuel South being at that time State Treasurer. The State House was burned November 4th, 1824. (See chapter on State Capitols.)

In 1828 there was "an Act to incorporate the Lexington and Frankfort Turnpike or Railroad Company." The road was to be fifty feet in width, on which there was to be built an artificial road, at least twenty feet in width, of firm, compact and substantial materials, composed of gravel, pounded stone or other small hard substances, in such manner as to secure a good foundation, and an even surface. Gates were to be erected not closer than five miles apart.

Lewis Sanders, Jr., was elected county attorney for the year 1828. The court allowed one dollar per day for an ox team, when used on the county road.

During the year 1828, the bridge at Hardinsville, between Franklin and Shelby was rebuilt by order of the county court. George Gill was the contractor and builder.

In 1829 the county court elected Mason Brown, County Attorney to take the place of Lewis Sanders, Jr. Mason Brown continued in the office for several years, and was very active and efficient in looking after the county affairs.

In 1830, John Brown was appointed Sheriff of the county, and John McIntosh was re-elected Jailer.

A State road was made in conformity to an Act of the Legislature from Frankfort to Ghent, Kentucky.

Patrick Major built a grist mill on Benson Creek opposite Buzzard's Roost.

On motion of Edmund H. Taylor, the county court granted him the right to establish a ferry from the west end of Broadway street, to the west side of the river below the mouth of Benson, at the same place which was granted to Christopher Greenup in 1805, and was also granted the right to establish a ferry from said Broadway street to the west side above the mouth of Benson Creek.

The members of the Legislature from Franklin County, from 1820 to 1830, are as follows:

John H. Todd, 1820.
Benjamin Taylor, 1821.
Edward George, 1822.
Humphrey Marshall, 1823.
William Hunter, 1824.
John J. Crittenden, 1825-29-30-31-32.
Lewis Sanders, 1826-1828.
James Downing, 1827.
The population of Frankfort:

THE HISTORY OF FRANKLIN COUNTY.

In year 1800.......................... 628
In year 1810.......................... 1,099
In year 1820.......................... 1,917
In year 1830.......................... 1,987
In year 1840.......................... 1,917
In year 1850.......................... 3,308
In year 1860.......................... 3,702
In year 1870.......................... 5,396
In year 1880.......................... 6,958
In year 1890.......................... 7,892
In year 1900.......................... 9,487

Daniel Weiseger, the grandfather of General Daniel Weiseger Lindsey, and John B. Lindsey, came to Franklin County in its very early history, he was recognized as one of the most substantial citizens of that period, for several years he was the clerk of the Franklin County Court, and for many years was connected in some way with every public improvement which was made in the city of Frankfort, and the county of Franklin; some of which improvements are still standing as monuments to his intelligence and integrity. In May, 1826, Daniel Weiseger was suggested as a proper person to be President of the Bank of the Commonwealth: "The Patriot said of him at that time, "Who is it that does not know Daniel Weiseger? He has grown with Frankfort; his moral character is above suspicion, his integrity proverbial. He had by his industry amassed a handsome property, most of it has been swept from him to pay the debts of friends, to whom he had lent his name as security. He has raised a large family of children, who are now supported by his unyielding industry; he has a high claim upon the town of Frankfort, nay the county and State, for his public spirit and liberality. His experience eminently qualified him for the duties of the office. Everything in the opinion of candid men conspired to recommend him as a proper person to fill the vacancy."

Daniel Weiseger died in Frankfort, February 22nd, 1829, and was buried in the Frankfort Cemetery.

CHAPTER VIII.

Course of Events from 1830 to 1840.

The rules governing Fiscal Court of the county in 1830 were as follows:

1st. The Jailer shall keep the court house clean, make fires and ring the bell at ten o'clock on each court day.

2nd. After the bell has been rung the Sheriff shall call the Justices, not present.

3rd. If three or more Justices attend, a court shall be formed, the oldest in commission taking the chair as President.

4th. The Sheriff shall attend and open court and see that good order is preserved during its sitting.

5th. Any person wishing to make a motion to the court shall by himself or attorney respectfully address the presiding Justice.

6th. The President shall keep a docket of all motions and those first made shall have precedence unless the parties or some of them be females, in which case their business shall be first in order. He shall propound all questions to the court and take their opinions thereon. He shall not have a vote, unless in case of an equal division of the court, and in that event, he shall give the casting vote.

7th. It shall be deemed a breach of good order for any member of the court to pronounce an opinion in his place or to hold any communication with parties in court, other than through the President, or leave their seats without his permission.

8th. The Clerk shall record the proceedings of the court as directed by the President and shall make no entry unless directed by him.

The period from 1830 to 1840 was productive of more internal improvements for the County of Franklin than was any other decade during that century. It was an era of McAdam roads, railroads and slack water navigation. On April 8th,

1834, several gentlemen were elected and constituted a board of internal improvements for the County of Franklin, consisting of Jeptha Dudley, E. P. Johnson, Chas. S. Morehead, Jamerson Samuel and Philip Swigert.

In 1831, Massie Franklin was appointed a Captain of Patrols in the town of Frankfort, and Joseph Clark, who was a son of Matthew Clark, was appointed Sheriff of the county, in the place of his father, who died before his term of office expired; he came into court on several occasions and offered to qualify, and each time was refused. He appealed to the courts and in 1834 the Court of Appeals affirmed his appointment. In the meantime Lewis R. Major was appointed and acted Sheriff of the county. In this year Alexander W. Macklin was a constable of the county and John J. Marshall kept a tavern.

On December the 19th of this year, John H. Hanna, J. Dudley and J. J. Marshall conveyed to the county of Franklin, a lot on St. Clair street, known as the J. Dudley Plank lot; this is the lot upon which the present court house was erected in 1835.

In June, 1832, it was ordered that the plan submitted by Gideon Shryock for a new court house be adopted. Gideon Shryock was also the architect who drew the plans and was the general superintendent of the old Capitol building which was completed in 1829.

It was ordered that James Shannon, Chas. S. Morehead and Henry Wingate be appointed commissioners to superintend the erection of the court house. The building was completed in 1835, but the county did not pay for it, in full, until 1840. The structure was of stone, two stories high, with four stone columns in front. The court room, the Justices' office and Sheriff's office were on the first floor, the jury rooms were on the second floor. There have been only a few changes in it since that time, until 1909. A few years prior to 1909 there was a movement inaugurated to erect a new building, but the county had reached the limit of indebtedness as prescribed by the Constitution of the State. The Court of Appeals rendered an opinion on March 25th, 1909, which declared that the County Court could not issue bonds for that purpose, unless authorized by a majority of the votes in the county. After this decision the County Court undertook to repair the old building, at an expenditure of about $40,000. The back end of the old building was torn away and the side walls extended back thirty feet, and the offices for county officials are located on the first floor; the back rooms were constructed of concrete and these fire proof rooms used for the County and Circuit Clerks' offices. The top was taken off and the walls extended up about three feet and the court room located on the second floor, the court room is about the same size of the old room, but it is well ventilated with plenty of light. The plan of architecture is very old, but the building is comfortable and convenient and it is quite a handsome structure.

In 1831, there was an act of the Legislature to incorporate the trustees of Mount Pleasant schoolhouse in Franklin County; Scott Brown, Thomas Parker, Benedict Carlisle and John B. Crockett were the incorporators. At the same session there was an act to incorporate the Frankfort and Lexington Turnpike Road Company; John J. Crittenden, Samuel P. Weiseger, Churchill Samuels and Ambrose W. Dudley were some of the incorporators.

The turnpike company for the Georgetown and Frankfort road and for the Frankfort, Lexington and Versailles road were also incorporated at that session of the Legislature. The Legislature appropriated $25,000 with which to help build the Frankfort, Lexington and Versailles road.

In 1832, there was a ferry established by Swigert, Milam and Humphries across from the South end of Washington street, to what is now the city school property. In 1833, Rev. P. S. Fall was principal of the "Female Eclectic Institute" near Frankfort. Lewis R. Major owned a farm of 375 acres on the Lexington road, three and one-half miles from Frankfort, on which he had a horse mill and a distillery, at which he made one barrel of whiskey per day; this is the farm on which Col. Chas. E. Hoge resides.

The Lexington and Ohio Railroad which is now the Louisville and Nashville, was surveyed in 1830, the survey of the route showed the altitude of Lexington to be four hundred and thirty feet above that of Frankfort. On Oct. 22nd, 1831, the first sill for the laying of rails for this road was placed, in the presence of a large concourse of citizens and strangers. The road was built in 1832-3-4. It was completed to the top of the hill known at that time as the incline plane, which was about one mile from the city (it is now within the city limits) in 1834.

The road was opened for travel from Lexington to Frankfort about the first of January, 1835. Horse power was first used.

The Commonwealth, dated January 2nd, says, "On Tuesday last, the railroad was opened from the City of Lexington to the head of the incline plane which is about one mile distant from town. Two cars filled with gay and delighted passengers traversed the whole line with great ease and celerity. On the arrival of the cars at the head of the plane a salute was fired by the citizens in honor of the event. The first cars were drawn by horse power. The locomotive engine designed for this road was brought to Frankfort by the boat "The Argo," in a short time after the road was opened for transportation. On January the 31st, the Commonwealth stated that the locomotive arrived at the head of the plane on Tuesday morning, January 25, having performed the trip from Lexington in two hours and twenty-nine minutes. It was now permanently placed on the road. In a few days Frankfort and Lexington will be only one hour a part. Frequent accidents occurred on the road, caused, largely by the insecure method of tieing the rails, which consisted of a thin piece of iron about three inches wide and about one-half of an inch thick, spiked to large stones laid lengthwise, sometimes one of these iron bars would become detached at one end and would run through the floor of the car, and sometimes on through the top of the car. On March 23rd, 1836, a very serious accident occurred about two miles east of Frankfort, the locomotive with the tender was thrown off the track and precipitated over the embankment which was about thirty feet high, and carrying with it the passenger car. A Mr. Tinder, of Woodford, and Mr. Willson, of Madison, Ind., were instantly killed and a child of Mr. Tutt died a short time after the accident. Nearly all of the passengers were injured, four of whom were dangerously so. The cause of the accident was attributed to the great speed at which the train was going, all the passengers united in the statement that the car was moving with very rapid velocity varying in their estimates at from twelve to fifteen miles per hour.

The contractors while constructing this road worked about seven hundred men, with the necessary teams, carts and machinery; some sections of it have been preserved in the Kentucky State Historical rooms. The construction and operation of it was the beginning of a new era in the County of Franklin and the City of Frankfort. The company had a great deal of trouble in securing their right of way and it was only secured after many months of costly litigation.

The running of steam cars was of great interest to the people of Franklin county, they would go for miles to see one pass. After the line was completed from Louisville to Frankfort, one of the first passenger cars came up on Sunday morning, it passed the North Benson Baptist church while the Rev. Frank Hodges was preaching, when his congregation got up to see it, he announced that the congregation was dismissed for a few moments and he went out with his auditors to see the train; after it had passed, they all went back and the preacher finished his discourse.

Steamboats did a flourishing business on the Kentucky river during this period. The Argo was designed and built for the Kentucky river trade and it made regular trips between Frankfort and Louisville. It was in commission from about 1832 to 1840. The new light draught upper cabin steamboat, Plough Boy, was placed in the Kentucky river trade in 1834, with J. C. Harris as captain. The Clinton was placed in the same trade about the same time. The Eagle was placed in the Frankfort and Louisville trade in 1837. The John Armstrong and The Frankfort, both of them new boats, which were built especially for the Kentucky river trade, were placed in the Frankfort and Louisville trade in 1839. The lock and dam in the Kentucky river, known as lock No. 4, was built by the Commonwealth of Kentucky during this decade. It is located a few hundred yards below the city limits. The lock walls measure two hundred feet in length and thirty feet perpendicular. They were finished in the very best style, the material is of gray limestone, quarried in the immediate vicinity. The lock with the dam cost the State $120,000. The dam affords slack water navigation for steam boats of 200 tons, for fifteen miles above Frankfort. The lockage was completed and navigation opened February 18, 1840. By act approved March 22, 1880, Kentucky granted to the United States government all rights to control the navigation and improvement of the Kentucky river.

During this period of her history Frankfort was known as a manufacturing center. Almost everything was manufactured by her enterprising citizens. Some of the things made at that time are as follows:

Glass, shoe brushes, counter brushes, hacklers, files, log chains, harrow teeth, ox rings, staples, pot hooks, drawing chains, axes, sixth chains, streaches, hoes, plough shares, irons, grid irons, scrubbing brushes, plough clevices, whitewash brushes, whet stones, copper hooped cans, wash coolers, stillyards, cut nails, brads, boxes, boxes for sardines, tomb tops, monuments, bagging, rope, jeans, linsey, iron and castings, flour, meal, pork, all kinds of lumber of every description, pork barrels, lard kegs, wagons, carts, steamboats, etc. A. W. Dudley manufactured carpet filling and chain, spun cotton, candlewicks, bats, twisted thread, etc. In 1833 Thomas McGain manufactured stoves, stove pipes and tallow candles. In 1836 John D. McGee and John C. Melcher put a sheet iron manufactory in operation. They manufactured stoves and all kinds of tin ware. Their establishment was on St. Clair street, two doors north of Main street.

During the same year the Franklin Paper Mill, three miles from Frankfort, on main Elkhorn, was placed in operation. This mill was run by E. H. and S. Steadman. They manufactured every description of paper of the best quality. They shipped the manufactured products from this mill to all sections of the country. They paid good prices for clean cotton and linen rags.

In 1837, Mr. David McChesney established a coach manufactory in Frankfort, which proved to be a very successful business for many years. There was also a chain factory in operation in 1838. It was located on Montgomery (Main) street, nearly opposite the Weiseger House. It was run by Ambrose C. George.

Cholera made its appearance in Frankfort on June 26, 1833. The first person to die in the city was a negro, the property of Mr. Philip Swigert, but there had been several deaths in the county prior to that time. Within three weeks after that seventeen persons died in Frankfort of that dread disease; three white and seven colored died in North Frankfort, and four white and three colored in South Frankfort. During this epidemic there were about one hundred and fifty deaths in the county.

Margaret Arnold Cardwell, the youngest daughter of James Arnold, and the wife of John Cardwell, died of cholera at her home opposite the mouth of Glenn's Creek in August, 1833. Tradition of the family says that she was a very handsome woman, and that she was stronger than any ordinary man. She could stand with both feet in a half bushel measure and shoulder a sack with two bushels of wheat in it.

In 1833 there was an act providing for the election of a State Librarian and prescribing his duties, and appropriating $500 per year, for a period of five years, with which to purchase books, the purchase to be made by the Librarian under the directions of the Court of Appeals.

In the year 1834 an arsenal was built on the northeast corner of the public square. James Davidson, Thos. S. Page and Edmond H. Taylor were the commissioners who constructed it. A gun house, situated on the public square, was pulled down and the material used in constructing the arsenal. The cost of the erection was two thousand dollars.

The 4th of July, 1834, was a great day for Frankfort. The celebration was had at Cove Spring. Four thousand people were present. Four fat beeves were barbecued, and one hundred and forty lambs and shoats. There were bacon and hams without number, and all other articles needful for a sumptuous feast. John J. Crittenden read the Declaration of Independence, and Chas. S. Morehead was toastmaster. There were people present from forty-two different counties in the State, besides many people from other states. Feasting and speechmaking continued throughout the day. A New Englander, styling himself "a Yankee," said in a letter dated July 3, 1834: "I rode from Lexington to this place today and have been gratified for the first time since I left my native land with a view of New England scenery, its rocky hills, its lofty precipices, its deep luxuriant valleys, and its winding streams. Frankfort is fairly wedged in among the hills, except on one side, where the river meanders. But the town makes up for the oddness of its locality by its pleasant scenery and pleasant society. Tomorrow there is to be a great public festivity in this place called a barbecue. I anticipate great pleasure in being present. As you are not acquainted with anything of this kind I shall favor you with a description. This species of festivity had its origin in this State from circumstances connected with the history of the first settlement. The sparseness of the inhabitants, and at the same time their social disposition, led to neighborhood meetings, for the purpose of pleasure or of discussing local politics. The houses being too small to accommodate a large company, the only alternative was to seek a pleasant grove in the vicinity of a cool spring. Here rude tables were covered with the rich viands of the county, and after the repast was ended the young joined in a dance, while the old became spectators of the lively scene."

On Friday evening, July the 4th, he said: "I have just returned from the barbecue, much amused and much fatigued with the day's excursion. It is raining in torrents. You may just fancy yourself in my company and we will take the trip over again. Without wading a mile through mud and water, I will place you at once upon the ground. You wonder at the multitude of people. I suppose there are three or four thousand. You notice that inclosure with a crowd of anxious looking men around it—that is the bar, and within are several hogsheads of that famous beverage called mint-julip. This is made by mixing in proper proportions sugar, water, ice, mint and old whiskey, but I will not go into further particulars on the subject.

"A call is made for a speech. As might be expected, this call is for John J. Crittenden. He is a favorite, and he well deserves to be a favorite son of Kentucky. His personal appearance is good, his countenance, though dignified, is always lighted with a smile, and he possesses that peculiar power in oratory which can charm the learned and ignorant at the same time. His voice, though commanding, is rich and mellow in its tones, and a multitude would stand by the hour gazing on his glowing countenance and hanging with breathless silence on his words as they leap apparently unbidden from his lips."

On February 25th, 1834, Hon. John Breathitt, Governor of Kentucky, died in the city of Frankfort, of pulmonary consumption. By his request his remains were buried in Logan County. The procession was formed at an early hour, and moved from the capital to the Governor's mansion, where it was joined by the military. The religious ceremonies were performed by Dr. Noel and the Rev. Thornton Mills, after which the procession moved in the following order: 1st. The military. 2d. The joint committee on arrangements. 3d. The acting Governor and Secretary of State. 4th. The physicians. 5th. The Rev. Clergy. 6th. The pall-bearers, consisting of four members of the State Senate and eight members of the House, with the corpse. 7th. The relations of the deceased. 8th. The Senate, preceded by its Speaker and Clerk. 9th. The House of Represenatives, preceded by its Speaker and Clerks. 10th. The government officials. 11th. Citizens and strangers. The procession was the largest which had ever been seen in Frankfort. All the business houses were closed and great sorrow prevailed. After arriving at the farthest limit of South Frankfort the procession returned. The corpse was attended by citizens on horseback until it arrived at the county line, where a number of citizens of Anderson county received it and accompanied it to the Mercer county line.

In 1834 The Frankfort Lyceum was organized, with Charles G. Wintersmith as secretary. In 1835 John J. Crittenden resigned the office of magistrate. David Waits was appointed Sheriff, and John Buford was elected Jailer. In 1837 John D. Woods was appointed police judge of Frankfort. There was a never failing stream of water on the corner of Ann and Broadway streets, near where the Kendall property now stands.

In 1838 Edward S. Coleman was appointed Sheriff and Morgan B. Chinn became Jailer. In 1839 John C. Herndon became the County Attorney, and in 1840 John Watson became the Sheriff.

In 1837 small pox became prevalent in Frankfort, and in some sections of the county during that summer deaths occurred from its ravage. On Sunday morning, July 23, 1834, the middle arch of the St. Clair street bridge, which was then in the course of construction, gave way and all that part of the structure was precipitated into the river. The damage was so great that the company had to construct entirely a new bridge. On December the 26th, 1835, the middle span of the bridge fell a second time, the structure had been completed and had been in use just eight days when it fell, two wagons with their drivers and teams and six colored men were on the bridge at the time it fell. The wagons and teams were lost and two colored men were killed. One of the negroes belonged to Mr. Williams and was instantly killed. The other, the property of William S. Waller, died in a short time after the accident. In 1835 there were three newspapers published in Frankfort, to-wit: The Commonwealth, The Frankfort Argus, and The Cross. In 1837 there was a weekly paper edited and published by F. D. Pettit and J. H. Mayhall, which they called the Frankfort Farmer.

There was an act of the Legislature approved February 28th, 1835, which incorporated the town of Frankfort. This act defined the powers and duties of the officers of Frankfort, and granted many powers to the chairman and board of trustees. Prior to this date the town had been governed by the laws enacted by the Virginia Legislature, and under which the town of Frankfort was established.

In February, 1835, Samuel Q. Richardson, a prominent lawyer of Frankfort, was shot and killed by John U. Waring on the steps leading to the second floor of the Mansion

House. The Legislature was in session at that time, and the killing of such a prominent man as Mr. Richardson created the wildest excitement. Samuel Q. Richardson had defended J. O. Beauchamp for killing Col. Solomon P. Sharp in 1825, at which time he severely criticised the conduct of John U. Waring, in reference to that assassination, and after the trial was over Waring threatened to kill Richardson, but he did not carry out the threat until ten years later. Waring waived his examining trial, but he made a long speech before the examining court justifying the killing on the ground that Richardson had made threats. Waring was committed without bail. He spent three years in jail and was tried three times. The first and second trials resulted in a hung jury each time. On the last trial he was acquitted. Richardson was not armed at the time he was killed. His remains were buried at Lexington, Ky.

The name of John U. Waring appears for the first time on the criminal records of the county in 1818. At every term of the court after that for a quarter of a century he appeared as a defendant. He was before the court on peace warrants, almost without number. John U. Waring was a lawyer of some ability. For many years he owned a farm, which was afterwards known as that of R. K. Woodson, located on the Kentucky river across from the Big Eddy, he had a fine vineyard on it; he owned property in Frankfort and Versailles. He was prosecuted for the crime by Mason Brown and Lewis Sanders, Jr. He was defended by Frank Johnson, John J. Crittenden and Thos. F. Marshall.

On Saturday, the 7th day of March, 1845, John U. Waring was killed in Versailles, Ky. The Frankfort Commonwealth said of him: "Mr. Waring was himself a man of desperation and violence. He it was who slew the late Samuel Q. Richardson and he had been engaged in many a bloody encounter; indeed we can scarce remember when he was not notoriously at deadly feud with reputable citizens and he was commonly regarded as an enemy of mankind, having made few friends and many bitter foes."

A postmortem examination disclosed the fact that the

bullet had passed through his head, down his throat and had lodged in his lungs. It also disclosed a further fact long suspected, that he wore a strong coat of mail made of steel; he was shot from the garret of Shelton's tavern, a rifle was found there bearing marks of recent use. It was thought by some, that the son of the Jailer of Woodford County killed him, as that young man left in a short time after the killing. It seems that no special effort was made to locate the assassin, as it was generally considered that the country was well rid of such a bad character.

The attorneys at law living in Frankfort and practicing their profession in 1835, were: Thos. B. Monroe, John J. Marshall, Victor Monroe, Chas. S. Morehead, James T. Morehead, Mason Brown, Samuel Todd, Benj. F. Hickman, John L. Blaine, John C. Crittenden, Wm. H. Todd, Humphrey Marshall, Jr., Thomas N. Lindsey, William G. Talbott, William Owsley, Uriel B. Chambers, Austin P. Cox, O. G. Cates, John J. Crittenden, J. Swigert, James G. Dana, Benjamin G. Burks, Richard F. Richmond, Chilton Allen and Landon Thomas.

At an election of Trustees for the town of Frankfort in 1836, Philip Swigert was elected chairman, J. J. Vest, A. G. Hodges, G. E. Russell, Joseph W. Allen, James Shannon and Austin P. Cox were elected trustees and John C. Herndon was elected clerk.

In 1836, the high school which had been taught by the Rev. Wm. Purvance and the one taught by L. B. Nash were merged into one, which was called the Frankfort Academy. Mr. B. B. Sayre was one of the teachers in this academy; he afterwards became one of the most celebrated teachers in Kentucky. His influence has been felt, perhaps, more than any other one man who has lived in the State. He came from Virginia about 1835. He taught for many years. Pupils from all sections of the country came to him. For some years he taught where the Episcopal church now stands. From about 1842 to 1848, he taught in the building now known as the Lindsey law office on the corner of Main and St. Clair streets. He afterwards taught where Mr. J. A. Scott resides. He went to the Kentucky Military Institute in 1863, but taught there only a short time. He died in Frankfort April 28th, 1879, and is buried in the south west corner of the Frankfort cemetery. A few men of note who were taught by him are as follows: Gen. George B. Crittenden, Gen. Thos. L. Crittenden, Col. Eugene Crittenden, Gov. T. T. Crittenden, of Missouri; United States Senator Geo. Vest, U. S. Senator J. C. S. Blackburn, State Senator James Blackburn, Mr. John B. Lindsey, Gen. D. W. Lindsey, Judge P. U. Major, Col. S. I. M. Major, and many other men who have been important factors in the government of both State and Nation.

The fourth of July celebration in 1836 was held at "Stony Point" (on top of Fort Hill); a barbecue dinner was prepared for the hundreds who attended. John F. Levy read the Declaration of Independence and B. B. Sayre delivered the chief oration. Col. Peter Dudley and Col. John Woods were the marshals of the day and had charge of the immense parade. Orlando Brown, Lewis Saunders, Jr., Chas. S. Morehead, Col. R. F. Richmond and Col. E. H. Taylor responded to toasts on that occasion.

A public dinner was given to the Hon. John J. Crittenden at Bellepoint (Todd's spring), July 23rd, 1836; about five hundred people were present. Toasts were responded to by John J. Crittenden, James T. Morehead, B. B. Sayre and others.

Hon. Daniel Webster and family arrived in Frankfort on Friday evening, May 31, 1837, and left for Louisville on the following Monday morning. The citizens of Frankfort joined in giving him a hearty welcome, and all were anxious to see a man of such prominence. He was received a few miles from town by a committee of citizens on horseback, who escorted him to the residence of the Hon. John J. Crittenden, whose house was his home while he stayed in Frankfort. On Saturday he attended a barbecue which was prepared on the banks of Elkhorn, with the expressed design of enabling him to see "Old Kentucky as she is." He there met with citizens of all parties who extended to him a hearty welcome. He made a speech on that occasion which won for him the admiration and good will of all who heard him. The day was one which was long remembered by the citizens of Franklin County.

The Fourth of July celebration for 1837, was held in the Capitol building. Orations were delivered by Thomas B. Stephenson and Col. Victor Monroe, after the orations the company repaired to Fort Hill where they partook of an excellent barbecue, after which several toasts were responded to. The Hon. Jas. T. Morehead presided as Toast Master.

Hon. John Brown died at his residence in Frankfort, Ky., on the morning of August 29th, 1837. He was the son of the Rev. John Brown and Margaret Preston. He was born in Virginia, September 12th, 1757, and for two years he was the assistant of Dr. Waddall in a private school, after which he became a student at Princeton College and was there when the college was broken up by the Revolutionary war. Subsequent to this he volunteered in a company for the purpose of aiding Lafayette in his military operations in Virginia, after which he entered William and Mary College and after leaving there he commenced the study of the law in the office of Thomas Jefferson. Upon completing his legal studies he emigrated to Kentucky in the winter of 1782, and he continued to live in Kentucky until his death fifty-four years later. He was prominent in the events which preceded the separation of Kentucky from Virginia and no one contributed more than he to procure for Kentucky the full benefits of an unobstructed use of the Mississippi river. In the year 1785, he was elected Senator in the Virginia Legislature from the district of Kentucky, and in 1787, the Legislature elected him a member of the old Congress, by that election he became the first member ever sent from the western country to the Congress of the United States.

Upon the formation of the new consitution he was elected one of the first Senators from Kentucky, which honor was three times, consecutively, conferred upon him by the State. He retired from public life about the close of the year 1805.

In the year 1838, there were two bridge companies incorporated, one with the expressed intention of constructing a bridge from Washington street to the south side near the mouth of Benson creek, and the other to build a bridge across from the foot of Ann street. There was also an act approved February the 1st, 1838, the preamble and a part of which is as follows:

"Whereas it is represented to the present General Assembly that it is the desire and intention of a number of individuals to establish a public school suited to the wants and conditions of all classes of the Commonwealth, in the town of Frankfort, and whereas the Frankfort Seminary has been pulled down and removed from the public square, thereby depriving the citizens of the only house of public instruction in said town as well as the entire loss of the proceeds of six thousand acres of land granted by the Legislature to the County of Franklin for seminary purposes; and whereas it is a matter of great importance to the public, that the town of Frankfort shall be supplied with water, as well for private as for public uses, and it is represented to the General Assembly that the same can be done by conveying it from the Cove spring in the neighborhood of said town; and that the security of the private and public buildings thereof would be greatly protected. Section 1—Be it enacted by the General Assembly of the Commonwealth of Kentucky, that it shall be lawful for Edmund H. Taylor, Philip Swigert, Thomas S. Page, Mason Brown and John J. Vest to raise by way of lottery in one or more classes, as to them may seem expedient, any sum not exceeding one hundred thousand dollars to be appropriated, one-half for the use and benefit of a city school in the town of Frankfort, and the other half for the construction of such reservoirs, pipes, conductors, and other works, that may be necessary and proper to convey the water from the Cove Spring into said town, in such manner and quantities as the aforesaid persons may think suitable to the convenience of the people of said town and the safety of the private and public buildings therein." The act further provides that the managers shall execute a bond to the Commonwealth for a faithful discharge of their duties, and their powers are defined. The amount to be raised was to be paid to the Trustees and expended by them.

The provisions of this act were carried out; that part in reference to the public school became the basis of one of the best public schools in the State, the interest on the money raised has been used to pay the running expenses of the city school for three-quarters of a century.

The proposed water works were completed in 1839, at a cost of about $38,000 and the city was supplied with water by reason thereof until the latest improved water works were completed in 1886. At a meeting of the Board of Trustees of the town of Frankfort held on the 4th day of November, 1839, it was unanimously resolved: "That this Board entertains the highest respect for the integrity and moral worth of John Moore, Esq., and that they hereby tender him the individual thanks of the trustees and the acknowledgments of the citizens of the town for the faithful, skillful and workmanlike manner in which, as contractor for the water works, he has introduced fresh water into the town of Frankfort."

The pipes were supplied by a never failing spring known as Cove Spring, sufficiently elevated to throw the water into any building in the town.

The city sold these water works to the Frankfort Water Co., in 1885, for the sum of $20,000 in cash and for other valuable considerations.

The said company erected upon one of the hills south of the city two reservoirs of an aggregate capacity of five million of gallons, the flow line of which was two hundred and fifty feet above the intersection of Broadway and St. Clair streets. The pumping machinery has a capacity of delivering into the reservoirs 2,000,000 of gallons in twenty-four hours. The supply of water is taken from the bottom of the channel of the Kentucky river some distance above the sewerage of the city. The water mains are of the best quality of cast iron, tested to withstand a hydrostatic pressure of three hundred pounds to the square inch.

The original cost of the construction of the said water works was $125,000, to which has been added many thousands of dollars for improvements. Frankfort boasts of the best water works in the State.

The Kentucky Historical Society was incorporated by act approved February 16th, 1838. The act names the incorporators, empowers them to elect officers, make by-laws, select time and place for holding meetings and defines their powers. The preamble sets out in full the object of the society.

This society was re-incorporated in 1880, and re-organized in 1886. It was not until 1906 that the State gave any substantial aid; at that time there was an act appropriating five thousand dollars per year and providing for stationery supplies for the society and providing for the publication of The Register Magazine of the society, the purchase of objects of historical interest, and the payment of a Secretary-Treasurer.

The winter of 1838, was as delightful as any one could desire, there were neither snows, heavy rains nor hard freezes.

Rev. Joseph J. Bullock, of Frankfort, was named by the Governor for the office of Superintendent of Public Instruction, in 1838. This was a new office created by the Legislature. Other appointments for Frankfort men made at that time by the Governor, were John M. Bacon to be police judge of Frankfort, General Ambrose W. Dudley, Quartermaster General of the State of Kentucky and Hon. Jas. T. Morehead to be president of the Board of Internal Improvement.

In the summer of 1838, the locust desolated the whole country, they blighted the forests, herbs and fruits of the whole county.

Mr. John Harvie died at Frankfort September 26th, 1838. He was born in Virginia; he lived in Frankfort about thirty years. He represented Franklin County in the Kentucky Legislature in 1835. He was a man of superior qualities of mind and heart. He was one of the very finest specimens of the "Old Virginia Gentleman," and that term applying as it did to him with all its force, conveys the most perfect idea of his life and character. He was the father of Mr. John and Col. Lewis Harvie, who lived to be very old men and who also belonged to that old school of Virginia and Kentucky gentlemen. They died in Frankfort about the close of the last century. Col. Lewis Harvie was small in stature; he was very courteous and no one doubted his courage. On one occasion Judge William Lindsay was discussing some proposition before a Legislative committee at the Capital Hotel, at which time he made a statement in reference to Col. Harvie and to which he took exceptions. He took his watch from his pocket and holding it before him, he said: "Judge Lindsay, I will give you just three minutes in which to take back the statement which you have just made." Judge Lindsay had not thought of offending Col. Harvie and he promptly said: "I don't want that much time, Lewis, I will take it back right now;" this response raised a shout of laughter from those present, and each of the participants in the controversy thought that the joke was on his opponent.

On May the 9th and 10th, the first giraffe ever seen by the people of Frankfort was placed on exhibition; at that time it was considered one of the most wonderful of living creatures. Thousands of people from all sections of the country came in to see it. It attracted the notice of the press to a very unusual degree.

In 1839, Mr. Joseph Flood and Miss Eliza Ann Major, daughter of Rev. John S. Major, were married. The Commonwealth said of her: "We know that the happy bride has made a most seasonable choice and she is truly fortunate who has obtained, in this time of unprecedented drouth, not a mere sprinkling, but a whole Flood for her portion."

Governor James Clark died in Frankfort on the 27th day of August, 1839. There was a meeting of the citizens at the court house; Col. James Davidson was called to the chair and Hon. J. J. Crittenden, Col. R. F. Richmond and Orlando Brown were appointed a committee to prepare resolutions. His remains were accompanied from the Governor's Mansion to the top of the plain, by a large concourse of citizens on foot, in carriages and on horseback, the whole being preceded by Capt. Lockwood's infantry company. At the top of the plain it was placed in a car and escorted to Lexington.

On Tuesday night, August 27th, 1839, the whole world was gazing at the great beauty of the heavens, the Auora Borealis was brighter than was ever known before. The Commonwealth said: "The truth is, the imagination could not embody in its conception such peerless splendor, and human language never had the power to describe it."

The fourth annual fair of the Franklin Agricultural Society was held near Luckett's Tavern, at the Forks of Elkhorn, commencing Wednesday, October 9, 1839. One of the first fairs in the State was held a short distance below Frankfort, near Leestown. The first mention made of it was in 1798, but evidently a fair had been held there some years prior to that time, and the grounds at that place were used for many years subsequent thereto. There was also a race course in connection with it. The exact location or length of same is not known, but it was used for many years. The county records show that there were several indictments against parties for unlawfully selling whiskey on the race course, and at the fair grounds. During the summer and fall large crowds of men and boys would congregate there on Sunday for the purpose of horse racing, foot racing, cock fighting and whiskey drinking, which would some times end in a free for all fight. These Sunday meetings continued until they became a nuisance and the police authorities put a stop to them. The Franklin Association held a fair there annually until a new race course and fair grounds were constructed near the Forks of Elkhorn, which were used for nearly half a century. The buildings on these grounds were destroyed by fire a short time prior to 1860. These grounds were located on the farm owned by Col. Steve Black in 1909, a short distance from the Forks of Elkhorn. The fairs held there were attended by people from all sections of the State. The race course was a mile in length and was one of the most noted in the State. Some of the best horses of that day were run on it. It was known as the Capital Course. The advertisement of this course in the year 1840 was as follows: "Capital Course Races."

Races over the Capital Course will commence on Wednesday, the 6th day of May, 1840, and continue four days.

First Day—Cooper Stake, a silver pitcher, value $100, and $100 entrance, mile heats, closed with the following subscribers: W. W. Bacon, J. W. Fenwick, Col. Wm. Buford, Capt. J. A. Holton, Sidney Burbridge, Capt. Wm. J. Harris and Benjamin Luckett.

Second Day—Weiseger Stakes, three mile heats, purse $300.

Third Day—Two mile heats, silver pitcher, value of $100.

Fourth Day—A post stake, free for all, $50 entrance fee.
A. W. LOCKWOOD,
Treasurer.
H. BLANTON, Secretary."

In 1836 the third annual fair of the Agricultural Society was held on October 10th and 11th, one mile and a half east of Frankfort, on the farm of Isham Talbott, deceased. The location was a very favorable one, having every accommodation, etc. A public dinner and addresses were some of the attractions named. This place is known as the Dudley farm and is owned by the State in connection with the Colored Normal School. In 1874 there was a fair held at what is known as Woodland Park. In the years 1875-1880, inclusive, fairs were held at the R. P. Pepper race course and were largely attended. The colored people had a successful meeting and a creditable fair at this place in 1909, and for several years prior thereto.

A very successful fair was held in 1909, about one mile above Frankfort, on the Saffell farm. The grounds were located between the Kentucky river and the Lawrenceburg road. Large crowds were in attendance and the fair was in every way a success.

The following were the members of the House of Representatives from Franklin County from 1830 to 1840:

John J. Crittenden, 1830-1831 and 1832.
John J. Marshall, 1833.
Jamerson Samuel, 1834.
John Harvie, 1835.
Dandridge S. Crockett, 1836.
James T. Morehead, 1837.
Charles S. Morehead, 1838-1839 and 1840.

The population for Franklin County in 1830 was 9,234; in 1840 it was 9,420.

CHAPTER NINE.

Course of Events from 1840 *to* 1850.

In Order Book "L," pages 22, 23, 24 and 25 of the Franklin County Court Clerk's office, there is a long report of Samuel Todd and S. I. M. Major, Commissioners, as to the condition of the County Clerk's office, giving the number and condition of books, deeds, mortgages, orders, wills, etc., also itemizing and giving the condition of all other records in the custody of the County Clerk. The report closes by saying, "The Clerk's office is a small, one story building, very uncomfortable and unsafe; there is but one room and the floor of that very open, the walls very thin and slightly plastered."

There was a large influx of foreigners, especially Irish, to the county of Franklin in the year of 1840; at this date William H. Holman was the proprietor of the "Tavern on the Hill," which was located on the cemetery property, about four hundred feet from the entrance to the cemetery grounds.

Henry Clay spoke in Frankfort on national affairs, Sept. 2nd, 1840. Robert P. Letcher was inaugurated governor during this year. The address of welcome on the part of the city was made by B. B. Sayre, Capt. Lockwood's infantry and Capt. Goram's cavalry, both of Franklin county were in the parade; "The old Thames cannon was brought out upon that occasion and spoke with her accustomed cheery voice." The Thames cannon was also known as the Burgoyne cannon. It is a relic of the revolutionary war and also of the war of 1812. It was captured at the Battle of Saratoga, from the British army under Gen. John Burgoyne, by the Americans under Gen. Gates, Sept. 19th, 1777, and afterwards was surrendered to the British by General Hull August 16th, 1812, and recaptured by General Harrison and his Kentuckians at the battle of the Thames, October 9th, 1813. The cannon was presented to Governor Shelby and afterwards presented by him to the State of Kentucky. In 1909, Gen. P. P. Johnson, Adj. Gen. of Kentucky, placed it in charge of Mrs. Jennie C. Morton, Secretary of the Kentucky Historical Society. It is one of the most valuable relics now owned by the State.

James Harlan, of Franklin County, was appointed Secretary of State by Governor Letcher September, 1840.

The Legislature of Kentucky authorized a lottery drawing in the City of Frankfort for the benefit of the Shelby College. The drawing was at the Weiseger House October 14th, 1840, at 4 o'clock p. m. The payment of prizes was guaranteed by security, to the State; whole tickets sold for $3 and shares in proportion; packages of twenty-six tickets were warranted to draw at least one-half the cost of them.

The assessed valuation of the property in Franklin County at this time was as follows: There were 217,920 acres of land, which was valued at $1,777,089. There were 1,240 males over 21 years of age. There were 2,593 slaves, which were valued at $982,400, and thirty-five stores valued at $114,740. The total valuation of all property was $4,096,666. Negroes made up about one-fourth of the assessed valuation of the county, the average assessment being $378.50. The barter and sale of negroes was greater than that of any other property, the newspapers of that period were full of such advertisements as the following: "For sale—A very likely negro woman; a first-rate cook, washer, &c., and three children. Enquire at this office." "Negro girl for sale—I wish to sell a likely negro girl who is a good cook, washer and spinner; she is also honest." "The subscriber, living six miles south of Frankfort, near South Benson meeting house, has a very likely and intelligent mulatto boy, twelve years old, for sale; persons wanting such a boy would do well to call and see him, as I will sell a bargain, for cash in hand."

Hon. Geo. W. Craddock came to Frankfort in 1840 as a representative of Hart County. After his term of office expired he located here and became one of the leading citizens and attorneys of the capitol city. He took an active part in the politics of the city and State. On one occasion a mass convention was held in Frankfort and several politicians tried to make speeches for their candidate, but the electors had converted themselves into a howling mob, and they refused to listen to any orations on that occasion. Judge Craddock finally arose and commenced his address by saying: "Gentlemen and fellow-citizens, hoodlums and——" After one prolonged shout the crowd settled down and gave the judge a very respectful hearing. He married a Frankfort woman and they raised a large family of children. He died in Frankfort in 1898.

In 1840 Mr. James G. Dana, reporter of the Court of Appeals, died at his home in the City of Frankfort. For many years Mr. Dana was the editor of the Commentator, a newspaper published at Frankfort. He was distinguished for his ability as a newspaper man and as a lawyer. For many years he was the official reporter of the Court of Appeals, and the reports of that day bear his name.

On the 15th of December, 1840, Maj. George Swingle died at his home in Franklin County in his 84th year. He was an acting major under General Washington in the revolution. He was never known to take ardent spirits.

Hon. John C. Breckinridge was a citizen and resident of Frankfort for several years. His law office was on St. Clair street next to Mrs. Watson's boarding house. Gov. R. P. Letcher was located in Frankfort in 1845. His law office was on the west side of St. Clair street.

Dr. Luke P. Blackburn was also located in Frankfort at that time. He and Dr. Churchill J. Blackburn were partners in the practice of medicine. Their office was in the building erected by Dr. W. L. Crutcher on St. Clair street.

Prior to 1851 nearly all the traveling through the country was either by stage coach or horseback. There was a stage which left Frankfort for Louisville every morning at 8. It took nine hours to travel from Frankfort to Louisville. The fare was $2. There was also a stage to arrive from Georgetown each morning. It returned at 2 p. m. There was one which left Frankfort for Madison three times a week; also one to Lexington and Harrodsburg each morning.

In 1841 there were steamboats run from Bowling Green by the way of Green and Barren river navigation, up the Ohio and Kentucky rivers to the capital, for the accommodation of the members of the Kentucky Legislature. This was considered a revolution in the mode of travel between the two great divisions of the State.

The steamboats which were in the trade between Frankfort and Louisville during this decade were the Tom Metcalf, Bob Letcher, and The Ocean. The Blue Wing was built expressly for the Kentucky river trade, and was placed in commission in 1845. The Sea Gull in 1847. The W. R. McKee in 1845. The Isaac Shelby, Fashion and Kentucky about 1846. Other boats in the Kentucky river trade since 1850 were: The Planet, Little Ben Franklin, Oliver Anderson, Little Mail, Gray Eagle, Blue Wing No. 1, Blue Wing No. 3, Dove No. 1, Dove No. 2, The Wren, City of Frankfort, Lancaster, Hornet, Hibernia, Fannie Freeze, City of Clarksville, Falls City, Park City, and Nellie. There were two steamboats built at the mouth of Steamboat Hollow, a short distance below the City of Frankfort. One was a sidewheel boat built in 1822 and was called the Plough Boy, and the other about 1830. It was built of locust and was called Locust Lexington. It was not used in the Kentucky river trade.

In the year 1841 there were no lights of any description on the streets of Frankfort, except such lights as were carried by pedestrians. The sidewalks were sadly out of repair, some were broken in places, sunken in others and covered by mud in many more. In many places there had never been any sidewalks constructed. Walking after night was exceedingly disagreeable, if not dangerous. The pavement in front of the Mansion House (McClure Building) was very bad. The postoffice was located there at that time, and it was almost impossible to get to the postoffice without wading ankle deep in mud and water.

The Frankfort common school system was adopted in 1840, and a tax of 45 cents on the hundred was authorized to be collected in 1841, and in November of that year the school went into operation. The following salaries were paid for the first ten months: Mrs. Price, for services and house, $750; Miss Mills, for services and house, $550; Mr. Harris, for services, $550; Mrs. Harris, $170, and Mr. Culter, $270.

THE HISTORY OF FRANKLIN COUNTY. 115

The number of children taught the first year was 230. The trustees were J. Swigert, Thomas S. Theobald, A. P. Cox, H. Wingate and Thomas B. Stephenson, and L. Hord was clerk. All of these parties were re-elected in November, 1842, and a tax of 12 cents on the $100 was voted.

In 1840 there was great doubt as to the exact location of the line between Franklin and Scott counties. By an act of the Legislature approved January 4th, 1841, Isaac Wingate and Willis Blanton of Franklin County, and two commissioners from Scott were appointed to re-establish the line. Doubt arose as to where the line ran on account of the removal of trees and other objects which marked the line in the improvement of farms, etc. The starting point was the "eight-mile tree" on the road leading from Frankfort to Georgetown, and to run thence in a straight line so as to intersect the big Buffalo road between the head of Cedar creek and Lecompts run. The report of the commissioners was filed and recorded in both Franklin and Scott counties.

In the year 1842 Philip Swigert, Henry Wingate, Orlando Brown, Austin P. Cox, James Shannon, James F. Dryden and Thomas B. Stephenson were elected trustees of the City of Frankfort. Philip Swigert was chairman of the board. In the same year the old jail property on Mero street was exchanged with Jacob Swigert for the ground on which the county and circuit clerks' office and the present jail were built and the contracts for building the county offices were entered into.

John Morris was Sheriff in 1841. Peter Jett was assessor in 1842. Oberson Lynn was Sheriff in 1843.

On May the 14th, 1842, Hon. Frank Johnson died in Louisville, Ky. He served many years in the State Legislature and several terms as a member of Congress from Kentucky. He was a distinguished member of the bar. He was the chief attorney for John U. Waring, charged with the murder of Samuel Q. Richardson in 1835. He was a resident of Frankfort for several years.

On June the 3d, 1842, Scott Brown died at his home four miles above Frankfort near the Kentucky river, in his 77th year. For many years he was a magistrate of the county and for two years he was Sheriff. He came to Kentucky from Virginia in 1790, and settled in the southern part of the county. He bore his part in the labors and hardships of the pioneer. He was an upright, honest and useful citizen, beloved and esteemed by all who knew him. He was not only a valuable and useful citizen, but he was a patriot and a soldier. He left several children, of whom Gen. Scott Brown and Judge Ruben Brown were a part.

On October 26th, 1842, a Whig barbecue was held in Frankfort, which was attended by between 10,000 and 15,000 people. The speakers' stand was in front of the old capitol building and the dinner was served on Market street. The meeting was presided over by ex-Governor Thomas Metcalf. Speeches were made by Col. Daniel Breck, of Richmond, Va.; Henry Clay, John J. Crittenden, Judge Owsley, Gen. Leslie Combs, Hon. Garret Davis, Hon. John White, at that time Speaker of the lower house of Congress, and Congressmen L. W. Andrews, Chilton Allen, William J. Graves and James C. Sprigg. Several other members of Congress were present. About 1,000 Whigs from Jefferson and Shelby counties walked through the country to Frankfort in order to be present on that occasion.

On Wednesday, January 4th, 1842, an earthquake was felt in Frankfort about 9 o'clock p. m., but no serious damage was done.

Daniel H. Harris was postmaster at Frankfort from 1840 to 1843. In 1843 Gen. William Hardin was appointed in his stead.

There was a very severe wind, hail and rain storm on Sunday, May the 28th, 1843; great damage was done to the whole country. A man by the name of Thomas was killed by a falling tree, and a tree also fell on the Presbyterian church near South Benson and very materially damaged it. This storm was long remembered in Kentucky as the most violent and destructive which ever desolated the State. The destruction to the growing timber was great; nearly every tree on some farms was blown down; fences were blown away by the wind or

THE HISTORY OF FRANKLIN COUNTY. 117

washed away by the water. The rain was heavier at Frankfort than it was in any other section of the State. It was ascertained by measurement that over six inches of rain fell, which was one-sixth of the entire quantity of rain which falls in Kentucky in a year.

Hon. John J. Crittenden returned to his home from St. Louis on July 4th, 1843. He came all the way by water. He thought the rapidity of his transit was wonderful. It took him two days and twenty-three hours (71 hours) from the time he stepped on the boat at St. Louis until he landed at his door in Frankfort. Fifty years later it would have taken him about fifteen hours to make the trip.

In 1843, A. W. Macklin built a mill dam across Elkhorn creek, nine feet high. This dam was built at the same place where Bennett Pemberton had built one many years before and which was washed away.

John M. Hewitt, who represented Franklin County in the Kentucky Legislature in 1855-1857, was charged before the Legislature with having prostituted his official position of Judge as a means of private revenge, and of being guilty of judicial tyranny that ought not to be tolerated in a free country. He was accused of being an extortioner, a claim shaver and usurer.

The Frankfort Commonwealth, dated July 2nd, 1844, said: "Mr. Clay (Henry Clay) was in Frankfort Wednesday and Thursday of last week, in fine health and spirits. It is understood he came to pay his respects to his amiable and accomplished friend, the favorite of every circle in which she is known, Mrs. Tubman, of Georgia, who entertained him with much courteous hospitality at her home during his late Southern trip."

In 1844, the Frankfort Bridge Company rebuilt the St. Clair street bridge. The Franklin County Court made an agreement with the bridge company to furnish six thousand dollars with which to help build the bridge, and in consideration of same the bridge company was to furnish free passage to all horseback and foot travelers of the county for all time. The bridge was completed in 1848.

The most rapid growth of Frankfort at any time in her history prior to 1900, was from 1840 to 1845. Its population was doubled during those five years.

In 1845 the "Grand Polka" and many other fashionable and beautiful dances were introduced in Frankfort. In that year P. & J. Swigert did a large and lucrative business in a pork slaughtering and packing establishment. On the 28th of November, 1845, seven hundred hogs were driven through Frankfort from Tennessee on their way to Cincinnati for slaughter.

In 1844 the Board of Magistrates of Franklin County, elected William A. Goram Jailer of the county, and in a short time thereafter he became very intemperate and in 1845 the Court, "for divers good causes to the Court appearing, it is ordered that William A. Goram be removed from the office of Jailer in and for the county of Franklin, and that Benjamin Luckett be appointed Jailer for said county." Mr. Goram was not satisfied with the order removing him. He took the case to the courts and the Court of Appeals on October 13th, 1845, held that the magistrates had no right to remove him. The Board of Magistrates at that time consisted of the following members, viz: Samuel B. Crockett, James Shannon, John Thompson, Franklin Chinn, Samuel Bristow, Samuel B. Scofield and Dandridge S. Crockett, was convened November 17th, and William Goram, by attorney, appeared, and offered to file the mandate of the Court of Appeals, and the Court said: "This day came again the parties by their attorneys, and the motion to enter the mandate being now fully heard and the court being fully advised, it is considered by the court that the motion be overruled." When giving the grounds on which the question was decided, the court said: "The governed can only preserve their liberty by a division of power, and making the several depositaries of authority guards and checks upon each other. In proportion to the concentration of controlling influence with a few or a single tribunal, however numerous, are the social and civil rights of man endangered. The late attempt of the Court of Appeals to seize upon the power confided by the Constitution of the State to the County Court relative to the office of Jailer impels us to protest against such usurpation and declare the grounds of our resistance." The Court further said: "We protest against the intermeddling of the Court of Appeals in the matter, and insist that they shall be restrained to their constitutional sphere of action." Further along in the opinion, the Court said: "If the distinction between executive and judicial were not palpable to the bluntest mind, by reference to the case of Taylor vs. The Commonwealth, 3 J. J. Marshall, page 401, it might be learned." The opinion closed with the following statement: "Believing that our rights have been invaded by another branch of the government styling itself the Court of Appeals, and that it is much safer to decline the exercise of all doubtful authority than to attempt to correct imaginary errors, we declare to the world that we will not record the mandate of the Court of Appeals." On the 8th of June, following, the Court of Appeals issued attachments against James Shannon, Dandridge S. Crockett, Samuel B. Scofield, Robert C. McKee, Franklin Chinn and Samuel Bristow, magistrates of Franklin County, returnable the fourth day of the term, for contempt in failing to attend the Court in obedience to its summons previously issued and executed, and showing cause why, as justices of the peace of Franklin County they had refused to enter and carry into effect the mandate of the Court in the case of Goram vs. Luckett, made at the fall term. The defendants were granted the right to execute a bond in the sum of one hundred dollars for their appearance on the day set. The attachments were executed on all of the defendants except Shannon, and they refused to execute the bond for their appearance and they were committed to the custody of Benjamin Luckett as Jailer of Franklin County. At that time a writ of habeas corpus could be issued by two magistrates. On the 20th of the month a writ of habeas corpus was issued by James Shannon and Robert C. McKee as justices of the peace, to the Jailer, commanding him to bring the body of Dandridge S. Crockett before them in the jail, and show by what authority he was imprisoned. Mr. Luckett appeared at the time stated and gave the stated cause of the commitment, but the Court deemed it insufficient and discharged the prisoner, and thereupon Dandridge S. Crockett and James Shannon issued similar writs for the other members of the fiscal court, and in that way released all of them. John M. Hewitt, George B. McKee and Robert C. McKee were the attorneys who represented the defendants; there was no prosecuting attorney present. On the the 20th of July, 1846, there was an order reinstating William A. Goram as Jailer of the county and at the same term of Court Goram resigned and Luckett was appointed.

The Legislature of Kentucky appropriated a sufficient sum of money to remove the remains of Daniel and Rebecca Boone from Missouri to Frankfort, Kentucky. Mr. Thomas L. Crittenden and Colonel Boone were the committee which was sent after them. Mr. Harry Griswold, who owned the farm in Warren County, Missouri, on which the pioneers were buried, refused to permit them to be removed and the committee had considerable trouble in securing them, though they had the written consent of the near relatives of the Boones. When the coffins were opened it was found that the large bones were perfect in size and shape, but of a very dark color and so far decomposed in substance as to have lost their strength and weight, to a considerable extent; a number of the small bones were rotten and could not be raised in form. Their coffins were entirely rotten except the bottom planks. The body of Boone had been buried about twenty-five years and that of his wife about thirty years.

The committee, with the remains, reached Frankfort in August and the re-interment was on Saturday, the 13th day of September, 1845. It was requested by the committee on arrangements that all business in the city be suspended and that all persons unite in the ceremonies. This committee consisted of the following citizens of Frankfort: Gov. R. P. Letcher, chairman; P. Swigert, W. Tanner, John P. Cammack, Robt. W. Scott, George W. Craddock, Landon A. Thomas, A. C. George, H. I. Bodley, John A. Holton, Keen O'Hara, John L. Moore, Geo. W. Graham, A. G. Hodges, James Davidson, John M. Hewitt, D. S. Crockett, Jno. Mayhall, Joseph Gray, Henry Wingate, John J. Vest, Jacob Beaverson, Lewis Sneed, E. H.

Watson, A. W. Dudley, Langston Bacon, C. W. Kenedy and James P. Page. Nearly every county in the State was represented in the vast assembly of people and also many from the Southern and Western States were present to pay the last funeral honors to the pioneers of the great western valley. The spot selected for the final resting place of Daniel and Rebecca Boone was very appropriate, no more beautiful one could have been found in all the great State of Kentucky. Situated on a high hill far above the Kentucky river, it commands an unobstructed view of the surrounding scenery, beautiful, grand, sublime; the Kentucky river wends its way between majestic hills and the spires of the classic old town are seen in the distance. The evergreens which stand above their last resting place constantly remind the wayfarer of the soul's immortality and these

> "Lofty Pines above their grave,
> Keep green the memory of the brave."

In speaking of the procession which followed the Boones to the cemetery, the Commonwealth said: "Of the people who composed the great body of the procession, it may well be said that the Saxon race in no clime or country could have been more nobly represented, whether for the brave appearance of the men or the splendid beauty of the women; they seemed indeed the suitable inheritors of this goodly land."

The Methodist annual conference was in session at that time and these two events filled every house in the city, both public and private. Every means of transportation was used to reach Frankfort; all the boats which were in the Kentucky river trade at that time were crowded to their utmost limit, and the excursion cars on the railroad and stage coaches from the interior brought thousands of people to the city.

When the first signal gun was fired at 10 o'clock, the large procession began to form and at half past ten, it moved in the following order:

General John T. Pratt, Marshal.
1   Company of Military.

Music.

Pallbearers.   Hearse.   Pallbearers.

2. Relatives and Companions of Daniel Boone and Wife. Marshal, Gen. Leslie Combs, with Col. Jessie Bayles and W. R. Herve, Assistants.
3. Officers and Soldiers of the Late War; L. Hord and John Watson, Assistans.
4. Committee of Arrangements; Orator of the Day and Officiating Clergy.
5. President and Members of the Frankfort Cemetery Company.
6. Governor, Suite and Officers of the State and U. S. Department.
7. Judges of the Superior and Inferior Courts and Officers.
8. Members of Congress and Legislature.
9. Trustees and Officers of the City; J. Swigert and Col. E. H. Taylor, Assistant Marshals.
10. The Rev. Clergy and Members of the Methodist Episcopal Church Conference; Dr. E. H. Watson, Assistant Marshal.
11. Masonic Order.
12. Independent Order of Odd Fellows.
13. City Fire Companies; Wm. M. Todd, Assistant Marshal.
14. Male and Female Sunday Schools and Teachers; Samuel Harris, Assistant Marshal.
15. Day Schools and Teachers; Gen. L. Desha, Marshal.
16. Military.
17. Music; R. H. Crittenden, Assistant Marshal.
18. Ladies and Gentlemen on foot.
19. Gentlemen on foot; Major E. H. Field, Marshal.
20. Strangers and Citizens in carriages.
21. Strangers and Citizens on Horseback.
R. Knott, Col. W. A. Goram and R. H. Reese, Assistant Marshals.

The hearse in which were placed the remains of Boone and wife was drawn by four white horses and decorated with evergreens and flowers; the pallbearers were Col. Richard M. Johnson, Gen. James Taylor, General Ward, Gen. Robt. B.

McAfee, Gen. Peter Jourden, Mr. Waller Bullock, Capt. Thomas Joys, Mr. Landon Sneed, Col. John Johnson, an early companion of Boone; Mr. Williams and Col. William Boone, a nephew of Daniel Boone. The hearse was preceded by the following military companies:

1. Cavalry Company of Woodford County, in Command of Captain Graddy.
2. Lexington Flying Artillery, Commanded by Capt. S. D. McCullough.
3. Versailles Artillery, Commanded by Capt. E. H. Field.
4. Danville Artillery, Commanded by Capt. S. S. Fry.
5. Lexington Old Infantry, Commanded by Capt. Happy.
6. Frankfort Cadets, Commanded by Capt. F. Chambers.
7. Frankfort Lancers, Commanded by Capt. Vest.
8. Capitol Guards, Commanded by Capt. A. G. Hodges.

These troops were all in new uniforms, and following which were the Masonic fraternities and Odd Fellows in uniform. The bishop who presided at the Methodist conference and the members of the conference were in the funeral procession. The opening hymn was read by the Rev. A. Goodell, of the Baptist Church, after the singing of which the venerable Bishop Soule, of the M. E. Church, led in prayer. Then came the orator of the day, Hon. John J. Crittenden, who "enchained attention by the spells of his magic eloquence—that he threw around his subject all the fascinations of his peerless fancy and unrivaled oratory, and when he ceased to speak the listeners still stood fixed to hear." The Rev. J. J. Bullock, of the Presbyterian Church, delivered the closing prayer, and Rev. P. S. Fall, of the Christian Church, pronounced the benediction. After the ceremonies were over the coffins were lowered into the grave and the pallbearers threw some earth over the remains. Hundreds of people then passed by, and each one threw a handful of dirt, and in that way assisted in filling up the graves.

The State, in 1860, appropriated sufficient money to erect a handsome monument, nicely carved, over their remains. This monument was completed in 1862. The panels were of Italian marble. It was built by John Haly, of Frankfort.

Vandals, as relic hunters, so defaced the panels that the monument was practically destroyed.

The Legislature of 1906 appropriated $2,000, which sum was supplemented by the Rebecca Bryan Boone Chapter of the Daughters of the American Revolution, making a sum sufficient to replace the panels. The work was completed in 1909, making it practically a new one. The new panels are of South Carolina marble, and they are an exact reproduction of the original.

The county seal was purchased in 1845.

The most memorable high water tides in the Kentucky river were in 1819, 1846, 1882 and 1883.

In 1845 the mill at the Kentucky penitentiary ground meal for a large part of the county; its capacity was forty bushels of corn per hour. The toll for grinding was one-eighth.

Clinton and Mero streets, between Washington and the river, were graded and paved in 1845, so that the water, then in a swampy section of the town, was drained to the river.

In 1845 the postoffice was moved from the Mansion House to a room on Lewis street, near Main, under the rooms occupied by the Yoeman Printing Company. B. F. Johnson was postmaster.

In 1844 Mrs. M. Train Runyan commenced teaching a private school for young ladies in Frankfort, which became famous in this section of the State, and which she continued to teach for about thirty-five years.

The Franklin Springs were sold in 1845. For more than half a century they had been famous as a watering place. They were located about six miles south of Frankfort. Col. R. T. P. Allen purchased these springs and established the Kentucky Military Institute there. This institution of learning became very popular, especially for Southern boys. Colonel Allen was a graduate of the United States Military Academy at West Point. He was an officer in the Florida war and was professor of mathematics in Transylvania University for three years, which position he resigned to organize the Kentucky Military Institute.

In 1846 the Legislature changed the line between Franklin

and Anderson counties, commencing at the mouth of Boones Branch in Little Benson, and from thence in a southwesterly course to Hogshead's old house, thence down Parkers Spring Branch to Little Benson so as to include the dwelling house occupied by Fielding L. Connor, but afterwards owned by James D. Parker, in the county of Anderson, and leaving the Presbyterian Church in Franklin County.

In 1846 the Legislature appropriated $50 with which to purchase books for the moral culture and instruction of the prisoners in the penitentiary. The fund was placed under the control of the Governor.

Franklin County furnished two companies for the Mexican war. One was Company C, First Regiment Kentucky Mounted Volunteers, under Capt. Ben C. Milam, and the other was Company B, Second Regiment Kentucky Foot Volunteers, under Capt. Frank Chambers.

The muster roll of Captain Milam's company is as follows: Ben C. Milam, captain; James H. D. McKee, first lieutenant; Richard D. Harlan, second lieutenant; John T. Roberts, Ben B. Bennett, Humphrey Evans, sergeants; John Swigert and Lewis J. Foster, corporals. The privates were James Herring and B. S. Gayle, buglers, and Joseph Robb, James Bates, Johnny Cavender, Cyrus Calvert, Robert Cochran, Nathaniel C. Cook, Clinton D. W. Cook, Benjamin Church, Richard Davenport, Zachariah Dougherty, James E. Evans, Bennett Edwards, B. S. Fields, A. W. Holman, Jeremiah Harrison, William Hassett, Fielding S. Hawkins, James F. Lee, Samuel C. Leonard, T. J. Macy, L. Martin, A. J. Mitchell, A. J. McDonald, William McLean, Ben Franklin Pearce, John H. Redish, George M. Shannon, John A. Snelling, J. J. Soward, John A. Scott, W. W. Stapp, W. C. Stockton, A. Wilkerson and John S. Semonis. The following were discharged from service on account of disabilities, to-wit: W. M. Robb, B. Utterback, E. T. Parrent, corporals; the privates were G. W. Bailey, R. B. Howard, D. Hancock, Thomas Harper, Joel Ashley, W. P. Jones, J. J. Kendall, J. D. McKee, S. Montague, J. G. Miles, F. M. Milam, S. McQueen, Samuel Mars, R. P. W. Noel, W. H. Price, A. B. Reed, W. H. Sudduth, and J. Wilson. Those who died in the service were James Bailey, W. J. Hall, Robert Latta, W. Newton, and W. Williamson. The following: J. F. Ellingwood, James Lester, and John Sanders were killed at the battle of Buena Vista February 23d, 1847. On January 22, 1847, the following members of this company were captured by the Mexicans, to-wit: John Swigert, James Herring, James Bates, Cyrus Calvert, Robert Cochran, Zachariah Dougherty, A. W. Holman, John A. Scott, A. Wilkerson, William Whitehead, and W. S. Wood.

The muster roll of Captain Chambers' company: Frank Chambers, captain; James Monroe, first lieutenant; Henry C. Long, William D. Robertson, and Samuel P. Barbee, second lieutenants; William F. Gaines, William Hardy, and Hanson S. Mayhall, sergeants, and Richard P. Evans, Clark Knott, James B. Davidson, and Ambrose W. Hampton, corporals; Thomas B. Heffner and George W. Chambers, buglers. The privates were George Allen, John Amer, Elias T. Bartlett, Samuel S. Bartlett, Benjamin O. Branham, Emil Brea, John J. Christopher, Patrick H. Chambers, John L. Collins, W. Williams, L. Craig, James W. Cummings, Daniel Easley, George W. Edwards, Charles R. Featherston, Richard A. Gayle, Abel P. Harris, Ruben A. Hawkins, William M. Hayden, John R. Hayden, William Henderson, David J. Herndon, Willson J. Jordon, James E. McGune, David McQueen, Moses S. Milam, Thomas J. Milam, William Morrison, John E. Moore, William W. Perrin, Almus W. Polsgrove, John Polsgrove, James N. Reed, William R. Satterwhite, James W. Sheets, Samuel Sheets, Norman Sidbottom, Robert Sheridan, James Sherrin, William Skyler, Walker Stephens, James D. Taylor, Lewis Tull, Thomas Webb, and James L. Williams.

Those who died in the service were Rowland S. Parker, Leander Ford, Thomas J. Chambers, Lafayette B. Frederick, James S. Johnson, and Francis Lecompte. Henry Wolf, William Blackwell, Samuel Bartlett, and Major Updike were killed at the battle of Buena Vista February 23d, 1847. Those who were discharged on account of disabilities were William K. Major, James R. Page, James E. Coleman, Merriat Young, James W. Harris, James Blazehard, Wesley Christopher,

Benjamin Robinson, John Taylor, Matthew L. Hazelett, Stephen Sesfield, Alexander Moss, Enoch Ford, and Thomas J. Todd. The deserters were John White, who deserted at Louisville, June the 13th, and James Crummery, who deserted at Matamoras, Mexico, August the 22d.

The trustees of the town of Frankfort appropriated $200 for the purpose of bringing the bodies of the Franklin County men, who fell at Buena Vista back home, and the county of Franklin appropriated a like sum for the same purpose. Maj. B. C. Milam went to Mexico after the remains of the men in his company and those of Captain Chambers. He met with Mr. Ruben A. Hawkins at New Orleans, who returned to Mexico with him to point out the graves of those parties whom he had buried there. Mr. Hawkins reached Frankfort with the remains of John Sanders, John Ellingwood, James Seston, Major Updike, L. B. Bartlett, Henry Wolf, W. Blackwell, J. J. Thorp, H. Edwards, A. Goodpaster, Enoch Burton, and Robert Latta. The bodies were received at the wharf by the returned volunteers, under Major Milam and Captain Chambers, and the McKee Guards, under Captain Crittenden. They were buried in the State ground at Frankfort on Thursday, the 16th day of September, 1847, with military honors. About 3,000 people from Franklin and the surrounding counties were present and took part in the ceremonies.

On July 27th, 1847, the burial of the remains of Col. William R. McKee, Lieut. Col. Henry Clay, Capt. William T. Willis, Adjt. E. P. Vaughn, Lieut. Joseph Powell, W. W. Bayless, William Thwaits, N. Ramsey, Thomas Weigert, Alex G. Morgan, C. Jones, H. Carty, T. McH. Dozier, H. Trotter, C. B. Thomas, and W. T. Green, the honored Kentuckians who were killed at the battle of Buena Vista, took place in the presence of a large concourse of people. The crowd was variously estimated from fifteen to thirty thousand. From sunrise to 10 o'clock a cannon was fired every hour from the battery stationed in the cemetery grounds, under the direction of Captain Goins. At 10 o'clock two guns were fired in quick succession, the signal for the ceremonies to begin.

Henry Clay, the venerable and distinguished father of

Colonel Clay, was present, and near him sat the little orphan children of Colonel Clay. Col. Richard M. Johnson was also present. He was a guest of the McKee Guards. The orator of the day was John C. Breckenridge, whose fine appearance and pleasing address added greatly to his reputation as an orator.

The bodies were removed from the rotunda of the State Capitol and placed in hearses which were arranged in a semicircle on the northwest end of the Capitol grounds. The right of the procession rested on Market street. It moved in the following order:

George W. Triplett, marshal, led the column.

1. Jessamine Cavalry, under Captain Worley.
2. Fayette Cavalry, under Captain Willson.
3. Woodford Cavalry, under Captain Thornton.
4. Mortonsville Cavalry, under Captain Edwards.

Marshal, Col. R. T. P. Allen, assisted by Capt. Thomas H. Taylor, adjutant of the day.

5. Clay Guards, under Captain Taylor.
6. McKee Guards, under Captain Crittenden.
7. Fayette Guards, under Captain Robinson.
8. Lexington Light Artillery, under Captain Happy.
9. Jessamine Artillery, under Captain Hill.
10. Keene Artillery, under Captain Coons.
11. Lexington Artillery, under Captain Cadwallader.

Music.

Marshall, E. A. Dudley, assisted by G. P. Theobold and John T. Roberts.

12. Committee of arrangements, with the officers of the cemetery.
13. Bodies of the dead, drawn in hearses built on cannon carriages, the cannons being shrouded in crepe. The gun taken at Cerro Gordo and the "Thames Piece" were mounted for the occasion. The carriages were hung in black. The hearse which contained the body of Colonel McKee was built on a brass cannon in the possession of the Lexington Legion, and was drawn by four white horses. Following this was the hearse containing the remains of Lieutenant Colonel Clay; the re-

mains of Captain Willis came next, Adjutant Vaughn next, etc., the whole attended by pallbearers.

14. Lexington Rifles, under Captain Jouett.
15. Families and relatives of the dead.
16. Ministers of the gospel.

Music—Band from Newport Barracks, at that time recognized as being one of the best in the United States.

Marshal, Col. James Davidson, assisted by J. H. Slaughter.

17. The Second Kentucky Volunteer Regiment, under Major Fry.
18. The Kentucky Volunteer Cavalry, under Colonel Marshall and Colonel Field.
19. The First Regiment of Kentucky Volunteers, Louisville Legion, under Colonel Ormsby.

Twenty officers of the United States army and soldiers of the Mexican war.

Music—Col. H. C. Pindell, Marshal.

21. The Governor and suite.
22. Officers of the State and United States government.
23. The Sons of Temperance.
24. Independent Order of Odd Fellows.
25. Masonic Fraternity.

Marshal, Captain Anderson.

26. Students of colleges and various departments of learning.
27. Literary societies.
28. Fire companies.

Marshal, Captain J. W. Russell.

29. Citizens on foot.

Chief Assistant Marshal, Landon A. Thomas.

30. Citizens in carriages.

At half past eleven the procession was formed and moved through the principal streets of Frankfort to the cemetery. A gun was fired every five minutes while the procession was moving.

John Swigert, John Scott, and W. Holeman, members of Capt. Milam's company, were captured near Encarnacion by a Mexican force. In July, 1847, they escaped from their guard, and after many perilous and thrilling adventures reached their homes in Frankfort.

The town of Bridgeport, in Franklin County, was incorporated in 1848. John Jenkins, Frederick Robb, and H. Edwards were appointed trustees. The act provided that the grounds laid out should not exceed fifty acres.

Pleasant Hill, located on Main Elkhorn, near the mouth of Johns Branch, in 1848, elected trustees as follows: Lewis C. Sullivan, Alexander B. Bacon, John T. Hawkins, James M. Graham, and John F. Graham.

The Frankfort and Lawrenceburg road was incorporated in 1847. Franklin County was authorized to take stock in it.

The telegraph line between Louisville and Frankfort was completed February 25th, 1848. The first message ever received at Frankfort by telegram was the announcement of the death of ex-President John Quincy Adams, which was received at 9 o'clock a. m. February 25th, 1848. The line to Louisville was completed several days before the line to Lexington.

The use of gas for illuminating purposes was introduced in Frankfort in September, 1848.

President-elect Gen. Zachary Taylor paid a visit to Frankfort on the 19th of February, 1849. He came up on a boat and was met at the wharf by the joint members of the Kentucky Legislature, the old Mexican soldiers, and a large concourse of citizens. His visit was especially to Governor Crittenden, who was at that time Governor of the State.

In June, 1849, there was a great religious revival in Frankfort. Several hundred people joined the various churches of the city.

Samuel Crockett was Sheriff of Franklin County in 1849, and T. N. Lindsey was elected a member of the constitutional convention from the county.

The Benson bridge, near the mouth of Benson Creek, was built in 1849.

William T. Herndon was appointed Sheriff in 1850.

The members of the Frankfort bar in 1850 were Lysander Hord, Thomas N. Lindsey, Landon A. Thomas, S. F. J. Trabue, P. U. Major, John C. Herndon, Robert Henry Crittenden,

James Monroe, Philip Swigert, Richard C. French, Thomas Hart Taylor, Jno. M. Hewitt, Ben Monroe, James Harlan, William Harlan, T. P. A. Bibb, O. G. Cates, W. B. Reed, G. W. Craddock, C. S. Morehead, R. P. Letcher, T. D. Tillford, Austin P. Cox, Mason Brown, A. S. Mitchell, and Andrew Monroe.

The physicians were W. T. Price, E. H. Watson, Dr. Phythian, O. S. Willson, Churchill J. Blackburn, Luke P. Blackburn, and Alex M. Blanton.

Franklin County members of the House of Representatives of Kentucky from 1840 to 1850 were:

Charles S. Morehead, 1840, 1841, 1842, and 1844.

James Milam, 1843.

James Harlan, 1845.

William D. Reed, 1846.

Landon A. Thomas, 1847.

John A. Holton, 1848.

James Monroe, 1849.

Lysander Hord, 1850.

The population of Franklin County in 1840 was 9,420, in 1850 it was 12,462.

The number of slaves in 1840, 2,846; in 1850, 3,365.

The population of Frankfort in 1840 was 1,917; in 1850 it was 3,308.

CHAPTER X.

Course of Events from 1850 to 1860.

In the year 1850 the Kentucky river was under the control of the State; there was a resolution by the General Assembly "That the military monument which had been made under the direction of the committee appointed for that purpose and which is to be erected in memory of the brave officers and soldiers who have fallen in the defense of the honor of their country, be permitted to pass through the locks of the river without payment of toll." This military monument was erected in 1850, the statue of victory on the top of it was raised to its place on July 1st, 1850.

In 1851 the Legislature directed the Governor of Kentucky to purchase from the Frankfort Cemetery Company lots Nos. 131-132-143-144-154 and 155 in which to bury the remains of Kentucky's illustrious dead, the price for same was six hundred dollars.

There was an act in 1851 appropriating eighty dollars with which to bury some Kentuckians who were killed at the River Raisin. In 1848 Col. Edward Brooks, acting under the authorities of the town of Monroe, Mich., delivered the remains of fifteen Kentuckians who fell at the battle of the River Raisin, and by resolution, the Governor of Kentucky was directed to have them buried in the Frankfort Cemetery.

The sum of four hundred dollars was paid by resolution of the General Assembly, to Edward H. Nock, as compensation for painting the portrait of Governor Isaac Shelby. This portrait hung in the Legislative Hall in the Old Capitol building for more than a half century, but when the archives of the State were removed to the new Capitol in 1909 it was placed in charge of the State Historical Society, where it was given one of the most prominent positions in the Hall of Fame.

The State, by act of the Legislature, appointed Ambrose W. Dudley, E. H. Taylor and Philip Swigert, Commissioners to superintend the erection of an Arsenal, on any ground not

THE HISTORY OF FRANKLIN COUNTY. 133

less than one-half mile from the Capitol building. The sum of eight thousand dollars was appropriated and the Commissioners were directed to act "according to such plans and specifications as they may deem best suited for a building for said purpose."

By an amendment, the Commissioners named were authorized to select at their discretion the most suitable place within the town of Frankfort or in its vicinity, as to them may seem most eligible for the location of the Arsenal. The building was completed in 1850 and the military equipments of the State were removed from a small building on the State House square to the new Arsenal, during that year.

The incorporated towns of South Frankfort and Frankfort (North Frankfort) were consolidated by act of the Legislature approved March 4th, 1850. The most prominent men of South Frankfort in 1818 were Edward S. Coleman, Chairman of the Board of Trustees; David Graham, George Gayle, Larkin Samuels, George W. Graham, Israel Ellis, Hosea Cook, Henry Wingate, John Campbell, George Todd and Evan Evans; Sam South was chairman of the Board of Trustees in 1823; S. I. M. Major in 1825; John J. Vest in 1827; Rev. S. M. Noel in 1829; John J. Vest in 1831; Chas. S. Morehead in 1833; Littleberry Batchelor in 1834; O. G. Cates in 1837; Edward S. Coleman in 1841 and for several years thereafter. In 1845 Coleman's Tan Yard was in operation near Coleman's spring at the south end of Steele street; the buildings were one story with basements.

During the year 1850 the following incidents are noted: The Farmers' Bank was organized, the largest stockholders and organizers of this bank were James Harlan, John H. Hanna, J. Swigert, William Tanner, John W. Russell, P. Swigert, A. C. Keenon, A. G. Hodges, John C. Herndon, H. I. Todd and S. Robinson.

James M. Todd was appointed postmaster at Frankfort.

On August 8th, the cornerstone of the Episcopal Church was laid, the address was delivered by Rev. Mr. Craik of Louisville, Bishop Smith, Rev. Messrs. Claxton of Madison, Ind.,

Elwell of Shelbyville and Norton of Frankfort assisted in the ceremonies.

Cholera made its appearance in Frankfort again, during the year, but there were only a few deaths from its effects.

The publication of a religious paper known as "The Methodist Monthly" was commenced in October, the Rev. T. N. Ralston was the editor. He was assisted by Rev. G. W. Bush and W. H. Anderson.

Mr. Joseph Belt, who served five years and seven months in the American Army during the War of the Revolution, died, domiciled in Franklin County, September 10th, 1850. He was ninety-nine years old at the time of his death.

Col. Richard M. Johnson, who had been Vice President of the United States and who had held many offices of trust and who was known as one of the greatest men of that time, died in Frankfort and was buried in the Frankfort Cemetery, November 12th, 1850. The funeral services were held in the House of Representatives. An immense crowd of citizens and strangers were in attendance. Rev. Stewart Robinson preached the funeral discourse. "The procession was long and imposing, the Masons and Odd Fellows especially making a fine appearance." Minute guns were fired as the procession entered the cemetery and until the ceremonies at the grave were concluded. Obituary addresses concerning Col. Richard M. Johnson were published in pamphlet form. The following Legislature authorized Mason Brown, John M. Huett, Edward H. Taylor and William Tanner, Commissioners with authority to contract with Robert E. Launitz for the erection of a monument to his memory in the Frankfort Cemetery, and for which nine hundred dollars were appropriated, and for this small sum the Commissioners secured one of the most beautiful and artistic monumental structures that was ever erected on the Western Continent, up to that time.

The first money appropriated by the County Court for the purpose of macadamizing the county roads was placed on the Glenn's Creek road in 1851. The Frankfort and Lawrenceburg turnpike road was built during this year. The county of Franklin owned a large part of the stock in this road when it was completed. At the close of the year 1851 there were seventy-four public roads in the county, all of which were under the supervision of County Surveyors and were repaired by warning in the hands assigned to their respective roads.

After the adoption of the Constitution of 1849, the first election held under the new Constitution was in 1851, at which time John C. Herndon became the first County Judge of Franklin county; Alexander H. Rennick was the first clerk elected by the people; William T. Herndon the first Sheriff; John R. Graham, Coroner; Benjamin Luckett, Jailer; William M. Bristow, Assessor, and Lysander Hord, for some reason was appointed County Attorney. Samuel I. M. Major was elected Surveyor, but his election was contested by William F. Graham on the grounds that Major was not of age. The Court held that said Major was not twenty-one years of age and consequently could not hold the office, the Constitution having provided that a man was not eligible until he was twenty-one; a new election was ordered. The County Judge's salary was fixed at two hundred and fifty dollars per year. On May 29th, 1851, the first passenger train of cars from Louisville arrived upon the banks of the river opposite Frankfort; this was an important era in the history of Frankfort and Franklin county and the public-spirited citizens of the county celebrated the event. The railroad bridge across the river at that point was completed during that year, the contract price for its construction was originally $27,000, but some changes were made and the amount was increased to $30,000. During this year Joseph Patterson, a civil engineer, surveyed a route for a railroad from Frankfort to Harrodsburg, the distance being thirty-two miles and one thousand and forty-feet to the railroad junction on the west side of the river. His estimated cost was $26,232 per mile. The proposition as to whether the county of Franklin would vote the appropriation of $225,000 as her part of the expense of building the road failed to receive a majority of the votes.

Henry Clay died in Washington City on the 29th day of June, 1852; out of respect to his memory, Governor Powell ordered all the public business of the State to be suspended and the offices closed and the buildings to be clothed in mourning. The City Council was convened in extraordinary session and resolutions passed; the citizens of Frankfort and vicinity held a mass meeting at which appropriate resolutions were passed.

During this year Mr. David Meriwether built the Meriwether Hotel, on the corner of Broadway and Ann streets. For many years this hotel was the political headquarters for the politicians of the State.

The Frankfort Woolen Mills were incorporated in 1852, J. M. Lancaster, John H. Hanna, Jacob Swigert, Nathaniel Hart, P. Swigert, John Watson, S. Brownwell and William L. Vance were the incorporators. The capital stock was placed at one hundred thousand dollars.

General Winfield Scott, a candidate for President of the United States, visited Frankfort in the month of September; a reception committee met him at the train and escorted him to the Capitol building, where he addressed the assembled multitude on the political questions of the day; a public reception was held at which a large number of people met him. At that time Franklin county was nearly evenly divided between the Democrats and Whigs. Pierce, the Democrat, received 759 votes and Scott, the Whig, received 833 votes in the county.

Joshua McQueen, a Revolutionary soldier, died at his home near Frankfort on April 3rd, 1853, at the age of 106 years. He was appointed sergeant by General Washington, which position he held during the war. He left surviving him a large family of children, grandchildren and great grandchildren. On December 11th of the same year James Brisco, in his 94th year, also died. He was a soldier and seaman of the Revolution. He was at the siege of Yorktown and the surrender of Cornwallis. He served as boatswain under Commodore Taylor. At the time of his death, Cornelius Fenwick was the only surviving Revolutionary soldier in Franklin County.

Ben F. Johnson was appointed postmaster at Frankfort in May, 1853. He succeeded James M. Todd, who resigned.

In December of this year the Capital Hotel was opened to the public and for more than half a century it has been one of the leading hotels of the State.

William T. Herndon was re-elected Sheriff of the county in 1853.

John M. Harlan, who has since become one of the Justices of the Supreme Court of the United States, was appointed Notary Public in and for the county of Franklin, March 20th, 1854, and during the same year he was elected City Attorney for the city of Frankfort. In 1855 he was one of the Sons of Temperance, and in 1856 he was re-elected City Attorney; in 1858 he was elected County Judge of Franklin County; in 1859 he made the race for Congress in the Ashland District, but was defeated by a small vote, during the same year he was appointed Adjutant General of the State of Kentucky, and in 1877 he was appointed Justice of the Supreme Court of the United States.

Ex-President Millard Fillmore visited Frankfort in March, 1854. He was entertained at the Capitol Hotel. Hon. John J. Crittenden presided. Addresses were made by Col. Thomas L. Crittenden, Gov. C. S. Morehead, Governor Powell, Gov. Crittenden, Gov. Letcher and Colonel Brown.

The year 1854 was the most disastrous year ever known to the people of Frankfort and Franklin County. The drought was so severe that practically nothing was raised in the way of farming products, the heat and drought were the severest ever known in Franklin County. The Kentucky river was ten feet lower than it was ever before known. The farmers had to haul water for miles; that period has been known since then, as the year of the great drought, and it has also been known by the people of Frankfort as the year of the great fire. The greatest conflagration ever known to the people of Frankfort occurred on April 29th. The fire commenced near the center of the square on St. Clair street between Broadway and Main streets. It burned every house up to and including the house on the corner of Main and St. Clair, and extended up Main street to Lewis street and down Lewis, about two-thirds of the square. There were twenty-four houses consumed, seventeen of which were brick. It was the business portion of the city which burned. A large part of the property was occupied by tenants, most of whom lost their entire stock of goods.

The election of county officers for Franklin County in 1854 resulted in the election of J. C. Herndon, County Judge; A. H. Rennick, County Clerk; H. I. Morris, Sheriff; P. U. Major, County Attorney; R. A. Brawner, Jailer; J. J. Smither, Assessor; J. R. Graham, Coroner; W. F. Graham, Surveyor; John W. Pruett, Constable of the Frankfort District, and James Monroe, Police Judge of the City of Frankfort. There were 528 votes in favor of a road tax and 847 against it.

The General Assembly of Kentucky by resolution in 1854, directed Gov. L. P. Powell to have the remains of Gov. Charles Scott, Major William T. Barry and Captain Bland Ballard and wife, to be brought to Frankfort and re-interred in the grounds belonging to the State in the Frankfort Cemetery. The Governor named November 8th as the day for the ceremonies.

"The Commonwealth" of November 10th gives the following description of the proceedings: "Wednesday, the 8th day of November, 1854, was a great day in Frankfort, and one not soon to be forgotten. The last and distinguished honors provided by Kentucky for three men who had served her cause, in the council and in the field, and whose lives had contributed to the glory of her history, were paid with befitting circumstance, in the presence of an immense crowd of Kentucky's sons and daughters. Strangers began to arrive on Tuesday, and on Wednesday morning every avenue leading to our little city poured in a living stream. The public square, streets, sidewalks, hotels and private houses were soon swarming with the crowd. Among those present were a great many of Kentucky's noblest sons—men distinguished upon the field of battle and men distinguished in almost every department of public service and of life—in the Executive chair, in Congress, in the Legislature of the State, upon the bench, at the bar, at the bedside of the sick, in the sacred desk, in the editorial office, in mercantile pursuits, and in the mechanic arts. Kentucky beauty was well represented in maiden loveliness and matronly grace; and the whole blending together formed an immense concourse of just such men and women as would have swelled the hearts of the honored dead with gratitude and joy could their mortal eyes open upon them. The procession formed about 11 o'clock and slowly moved its long length towards the cemetery. In it we noted a number of the officers and soldiers of the War of 1812, and of the War with Mexico. A delegation of officers from the Louisville Legion, under command of Col. DeKorponay; a fine volunteer company from Georgetown, commanded by Capt. Grant; the cadets of the Kentucky Military Institute, commanded by Col. Morgan; several lodges of Odd Fellows; several divisions of the Sons of Temperance; the pupils of Mr. Sayre's High School, and an innumerable throng of citizens and strangers in carriages. The march of the whole was enlivened by excellent music from Arbogast's and Plato's Saxhorn Bands of Louisville, whose performances throughout the day added greatly to the enjoyment of the occasion. Upon the cemetery grounds a platform for the speakers had been erected near the beautiful tomb of the Trabue family, and facing a gentle slope which rose like an amphitheatre around it. Here the exercises were opened with prayer by the Rev. Dr. John D. Mathews. Governor Powell then introduced the further proceedings by a brief and appropriate address, and concluded by presenting to the audience Col. Thomas L. Crittenden, who delivered an oration of classic elegance and marked appropriateness upon the life and character of Governor Charles Scott. After music from the band Col. Theodore O'Hara was introduced and delivered a glowing, eloquent and ornate eulogy upon Major William T. Barry. To this succeeded a speech from Col. Humphrey Marshall upon the life and character of Major Bland Ballard—an effort marked by discriminating fidelity to truth, by great propriety and force of diction, and a nervous manly elocution, which won new laurels for the well-known orator. After the close of the speeches the remains were re-interred in the ground belonging to the State. Rev. Mr. Norton of Frankfort and Rev. Mr. Berkley of Lexington officiating in the closing religious services. The numbers who were present have been variously estimated at from three to five thousand persons."

The remains of Governor James T. Morehead were brought to Frankfort and placed in a vault January 5th, 1855. A committee of citizens from Frankfort met the committee from Covington at Louisville and under charge of the two committees the remains were brought to Frankfort. The remains were followed by a large number of citizens from the depot to the cemetery. The burial was with a great deal of ceremony on June 13th. General John M. Harlan was chief marshal. Many out of town people were present. James T. Morehead was born in Bullitt county May 24th, 1797. He was educated in the village schools and Transylvania University, studied law with John J. Crittenden; was elected Lieutenant Governor in 1832; upon the death of Governor Breathitt in 1834 he became Ex-officio Governor. After his term expired he resumed the practice of law in Frankfort. In 1837 he was elected to represent Franklin county in the Kentucky Legislature. He was United States Senator from Kentucky in 1841 to 1847. He was an excellent speaker and conservative statesman. His general information was extensive and varied. His library, embracing the largest collection then known of works relating to the history of Kentucky, was purchased by the Young Men's Mercantile Association of Cincinnati, O.

The granddaughter of Governor Morehead presented a splendid oil portrait of him to the Kentucky Historical Society. This portrait is said to have been made by Jouett. If it was not made by him, it was evidently the work of some other skilled artist.

In 1855 Henry Innis Morris was elected Sheriff of the county and he was re-elected in 1856.

A. W. Macklin & Co. did a large and lucrative business as pork packers at Frankfort. During the season of 1853-4 they slaughtered 10,042 hogs; during the season of 1854-5 they killed 10,311; in 1855-6 they killed 13,833. The largest number slaughtered in any one day was 804.

In the year 1856 the Rev. J. M. Lancaster was in charge

THE HISTORY OF FRANKLIN COUNTY. 141

of the Catholic Church at Frankfort; the Rev. John Theobald was in charge of the Baptist Church; the Rev. J. P. Saffold was in charge of the Presbyterian; the Rev. J. M. Bonnell of the Methodist; the Rev. J. N. Norton of the Episcopal, and Rev. P. S. Fall was in charge of the Christian Church.

Judge J. C. Herndon, County Judge of Franklin County, died at his residence in the city of Frankfort on the 18th day of March, 1856, at the age of 47 years. He was an industrious lawyer of considerable ability. For a time he had been a deputy in the County Clerk's office and had held a like position in the Circuit Clerk's office. He was at one time assistant clerk of the House of Representatives, and at another time he held a like position in the State Senate. He was the first man who ever held the position of County Judge of Franklin County, and he was serving his second term in that position at the time of his death.

At the special election held to fill the vacancy of County Judge, Mr. Reuben Brown was elected. He defeated Judge Lysander Hord by 78 votes. James Monroe was elected County Attorney at the same election.

The first bond issue of Franklin County was authorized by act of the Legislature approved March 10th, 1856, by which act the Judge of the Franklin County Court was authorized to issue bonds not to exceed two thousand dollars, to pay off the outstanding debts.

In the year 1857 Thomas M. Green was the editor of The Commonwealth, published at Frankfort, and S. I. M. Major was the editor of the Frankfort Yoeman. The political controversy became so bitter between them that Col. Green sent Col. Major a note dated at Frankfort, May 30th, in which he said: "I wish to know what place outside of the State a note from me will reach you." In answer to which Col. Major said he would be in Jeffersonville, Ind., on Monday, June 1st, at 8 o'clock p. m., at which time Thomas Buford, as the representative of Col. Green was there with a challenge for a duel. Col. Major selected Mr. John O. Bullock as his representative, and it was left to him to fix the time, terms and place of meeting. He fixed the time June 11th; place, the State of Virginia at or near the mouth of the Big Sandy river; weapons were to be the ordinary rifle known as the Kentucky or Western rifle carrying a ball not larger than sixty to the pound, the barrel of the gun not to exceed 38 inches in length; distance, ninety yards. Col. Green refused to accept the terms and the duel was never fought. During this year Jacob Harrod Holman died at his residence in Frankfort. He had been public printer for many years. At one time he was editor of the Commentator, and later he was the editor of the "Spirit of '76" and the "Kentuckian," all of which were published in Frankfort. In the year 1819 Holman fought a duel with Francis Waring, a practical duelist and a brother of the noted John U. Waring, who killed Samuel Q. Richardson in 1835. On the 4th of July, 1819, Francis Waring struck Holman's dog with a saber and killed it, following which a rough and tumble fight ensued, and out of which resulted the duel. Dr. Joe Roberts was the bearer of the challenge. William P. Greenup, son of Governor Greenup, acted as the personal friend of Holman. They met on the farm of Waring's brother-in-law, Rev. Silas Noel, about one mile and a half from Frankfort, and about one mile from where the original difficulty took place. At the first fire Waring fell shot through the heart. Holman also fell at the same time pierced through his hips, and from the effects of which he was a cripple for life.

The contest between the Democratic party and the American Whig or Know-Nothing party in 1857 was one of the warmest ever held in the State. The center of the political contest was at Frankfort. The two parties were evenly divided in Franklin County, there being only one vote difference in the race for State Treasurer. The contest in Frankfort was exceedingly bitter, rioting commenced in a short time after the polls were opened and continued throughout the day. The Americans undertook to prevent the Irish from voting. A mob gathered around the polls and when an Irishman came up to vote some one would call out, "move him," and immediately a shower of rocks, sticks, brick-bats and bottles would strike him. It was almost worth an Irishman's life for him to undertake to vote without some one, native born, with him.

The first fight of the day was when an Irishman by the name of Griffen came up to the court house to vote. When he got within about forty feet of the polls, a bully stationed there for the purpose of assaulting any one who was not American born, made an assault on him. A mob immediately gathered around them. Griffen's brother came to his assistance and when in the act of shooting, some member of the mob struck him in the head and seriously wounded him. The Griffens were rescued from the mob by Col. Lewis E. Harvie and other Democrats, who beat the mob back. Col. Harvie used his walking stick very freely and in return received several wounds, none of which were serious. Later in the day a German came to the polls, and some one called out "move him," and he moved without further invitation, but not quick enough to prevent him from being struck in the head with a rock by some member of the mob, and from the effect of which he came near dying. That afternoon, Judge Thomas B. Monroe, at that time United States District Judge, took an Irishman with him to the polls and when he started to vote, some member of the mob called out "move him." The Judge immediately drew a large knife, and, facing the mob, he brandished his knife and denounced the Americans as a mob and a set of bullies, and said that he would like to see any one prevent the Irishman from voting. The American party was badly defeated in Kentucky. Thomas M. Green, editor of the Commonwealth, in giving excuses for the defeat said: "The fact is that in this race we have had the whole power of the patronage of the Federal Government, the Roman Catholics, the Dutch and Irish, and the whole gang of those mercenary wretches who fight for those who are able to pay best and as might have been expected, we have been defeated by them."

The Bridgeport Female Institute was incorporated in 1858, John Mayhall, James Terry, Benjamin Exum, S. R. Hieronymus and Andrew Neat were the incorporators. For several years this was a very prosperous school and it did a great deal of good in that section of the county.

By resolution of the General Assembly in 1858 the Public Printer was directed to publish in the front part of the acts the names of the State officials. That record shows that the following Franklin County citizens were in office: Charles S. Morehead, Governor; Mason Brown, Secretary of State; T. P. Atticus Bibb, Assistant Secretary of State; James Harlan, Attorney General; Thomas S. Page, Auditor; James R. Watson, Assistant Auditor; James H. Garrard, Treasurer; Andrew McKinley, Register; John M. Harlan, Adjutant General; Albert G. Cammack, Quartermaster General; A. W. Valandingham, State Librarian; A. G. Hodges and John B. Major, Public Printers; J. H. Johnson and Samuel C. Sayre, Assistant Clerks of the House, and Patrick U. Major was Commonwealth's Attorney for the district. Out of the sixteen State officers named by the Public Printer, thirteen of them were citizens of Franklin County. About 50 per cent of the men who have been Governor of Kentucky have been citizens of Frankfort; some of them before and some after their terms of office. Prior to 1860, perhaps 80 per cent of the State officials were citizens and voters of Franklin County. To such an extent did the politicians of Frankfort dominate and control the politics of the State that it became a difficult matter for a man out in the State to be elected to an office, if Frankfort opposed his election. This state of affairs naturally aroused jealousy and engendered a feeling of bitterness against Frankfort. So acute did this feeling become that the people throughout the State, and especially the politicians, commenced accusing Frankfort of being the source of all their woes, political and otherwise. An article from the Louisville Democrat of March 4th, 1859, gives some idea of the feeling which had been worked up against Frankfort. The article reads: "The City of Frankfort, the Capital of the renowned Commonwealth of Kentucky, the abiding place of the famous or rather the infamous Hindoo Clique—the abode of political deviltry in general—the nursery of intrigue and corruption—in short the most God forsaken town that has escaped the hands of the destroying angel since the days of Sodom and Gomorrah—is down, is done for, has fallen, broke, smashed and assigned. For years the political tricksters have ruled the city with a rod of iron, and applied the lash with an unsparing hand upon all who would not lick the foot that kicked them. In power, they have ground to the dust an honest and unpurchasable handful of Democrats who have maintained their integrity through long and trying years of oppression. They have used the credit of the city, for the promotion of their own unhallowed ends, for the perpetuation of power in their own infamous hands; but now the day of reconing is come for lo,

> 'The desolater desolate,
> The Victor overthrown,
> The arbiter of others' fate
> A beggar for his own.'

"Frankfort has failed—her magnificent hotel, constructed on the credit of the city at a cost of $70,000—her extensive gas works, producing in the eloquent language of Judge McKee 'more stink and less light' than any other works of the kind in the world; her excellent water privileges—all have been mortgaged to Col. Hodges to prevent their immediate sale for the liquidation of bills contracted by the Clique, and to atone for the extravagance and folly of her selfish leaders. We sympathize with many of our friends in Frankfort, who may have big hearts and imperishable Democracy burning in their bosoms, may they survive the misfortune that threatens the city of their abode, and see the day when they shall bask in the sunlight of social and political freedom, as for the Clique, the devil has a mortgage upon them and the only wonder is, that he has not foreclosed it long since." This extreme feeling against Frankfort culminated in a joint resolution, appointing a committee of five from the House and three from the Senate to inquire into the expediency of removing the seat of government to Louisville or some other place. The Frankfort people have always been ready to fight each other on any and all propositions except that of Capital removal; on that one question they have always been a unit, and they have at all times been able to secure enough help out in the State to prevent the removal. Henry Clay made a strong and bitter fight against Frankfort and the Frankfort people never forgave him, and for half a century after his death, the Frankfort people have had no love for Lexington. George D. Prentice, the brilliant editor of the Louisville Journal, made a strong effort in 1843 to remove the Capital to Louisville. The controversy between him and Senator Rodes Garth from Whitley county, over the removal question, was the greatest sensational event of that session of the Legislature. Mr. Prentice said in his paper: "It is understood that this functionary (Senator Garth) has sent home for a clean shirt, and actually made arrangements with a servant for the washing of his pocket handkerchief. It is said, not the half, was told by our correspondent concerning this disgusting object." In response, Senator Garth said, on the floor of the Senate: "I pronounce that publication as slanderous and utterly false—a lie from beginning to end, sir. What do honorable Senators on this floor think of this dirty villian charging that I have hired a servant to wash my handkerchief, leaving the impression to go forth to the world that honorable Senators wash their own handkerchiefs, such a sooty, black-hearted calumniator disgraces and would disgrace the veriest brothel in our land and sink into infamy even a negro quarter, and, sir, we are now called upon to remove the seat of government to Louisville, the residence of this infamous journalist who detests virtue, abhors integrity and honor, and who endeavors to reduce reputable Senators and Representatives of the State of Kentucky to his own level of degradation and infamy. Slander, detraction and billingsgate is the proper food his appetite craves and desires to feast upon."

Harry I. Todd was elected Sheriff in 1859; James C. Coleman was elected Coroner; James W. Tate, School Commissioner; James Allen, Jailer, and D. W. Lindsey, City Attorney of the City of Frankfort. Peter Jett contested the election of William F. Parrent as Assessor. The contest board was composed of John M. Harlan, George W. Guinn and W. E. Ashmore. They decided the contest in favor of Parrent.

There was an act of the General Assembly in 1859 which authorized the Governor to cause a pavement to be laid on the east side of the (old) Capitol square, the work not to exceed in cost the sum of $800.

The Franklin County members of the House of Representatives from 1850 to 1860 were Lysander Hord, 1850; Andrew Monroe, 1851-53; John M. Hewitt, 1855-57; Thomas N. Lindsey, 1858-59; John Rodman, 1859-60.

John C. Harrison was sent to the Frankfort station by the Methodist Episcopal Conference in 1857, and the Rev. Joseph Rand in 1859.

There were 180 deaths in Franklin County in the year 1859. During the same year there were 275 children born; there were 51 marriages; the death rate was 1.42; the population of the county in that year was 12,715.

CHAPTER XI.

From 1860 to 1870.

In the year 1860 William H. Sneed was elected County Attorney, Harry I. Todd was re-elected Sheriff, Henry R. Miller, Jailer, and R. Gillispie, School Commissioner.

In 1861 Franklin Chinn was elected County Judge, to fill out the unexpired term of John M. Harlan, who resigned on May 4th. Judge Chinn defeated Robert H. King, candidate on the union ticket by only three votes.

During the year a great many barbecues were given in different sections of the county and many speeches were made on behalf of the union sympathizers, who were using extraordinary efforts to prevent the State from withdrawing from the union. On July 27th one of the largest of these barbecues was held at Julian's woods on the Louisville road. The people of Franklin and the surrounding counties formed a procession on Montgomery (now known as Main) street, reaching from the Capital Hotel to Hon. John J. Crittenden's residence, many citizens were in carriages, some were on horse back, but the great mass of the people were on foot. They marched to Julian's woods, where public addresses were made by a number of the best speakers in the State. Several thousand people were present and great excitement prevailed. Richard C. Anderson, the union candidate for Representative, was elected to represent the county. Brigadier General Robert Anderson, of the United States Army, "The hero of Fort Sumpter," was a cousin of Richard C. Anderson. On September the 6th, General Anderson visited Frankfort. There was a public reception at the Capital Hotel in his honor. The people of Frankfort were profuse in the social attentions paid to him during his stay.

The preachers located in Frankfort at this time were: J. M. Lancaster, of the Catholic Church; John Theobald, of the Old School Baptist; J. E. Spillman, of the Presbyterian; T. C. McKee, of the Baptist; William McD. Abbott, of the Methodist;

J. N. Norton, of the Episcopal, and W. T. Moore, of the Christian Church.

Judge P. U. Major, who was the Democratic candidate for re-election to the office of Commonwealth Attorney, at the August election, 1862, withdrew from the race, the day before the election and John L. Scott, the union candidate, was elected. W. R. Franklin was elected Circuit Clerk, Jacob Swigert, County Judge; W. A. Sneed, County Attorney; A. R. Rennick, County Clerk; J. A. Crittenden, Sheriff; Harry B. Miller, Jailer; Wm. F. Parrent, Assessor; Joseph H. Bailey, Surveyor, and John Whitehead, Coronor. In a short time after the election W. H. Sneed resigned as County Attorney to accept the position of Lieutenant in the Volunteer Infantry, and Eugene P. Moore was elected to fill out the unexpired term.

Francis, a slave, was charged, in 1860, with the offense of trying to poison the family of Hiram Berry. Several members of the family came near dying. She was tried in July of that year, and found guilty. The judgment of the court was, "It is adjudged that the defendant be taken to the jail of this county and there safely kept until the 7th day of September next, on which day between sunrise and sunset the Sheriff of this county shall hang her by the neck until she be dead." The judgment was executed at the time stated.

Gov. Robt. P. Letcher died at his home in Frankfort, January 27, 1861. The Legislature adjourned and went in a body from the State House to his late residence. The procession to the cemetery included members of the Legislature, the State Officials, Judges of the Court of Appeals, and a large number of citizens and strangers. It was preceded by the Frankfort Brass Band. Robt. P. Letcher was a native of Garrard County. He served seven years as Representative of Garrard in the Kentucky Legislature and ten years in Congress. He was elected Governor in 1840 and after that he became a citizen of Frankfort. He was defeated for Congress in the Ashland District, by John C. Breckinridge in 1853.

S. N. Hodges, a prominent attorney of Franklin County, was charged in 1862 with the killing of F. Perry, which tragedy occurred on the court house steps in the city of Frankfort. At the trial the proof was conclusive that Hodges acted in self-defense and the jury returned a verdict of "not guilty." One of the darkest periods in the history of Franklin County was that during the years 1861-4, when the dark clouds of Civil War had settled over the county. Not only were the people of the county disturbed and unsettled, but almost every family in the county had to give up one or more members of the family, to one side or the other, and in many instances brothers were divided; one casting his lot with the South and the other with the North. There were sixty-three men from Franklin in the Confederate Cavalry and one hundred and fifty-two in the Federay; one hundred and fifteen in the Confederate Infantry, and eighty-three in the Federal. That is, there were one hundred and seventy-eight volunteers on the Confederate side, and two hundred and thirty-five on the Federal side. In addition to these 413 there were as many as seven commissioned officers ranking higher than First Lieutenant on the Confederate side, to-wit: Thos. B. Monroe, and Ben Monroe, Majors; Preston B. Scott and John O. Scott, Surgeons; B. J. Monroe, T. B. Monroe and W. D. Acton, Captains. On the Federal side there were nineteen commissioned officers ranking higher than First Lieutenant, to-wit: D. W. Lindsey, Colonel in 22nd Kentucky Volunteer Infantry, and afterwards Inspector General of Kentucky; George Monroe was Lieutenant Colonel in the same regiment; Orlando Brown, Jr., enlisted as a private, he was promoted to Adjutant, then Major and afterwards to Lieutenant Colonel; Joseph W. Roberts went from private to Major, and then became Adjutant of his regiment; John B. Campbell enlisted as a private, was promoted to Corporal, and then Sergeant Major; Thomas L. Crittenden was Major General; Geo. W. Monroe was Brig. General; James R. Page and John G. Keenon each held the commission of Major; John M. Bacon was Lieutenant Colonel, and in the Spanish American war became Brig. General; Robert H. King, Lieutenant Colonel. Those who held the commission of Captain were William W. Bacon, Frank A. Estop, William K. Gray, Jacob Swigert, Daniel Garrard, Henry J. Sheets, Lewis Finnell and Albert G. Bacon.

Captain Daniel Garrard and Captain Albert G. Bacon were killed in battle. In the life of Gen. Forrest, page 32, is this statement in reference to the death of Captain Albert G. Bacon, who was killed on the 28th of December, 1861, "Beyond Sacramento the Union officers succeeded in rallying a squadron of the fugitives and turned upon their pursuers in a desperate and bloody combat, hand to hand. Forrest, still in advance, found himself confronted by this determined detachment of the Union Cavalry, and at such headlong speed was he running towards them, that before he could check his horse he was in their midst engaged in a desperate fight for his life. The Confederate, Captain Merriwether, close at his heels fell, instantly dead, from a pistol shot through the brain. Assaulted from all sides Forrest's skillful left hand stood him in good need. Before they could strike him down a quick thrust from his saber brought Captain Bacon down mortally wounded."

Out of the 115 Volunteer Infantry from Franklin County, who cast their lot with the Southern Confederacy, there were only 36 of them who ever returned to their homes, the others having been killed upon the battle field or died in prison. The 36 who returned, had 52 scars made by Federal bullets during their four years service. To tell of all the heroic deeds and gallant conduct, of all the privations, toils and suffering borne with Spartan-like fortitude by the men from Franklin County, who fought, some for the north and some for the south; to tell of the different actions in which they took part, of the blood which was shed, of the lives which were sacrificed, would extend this work beyond its present scope. A single instance from each side is given, merely to illustrate the fact that brave men went out from Franklin County, upon each side of that great struggle.

In that memorable charge made by Breckenridge at Murfreesboro, on the 2nd day of January, 1863, where the courage and endurance of men were tested to the extreme, R. K. Woodson, Jr., of the 2nd Ky. Reg. Hanson's Brigade, though only a private in the ranks, displayed that desperate courage which was the charteristic of the Franklin County soldiers. Three color bearers were successively killed, when the third one fell, Woodson seized the flag and while bearing it in advance of his comrades, he gave his life for the cause which he thought was just.

Lieutenant Lewis Franklin Todd (Federal) lost his right arm at Chaplain Hill. His distinguished service and severe wound entitled him to an honorable discharge from further service, but as soon as his wound permitted he rejoined his command and on the same day that Woodson died, he, too, gave his life at Murfreesboro for the cause which he thought was just, and though engaged in deadly conflict against each other, on that fatal day, they rest at last in the same consecrated ground at Frankfort. At the battle of Murfreesboro, Kentucky had seventeen regiments of Confederates and fourteen regiments of Federals.

On account of the threatened invasion of the State by General Bragg, J. H. Garrard, provost-marshal of Frankfort, gave notice for every able bodied male citizen of the city of Frankfort to report at the Court House on Monday morning, August 18, 1862, between eight and nine o'clock to enroll themselves for the defense of the city.

From September 3rd to November 5th, 1862, the publication of "The Commonwealth" was suspended. It was during that time that Gen. Bragg and his army were at Frankfort. The Union men, as a rule, fled with the Union soldiers. Gen. Bragg gave orders that no private property was to be destroyed or disturbed, but the goods purchased by him were paid for in Confederate money. The Frankfort Woolen Factory was the greatest loser. The Confederates took seventy-four thousand nine hundred and sixty yards of Kentucky Jeans for which the company had expected to realize as much as one dollar and fifty cents per yard, but instead received only one dollar per yard in Confederate money.

In the issue of November 5th, Mr. William Wallace Harney, editor of "The Commonwealth," said, "Pressing business demanded the presence of the proprietors and editor of this paper in Louisville. The atmosphere of Frankfort, usually so good, was becoming decidedly unhealthy and a little jaunt was earnestly recommended. It was a coincident, perhaps worth mentioning, that just about the same time a squad of Rebel Cavalry was expected in Frankfort. Knowing their principles and necessities, we were of the opinion that they might want us 'to let them a loan' and we were hard up. The proprietor, with proper discretion, left Frankfort in time, but the editor, with a fool hardiness which gave him a claim on Dr. Rodman of a certain State institution, remained to issue a final paper to our subscribers, giving a summary of the latest intelligence. Congratulating himself upon the admirable editorials and newest news he proposed to lay before his readers, he was walking comfortably up the street, when he beheld a sight. It was several creatures, to his optics about forty feet high with guns eighty feet long, in butternut jeans, one with a dirty white handkerchief on the end of a stick and he knew by the butternut and the dirt they were the Southern Confederacy. He was greatly encouraged by learning through a friend, that a list of a hundred names of persons to be arrested had been sent to Col. Scott in which the letters composing his name figured. As an example of his modesty he was quite willing to transfer the compliment to any one else, but it seemed that there was a great deal of modesty in the market just then and the article was not to be disposed of." Frankfort was captured and held twice during the month of November, by each party.

Lieutenant John J. Roberts was in charge of the defense of the city. One of his men was fatally wounded and Captain Garriott of the Southern force, was shot in the side and one of his company was also wounded. After Captain Garriott fell, the Confederate force gave way and the Union force took charge of the city.

From October 14th, 1862, to November 19, of the same year, twenty-eight Federal soldiers died in the local hospital at Frankfort.

When Gen. John H. Morgan made his raid through Kentucky, in 1864, Gen. D. W. Lindsey, who was at the time commander of a division under Gen. U. S. Grant in the South, was requested by Gov. Bramlette to return to Kentucky and organize the home guards as a protection for Frankfort, where there was stored large quantities of commissary and quartermaster stores. In the organization which he made, Ed Keenon was made Col., Thomas J. Hutchinson, major of the first battalion and John A. Crittenden, Adjutant. The two companies, one under Buck Keenon and the other under A. J. Graham, were ordered out to protect the arsenal and a large number of Ballard rifles, then on the cars in the city. A division of Morgan's command under Col. Clark was ordered to Frankfort to capture the arms and other munitions of war stored at Frankfort. Governor Bramlette, Gen. D. W. Lindsey, Gen. John M. Harlan and Col. George B. Monroe were in command when the attack by Col. Clark was made on June 10th. Mr. V. Berberich, who had charge of one of the guns located on Fort Hill, fired the first shot. A great many shots were fired but the casualties were few. Major Hutchinson was shot in the mouth; Corporal John M. Coleman was wounded in the breast. None of Col. Clark's men were killed. The spirited resistance made by the home guards prevented the capture of Frankfort at that time.

ROSTER OF SOLDIERS FROM FRANKLIN COUNTY IN THE REBELLION.

FEDERAL CAVALRY.

List of Company "B," 3rd Kentucky Cavalry: Captain, Albert G. Bacon; Captain, Robert H. King; Lieutenant, John J. Roberts; Sergeant, Baxter P. Gray; Sergeant, G. S. Innis; Sergeant, Walter W. Winter; Sergeant, Bunnias Malcomb; Corporals, Charles B. Wallace, Robert Innis, John Church, William Campbell, Thomas W. Hockinsmith; Privates, Salmon Harlow, Solomon Steele, Samuel McCurdy, Alexander Cohen, Turner Rogers, John Abrahams, John F. Clubbe, Geo. Fleming, Oliver H. P. Garnett, Thaddeus Hawkins, Allen K. Prime, Thomas Petty, David Rogers, John Steele, Hugh Tyler, Edward A. Wallace, Wm. Wells, Hiram Shannon, Willis Roach.

Company "C," 9th Kentucky: Robert L. Henry, Chas. F.

Fleming, John L. Dailey, Chas. M. Christopher, Jacob N. Boots, John C. Baker, Preston Bramlett, Edward F. Bacon, Wister Bolden, Wm. H. Christopher, Mason B. Christopher, Thomas F. Fightmaster, Willis H. Hosler, Cassius M. Hall, David C. Hoover, James A. Hardin, Edward Hudson, Thomas S. Hosler, Alexander C. Henry, Preston Hampton, Thomas W. Hancock, Lucien B. Hawkins, James W. Kinkade, Franklin R. Moss, John C. McGinnis, William B. Newton, Henry J. Newton, John Newton, Wm. H. Oliver, Geo. M. Perry, John K. Pallett, Robert H. Pallett, Albert N. Smith, Bush Sacra, Reuben Wallace, Leander Wise, James Wise, Wirt Yancy, Angus McMullen, Ashley Buffin, Jr., Thomas T. Saterwhite, deserted.

Company "E" 9th Kentucky Volunteers.

Captains, Henry J. Sheets, James R. Page; Lieutenants, Thomas Mahoney, Thomas M. Page, Richard H. Parrent; Sergeants, Wm. H. Stanley, John B. Dryden, George Finnell, Wm. H. Hutcherson, John W. Daniels, Jessie Whitehouse, John B. Richardson, Richard H. Mitchell; Privates, Gibson F. Graham, William Lillis, Daniel Sheehan, John Conner, John Harrod, Richard Bradley, Richard Gaines, Joseph Bohannon, Wm. Duke, Francis Goins, Robert Agee, Benjamin Armstrong, Wm. Brown, Daniel Burchfield, Andrew Burchfield, Fielding Bransom, Dennis Burns, John H. Bohannon, Benjamin Brown, Morris Caples, James Conner, William Craik, Henderson Crutchfield, John W. Cox, Richard Entwistle, Walter Flarity, Bartholomew Fisher, Presley O. Gaines, Squire Hicks, James M. Holder, William Hutcherson, Henry Hogan, Peter Harmon, David Kirkpatrick, Charles Mitchell, Henry Masters, Chas. H. Moss, Hawkins G. Mitchell, Braczellear B. Morris, Elisha M. Merchant, William McCauliff Alexander McEwan, Manlius T. Mitchell, Robert Owens, Andrew J. Polley, Joseph T. Prime, John Sheehan, Chas. P. Shea, John Sullivan, Thomas Tully, Joseph Vogt, Richard Vaughn, William Watkins, John S. Williams, Benjamin M. Jolly, John Dean, Charles Snellen, Joshua Warren, Samuel Armstrong, William T. Alexander, Sandford Goins, John W.

Peiffer; Deserters, Willis Sheets, Thomas Gayle, David Hockinsmith, John W. Hancock and Thomas Tooly.

ROLL OF FEDERAL VOLUNTEER INFANTRY.

COMPANY "A" 22ND KENTUCKY.

William Gainey, William H. Milam, William T. Walls.

COMPANY "F" 22ND KENTUCKY.

Captain Daniel Garrard, Jr., killed at Chickasaw Bluffs. Captain, William W. Bacon; Lieutenants, William H. Sneed and Richard F. Frayne; Corporals, David C. Bledsoe and Benjamin Merchant; Privates, Henry Cecil, John F. Henderson, Cornelius McCarty, Jeremiah Tyre, Geo. W. Willis, Thomas E. West, John West, Chas. Boucher, Henry K. Brawner, Harrison Cohorn, Theodore F. C. Polk, Charles Shaw, Wiley Smith, John Seal, Charles Rossen, Orlando Brown, Jr., William Bledsoe, John Buffin, Dennis Bergin, James Baldwin, John B. Campbell, James Hollywood, James Lunsford, Enoch Marshall, Christopher Merchant, Nathan Nolan, Joseph North, Geo. B. Pitman, Byran J. Quin, Joseph W. Roberts, Alexander Snelling, James A. Shea, James T. Shaw, Leonard L. Wells, Joseph Montgomery, Geo. W. Feitmaster, Robert Semones, Geo. W. Merchant, John Walker; Deserters, Alexander Burns, Daniel Smither, Reuben West.

COMPANY "I" OF 22ND KENTUCKY.

Captains, Frank A. Estep and William K. Gray; Privates, James Linton, Peter Brawner, John R. Gore, Isaac C. Mitchell, Spillman C. Owens, Hiram Shannon, Jacob Swigert, Jr., Frank Updike, John B. Walker, Edward B. Coleman, John B. Veach, James M. Pearson, Henry R. Bradley, Geo. W. Crumbaugh, Litz Combs, John M. Gayle, Leonard Striff, John Sullivan, Geo. W. Tweedie, Samuel F. Eperson, John R. Burke, Geo. W. Chinn, Henry Gergle, John Hoppell, Robert Hatcher, Charles

Marshall, William Howe, Thomas Abrahams; Deserters, Geo. W. Easly, Jessie Gibson.

ROSTER OF CONFEDERATE SOLDIERS IN THE REBELLION FROM FRANKLIN COUNTY.

Cavalry—Company "C" 9th Kentucky—Morgan's Command.

Lieutenant, A. J. Church; A. W. Macklin, T. B. Wilkinson, George Wilkinson, Terry Freeman, Thomas Freeman, Mason B. Lucas, T. W. Scott, Joel E. Scott, Joseph Bell, Jack Head, Moffett Crutcher, Louis Crutcher, William Crutcher, killed at Columbia; E. O. Hawkins, W. Price, W. H. Church, Robt. C. Church, Frank Chinn, Thomas E. Dailey, Ed. McLaughlin, Dan Hodges, Geo. Holloway, Geo. Scarce, John Sheets, William Sheets, Ben Sheets, William Updike, Ben Hockersmith, Theo. Hockersmith, Jessie Hockersmith, Robert Sheets, Wheeler Winter, John Bryant, John A. Lewis, W. J. Lewis, John Howe, John Harrod, James Harp, Merrett Williams, Jessie Tillett, Black Mitchell, Thomas Hopper, Joe Gibson, Joseph French, Sidney French, Robert Jones, William Duvall, Byron Montgomery, Aquilla Talbott, Howard Steadman, Loyd Wingate, Cyrus Wingate, Dr. Ben Duvall, Surgeon.

FRANKLIN COUNTY MEN IN CONFEDERATE INFANTRY.

Infantry—Company "E" 4th Kentucky.

Major Thomas B. Monroe, killed at Shilo; Reg. Surgeon, Preston B. Scott; Captain, Ben J. Monroe, killed at Shilo; Lieutenant, George B. Burnley, killed; Lieutenants, Isham T. Dudley, Robert A. Thompson; R. L. Russell, Thomas T. Price, Sam W. Shannon, Alfred Clark, George W. Lawler, Wm. T. Price, S. S. Stringfellow, Ben Baxter, John T. Cardwell, Joe Cole, James G. Crockett, Cornelius Duvall, J. K. Exum, Dan C. Graves, John J. Graves, killed at Chickamauga; W. W. Hawkins, killed at Chickamauga; Dennis Haly, Wm.

Howe, W. H. Hieronymous, Chas. Howe, Dodridge A. Jett, died in prison; W. L. Jett, Dennis McSweeney, Frank A. Monroe, Jessie R. Middleton, Wm. W. Menzies, John W. Miller, Andrew J. Witt, William J. Watkins.

Company "K" 5th Infantry.

Captain, W. D. Acton, Lieutenants, J. T. Gaines, D. S. Crockett, J. C. Robb; H. S. Green, Ben F. Rogers, James Yount, William Ellis, Neill Hackett, Felix Long, James B. McQueen, N. L. Moore, James D. Moore, William M. Robb, John Roberts, Alex Sheets, Presley Sandford, Jerry Spaulding, J. K. Tracy, Jacob Williams, W. W. Wright, James Lowery, Jack Pattie, C. H. Menzies, James McQueen, Tom Hawkins, William G. Crutcher, William Glore, Ben Hickman, Henry Marshall, Lewis Moore, Thomas Powers, Harry Roberts, Sam Sheets, W. N. Shelton, John W. Smith, Jerry Tracy, Henry White, James Wright.

Company "G" 6th Infantry.

Ben F. Dickerson.

Company "A" 2nd Infantry.

John A. Scott, Surgeon; A. G. Montgomery, Thompson Scroggins, John S. Stout, Samuel S. Willson, Pias Pulliam.

Company "B."

William H. Duvall, Marine Duvall.

Company "C."

George Sebree.

Company "E."

J. T. Atkins, Walter Bradley, F. M. Chambers, John Crutcher, Andrew Carter, Robert Carter, J. W. Cunningham, W. C. Church, Joseph Dailey, Willis Hensley, E. P. Mershon, John W. Payne, James Plasters, John Pulliam, J. W. Robinson,

Sam Sheets, Ben Sheets, John T. Sebree, J. O. Sebree, George Sebree, Robert Sebree, Ben Wright.

Company "H."

Alex G. Brawner, Thomas P. Brawner.

Company "I."

Lieutenant, S. S. Collins; John P. Aubrey, Ben F. Brown, E. J. Collins, Geo. W. Cheney, James Paxton.

Dr. Wm. C. Sneed died November 20, 1862. For twenty-five years he was a successful practitioner at Frankfort. He stood high in his profession and he was known as a man of integrity and honor. He contributed many valuable articles to the leading medical journals of the country. For some time he was president of the State Medical Society. His history of the Kentucky penitentiary was so well written that the Kentucky Legislature had it published at the expense of the State.

Hon. James Harlan died at his home in Frankfort, February 18, 1863. He was the father of Justice John M. Harlan. He was Attorney General of the State for many years and was one of the most prominent lawyers and politicians in the State. He was elected to the U. S. Congress, where he attained high rank. He was afterwards Secretary of State, Attorney General and District Attorney of the United States, which position he held at the time of his death. He was a man of distinguished ability.

One of the greatest men, if not the very greatest man, who ever claimed Frankfort as his home, was the Hon. John Jordon Crittenden, who died at his residence in Frankfort, on July 26th, 1863.

"The Commonwealth" said of him, "Thus has passed from the earth the last of the great men of post-revolutionary times, who kept alive, in the presence of the whole world the great truth that man was capable of self-government. He survived his illustrious compeers, Clay, Calhoun and Webster and at the time of his death did not leave his equal behind him in the Nation and scarcely in the world itself. In all that constitutes true greatness he had no superior. Great without ambition for place or prominence. Patriotic without any selfish inducements, brave, virtuous and self-denying, from the instincts of his nature he was the model of a citizen, a patriot and a gentleman. The great Kentuckian is dead. Millions of Americans, both North and South, will hear this announcement with profoundest sorrow, while to his own native Kentucky the news will come with a sadness that will make her feel as if she stood alone in the blast to mourn the loss of her well beloved son."

The Governor issued a proclamation dated at Frankfort, July 27th, in which he said: "When a great man dies a Nation mourns. Such an event has occurred in our midst, in the death of the Hon. John J. Crittenden. Kentucky's longest tried statesman in her public service, a man faithful to every trust, one who has added, by his talents and character, to the fame of the Nation and has pre-eminently advanced the glory and honor of his native Kentucky. It is fit and proper that all testimonies of respect and affection should be paid his remains by all in authority as well as by private citizens. I therefore earnestly request that all places of business shall be closed on Wednesday next, from the hours of 10 o'clock in the morning until 5 in the afternoon and hereby direct all the public offices in Frankfort to be closed during the entire day, and I appoint Gen. John W. Finnell, Col. James H. Garrard and Col. Orlando Brown a committee to make suitable arrangements for the funeral.

By the Governor.

J. F. ROBINSON.

D. C. WICKLIFFE,
    Secretary of State.

Hon. John Jordon Crittenden was born in Woodford County in 1786. He was educated at Washington Academy and William and Mary's College in Virginia. He studied law with the Hon. George M. Bibb and commenced to practice the profession at Russellville, Ky. In 1811 he was elected to rep-

THE HISTORY OF FRANKLIN COUNTY. 161

resent Logan County in the Kentucky Legislature. He served six terms from that county; the last term as Speaker. During his last year in the Legislature from Logan County, he was elected to the United States Senate, and was the youngest member of that body. He moved to Frankfort in 1819. He was elected to represent Franklin County in the Kentucky Legislature in 1825-29-30-31 and 1832. He was the recognized leader of the Old Court party in the controversy between the Old and the New Court. In 1835 he was re-elected to the United States Senate and he remained there until President Harrison appointed him Attorney General of the United States. After the death of Mr. Harrison, he resigned and was elected to fill out the unexpired term of Henry Clay in the Federal Senate. In 1843 he was re-elected to the Senate but resigned in 1848 to make the race for Governor. He also resigned the position of Governor in order to accept the appointment of U. S. Attorney General, under President Fillmore. After the expiration of his term he was again elected to the Federal Senate. He was serving his second term as a member of the lower House of Congress, from the Ashland District, at the time of his death. He was the recognized leader of the Peace party, and he did all that he could to prevent the war between the States. As a man he was loved and honored, and as a statesman he was held in reverence by the people of his State and Nation.

In 1863 H. M. Bedford was elected to represent the county in the Kentucky Legislature, and H. B. Innis was elected Sheriff. In November, Gen. D. W. Lindsey was appointed Inspector General of Kentucky, which gave him the rank of Major General and Acting Commander of all of the military forces of the State.

During the summer of 1863 Knight's bridge across Elkhorn was built by John Gault, contractor.

In 1864 Harry B. Innis was re-elected Sheriff, John R. Graham was elected School Commissioner, and William Craik was appointed Jailer in the place of R. H. Miller, resigned. In the month of August guerrillas became troublesome in the county. On the 22nd they went to John Steadman's store at

Steadmantown and took what they wanted; they also went to the house of Zachery Lewis and made a search for money. They took a horse from Lawson Noel and terrorized many other citizens. One of the guerrillas was known to be Hugh Harrod, a deserter from the company of Capt. R. B. Taylor, and probably all of them were deserters from the Union Army.

On January 24th, 1865, a band, commanded by a man named Taylor, was at Bridgeport and robbed the stores and citizens indiscriminately, and the following night the same band visited and robbed Farmer's store at Farmdale.

By order of Steve Burbridge, on the afternoon of November 2, 1864, eight men were brought from Lexington to Frankfort, and on that same afternoon four of them were taken to a vacant lot in South Frankfort, corner of Todd and Shelby streets, and shot in retaliation for the death of a man named Graham, who was killed at Peak's Mill. On the 3rd, the other four were taken to New Castle and executed for the two negroes who were killed there by John Marshall.

The official returns of the Presidential election in 1864, show that Lincoln was not popular in Franklin County as a presidential candidate. He received 253 votes and McClellen received 689 in the County.

O. G. Cates died on May 10, 1865. He was a resident of Frankfort for many years. He was a lawyer of ability. During the administration of Gov. Owsley, he was appointed Attorney General of Kentucky and served with distinction. He was afterwards President of the Board of Internal Improvements, which office he filled with fidelity to the State and honor to himself. He was buried in the Frankfort cemetery.

On June 12, 1865, an explosion of a locomotive boiler occurred at the Frankfort station, which caused the instant death of three men and the injury of ten others, six of whom were fatally injured. The station was almost a total wreck, the walls were knocked down and the roof torn to pieces. The sand box fell through the roof of Mrs. Campbell's residence on the north side of the street, and several other houses were materially damaged. Those who were instantly killed were, William Brown, of Frankfort; William Carroll, of Lexington, and

Louis Pumphry, of Louisville. Those who afterwards died from the effects of the injuries were John Henderson, Jr.; a young son of John E. Miles; Mike Fox; a soldier by the name of Kelly; J. W. Hunter and a boy named Cornelius. The cause of the explosion was never satisfactorily explained.

In 1865, James Harlan, Jr., was elected to represent the county; Richard A. Bohannon was elected Jailer and Stephen D. Morris, County Attorney. In October of that year, seven convicts made their escape from the Frankfort penitentiary. They put a ladder to the top of the wall and told the guard that they had been ordered to do so by the foreman, and in that way made their escape.

On Wednesday, November 22, 1865, the public building in which were situated the Governor's office, the Secretary of State, and the Clerk of the Court of Appeals, was destroyed by fire. The fire originated in the Appellate Clerk's office and the entire contents of that office were destroyed. All of the official and public documents in the office of the Governor and Secretary of State, together with the Governor's private law library and practically every thing else in those two offices were saved. The money loss was large, but the loss of records were of small consideration.

In 1866 gas mains were laid in South Frankfort and that section of the city was supplied with gas.

The oil portrait of Henry Clay, which hung in the Legislative hall of the Old Capitol for about half a century, was painted by William Fry, of Huntsville, Alabama. It is a full portrait of the "great commoner," life size, 7x11, and it is in every respect a fine painting. The likeness is good both in features and expression of the face and in the general appearance and attitude. "The noble figure stands out in bold relief upon the canvas as if endowed with life and animation, still charming and thrilling an audience with his golden and burning words."

Col. Robt. H. King died at his home in Frankfort, on June 9, 1866. He was Colonel of the 3rd Kentucky Volunteer Cavalry. He enlisted in the Union Army as First Lieutenant, in Capt. Albert G. Bacon's company, which was raised in

Franklin County; on the death of Capt. Bacon, at Sacramento, Lieut. King became Captain. He was afterwards commissioned as Major, and later as Lieutenant Colonel and afterwards breveted Colonel for gallant and meritorious conduct. He commanded a brigade in Sherman's "ride to the sea." Col. King possessed fine talents. He was a genial, social and gallant gentleman and was greatly loved by those who knew him. "He passed through the war unharmed, but early in the days of peace and in early manhood he fell a victim to that insidious foe which destroys more men than pestilence and war and which produces more sorrow than all other evils combined. He was buried in the Frankfort cemetery with military honors. The pall-bearers were Maj.-Gen. Thos. L. Crittenden, Gen. D. W. Lindsey, Brig.-Gen. George W. Monroe, Gen. John M. Harlan, Lieut.-Col. James T. Bramlette, Maj. James R. Page, Maj. John M. Bacon and Sergeon J. T. Hatchitt.

On May 7, 1866, a colored boy by the name of Charles made a criminal assault on a small white girl seven years of age. That night the negro was taken from the jail by a mob and hung. The hanging was done without any excitement or disorder. A merited punishment was sternly and speedily administered, an example was set which has been closely followed for half a century and which ought to be a sufficient warning to the negro race, and the white too, as for that matter, that the women and girls of Franklin County must be protected. During the half century which the negro has been free, not one of them has ever been tried in Franklin County by a legally constituted court for criminal assault, and doubtless during the next half century not one of them will be so tried. Such crimes arouse a natural indignation and the general public demands an immediate execution of the criminal, with the idea, that in order to thoroughly and effectively eradicate such crimes the punishment must not only be certain and severe, but it must also be speedily administered. On the night of January 30, 1868, a negro by the name of Jim Macklin, who had committed an assault on a young white woman near the State Arsenal, and had thrown her body down the embankment near the tunnel, was taken from the Frankfort jail and carried to the place where the crime was committed and hung. The results of this hanging created a great deal of excitement. The United States Court at that time had jurisdiction of such cases. Warrants were sworn out against some of the most substantial citizens of Frankfort, charged with being implicated in the hanging The United States Marshal arrested Michael Parker, John Owens, James Welch, Edward Cummins, Michael Buckley, Pat Sullivan, Mike Callahan, Dan Callahan, Pat Newman, Thomas Newman, Dennis Griffin, Ed Burns and L. Tobin and took them before the Commissioner of the United States Court for examining trial. Col. John Mason Brown prosecuted them and Judge G. W. Craddock, Judge P. U. Major and Major D. W. Carpenter defended. On motion of Col. Brown, Mr. L. Tobin was discharged, there being no evidence to implicate him. After a full hearing all of the defendants were discharged, except Michael Callahan, Daniel Callahan, Jim Welch, Edward Cummins and M. Parker. There was serious complaint against the manner in which Commissioner Vance conducted the trial of the accused parties; contrary to the advice of Col. Brown, he proceeded in a way which convinced the public that he was neither a lawyer nor an honest man.

Father Lambert Young, the Catholic priest, who was in charge of the Catholic Church at Frankfort, was subpoenaed as a witness against the defendants, but he refused to tell what had been told to him by reason of the fact that he was a Christian priest, and the court thereupon committed him to jail for contempt of court. The defendants were released on bail, but Father Young remained in jail until the 28th of July; after his release he wrote a card thanking his many friends for their kindness to him and in which he said, "None of these good citizens, I feel sure, are possessed with the idea that my refusing to testify on the trial of the Frankfort prisoners arose from any disposition to contemn the law, the Grand Jury or the Hon. Court. I truly revere the law and I respect its officers, and had it been possible for me to act otherwise than I did without doing outrage to my conscience as a Christian priest, and to my sense of honor as a man, I should certainly have promptly given the evidence demanded and thus have saved myself the misery of confinement in the county jail." Perhaps no man ever lived in Frankfort who was more universally honored and respected by Catholics, Protestants and the people generally than was Father Lambert Young.

In February, 1866, J. Swigert resigned as County Judge, and the Magistrates elected Judge Lysander Hord and at the following August election he was elected by the people; at that time A. H. Rennick was elected County Clerk; Eugene P. Moore, County Attorney; W. J. Chinn, Sheriff; E. H. Tole, Coroner; R. Hutchinson, Jailer; J. S. Hawkins, Surveyor, and Peter Jett, Assessor.

In October of that year Dr. James G. Hatchitt was appointed postmaster at Frankfort, in the place of William A. Gaines, resigned.

Hon. Mason Brown died at his home in Frankfort, on January 27, 1867, at the age of 68 years. He was the son of John Brown, the first Congressman from the Western Country. Mason Brown was a graduate of Yale College; after his graduation he entered the law office of John J. Crittenden, and subsequently graduated in the law school at Lexington. He formed a partnership with Hon. Ben Mills and subsequently with Governor Chas. S. Morehead and in conjunction they compiled a work of great value to the legal profession, known as "Morehead & Brown's Digest." He was known as one of the great lawyers of Kentucky. He was Commonwealth's Attorney for several years and was afterwards elected Judge of the Circuit Court and as such Judge he gained the distinction of being one of the greatest jurists in the country. He was Secretary of State during the administration of Governor C. S. Morehead, and he was United States District Attorney for the district in which he lived for several years, prior to his death.

In 1860, the Kentucky Legislature passed a resolution authorizing and directing the Governor of Kentucky to procure suitable gold medals, appropriately inscribed, to be presented to the surviving officers and soldiers of the Kentucky Volunteers, who were present and participated in the engagement between the Americans and British on Lake Erie on the 10th of September, 1813.

The Governor directed Mr. B. F. Meek of Frankfort, to design and make these medals. The medal was beautifully executed, of the purest virgin gold. Its circumference was four and seven-eighths inches and its weight thirty-one pennyweights. The obverse of the medal represented a naval engagement, executed with the minutest fidelity of detail. The rigging, smoke, battle flags and waves were graphically depicted, surrounding the design was the legend, "We have met the enemy and they are ours."—the memorable dispatch of the immortal Perry—with the date, "Lake Erie, Sept. 10th, 1813."

The reverse of the medal bore the inscription, "To . . . . By Resolution of the Kentucky Legislature, February, 1860," and inclosed by wreaths of oak leaves and laurel. At the time this medal was offered there were supposed to be only four Kentuckians living, viz.: Dr. William Talliaferro, James Artus, John Norris and John Tucker, but in 1866 two additional medals were ordered, one for Ezra Youngblood and one for Samuel Hatfield of Floyd County.

B. F. Meek was the owner of a jewelry store on Main street, where he did a successful business for a great many years. He was one of the makers of the Meek & Milam fishing reel, which became one of the most noted productions ever supplied to the sporting world. He took an active part in the business and political affairs of Frankfort. He was a man of integrity and was honored and respected by all who knew him.

On February 14, 1867, Benson Creek overflowed its banks and did a great deal of damage to that section of the county. Conway's mill, located at the falls of Benson Creek, about four miles from Frankfort, was washed away and totally destroyed; two spans of the county bridge, known as "Ganey's bridge," about one mile from the city were carried off by the flood; a man by the name of Alexander lost his stable, and a great deal of fencing was lost. At a court held in the following May $1,000 was appropriated with which to rebuild the

Gancy bridge; at the same session of the court $1,000 was appropriated for rebuilding the bridge over Main Elkhorn on the Owenton road; also a thousand dollars for building a bridge at the mouth of Benson, and $250 for building one over Leestown branch. The action of the commissioners in selling the upper stories, over the County and Circuit Court Clerk's offices was approved and confirmed.

In 1867 there were only thirty-six men in Franklin County whose income exceeded one thousand dollars per year, and only fourteen whose income exceeded two thousand dollars, and only nine whose incomes exceeded three thousand, and only five whose income exceeded four thousand dollars per year.

Franklin County lost by death more of its illustrious citizens during the decade from 1860 to 1870 than during any other like period of its history. To the long list of great men who died during this decade is added the names of Theodore O'Hara and Charles S. Morehead. While neither of them were actual residents of the county at the time of their death, yet the main part of their lives were spent in Franklin County, and the literary work which made them famous was done while they lived in Frankfort.

In the summer of 1867 the trustees of the Frankfort public school purchased a lot in South Frankfort, from Judge Geo. C. Drane, upon which to erect a public school building. During the following year Mr. John Haly, contractor, completed the building. It was a three story brick building with teachers' room, hat and cloak rooms, Superintendent's office, etc.

On November 12, 1867, Col. J. Stoddard Johnston became the editor of the Frankfort Yeoman. Prior to that time Col. S. I. M. Major had been editor and publisher. Col. Johnston was recognized as one of the best writers in the State. His strong editorials soon established the Yeoman as the leading journal of the State and as the organ of the Democratic Party.

P. R. Pattie was appointed Jailer in 1867, and Robert Lawler was elected Jailer in 1868 to fill out an unexpired term; Joseph Robertson was elected Sheriff in 1869.

In 1868 the Louisville and Nashville Railroad Company placed a floor for pedestrians on the railroad bridge. The floor was only five feet wide but it was of great convenience to the people of Bellepoint and the northwest section of the county. The completion of the bridge across the mouth of Benson that year gave the people of that section of the county easy access to the city of Frankfort. Prior to the completion of these conveniences the people in that section of the county were often prevented from reaching their County Seat for weeks and sometimes months, on account of high water and bad roads.

The annual Methodist Conference was held in Frankfort in 1868. It was presided over by Bishop Lovick Pierce. The Rev. H. A. M. Henderson was returned to the Frankfort station. The Rev. J. L. T. Holland was called to the Christian Church during the same year. The other preachers located in Frankfort at that time were Rev. J. N. Norton, in charge of the Episcopal Church; Rev. J. S. Hays, of the Presbyterian, and Rev. W. L. Jermane, of the Baptist. The ceremony of laying the corner stone of "St. John's in the Wilderness" took place on St. John's Day, June 24, 1867. It was witnessed by a large number of persons from that section of the county and from Frankfort. For quite a number of years after these buildings were constructed, the mission at that place was in a most flourishing condition, it embraced an orphans' home, a Sunday School and a place for public worship. It was located about five miles from Frankfort on the St. John's road.

At the January term, 1869, of the Franklin County Fiscal Court, $75,000 was appropriated to the Kentucky river improvement, and $10,000 for the bridges of the county, and in order to raise the amounts appropriated county bonds were issued.

Major Hall, so named in honor of Mayor S. I. M. Major, was completed in that year. It was located on Main Street where the City Hall now stands, fronting 66 feet and running back 138 feet. The first floor contained on one side of the main entrance a good restaurant and on the other a store room which was used for furniture. The upper story contained a large room which was used for a billiard room and an elegant suit of club rooms besides the hall. The size of the auditorium was 82x56. The seating capacity was 1,500. The drop curtain was a very superior painting representing the ruins of ancient Rome. The building was burned November 11, 1882.

On the night of the 19th of February, the upper portion of the center pier of the St. Clair street bridge fell. The passage of the bridge was closed for several months. The work to restore the pier was commenced at once, but on account of the high water at that season of the year, slow progress was made. It was late in the summer before it was again opened for vehicles.

The only death ever recorded in Franklin County from hydrophobia was that of Mr. John D. Sargent which occurred at his home in the country, March 22, 1869. About three months prior to his death he received a bite from a small dog, which attracted no attention and created no alarm because the wound was seemingly cured in a short time. Three days prior to his death he felt so unwell that he sent for a physician, who after a careful examination could not determine the character of his disease. A few hours later the disease developed such symptoms which rendered the mistaking it for any thing else, impossible. At every effort to gratify his extreme thirst he was seized with contraction of the throat and fearful spasms, requiring the assistance of several persons to hold him, until at last the dread of swallowing made him refuse everything offered to him. During the continuance of the attacks he made no effort to injure any of the many persons who were with him. It was a distressing and painful sight. The terror indicated in his face, the brilliant and protruding eyes, the agonizing convulsions and his loud cries for help impressed those present with the idea that his death was the most horrible one a man could die.

On the night of April 2nd, the whiskey warehouse situated on the north bank of the Kentucky river near the end of the St. Clair street bridge was burned with 3,500 barrels of whiskey, the estimated loss of which was $350,000. The warehouse belonged to George B. Macklin, and the whiskey was owned, to a great extent, by eastern parties, on which they had considerable insurance. The burning whiskey ran from the building on to the river in a broad stream, which burned with a bluish flame and which spread itself far out in the river and for a considerable distance up and down the river. The river on fire presented a most spectacular appearance. For several hours the bridge was in imminent danger. It caught fire several times but each time the flames were extinguished without material damage.

Capt. John A. Holton died at the homestead on which he was raised, near the Forks of Elkhorn, on the 13th of June. About 1804 he made his first trip on a flat boat, ladened with produce, from Frankfort to New Orleans. Prior to 1812 he made several other trips as captain of such boats, returning, as was the custom in that day, on foot, through the Indian country of Mississippi and Tennessee. He was one of the first to join Capt. Paschal Hickman's company in the War of 1812, and was one of the few survivors of that company at the massacre of the River Raisen. In this action Capt. Holton was wounded in the ankle and was taken prisoner. He was about the only man from Franklin County who after being wounded and captured escaped the massacre which followed the surrender of those brave men. After his return from the war he resumed his former occupation on the river and after the introduction of steam he became captain of a boat, first on the Ohio and Mississippi and later on the Kentucky river. He was a very popular and successful officer. In 1848 he represented Franklin County in the Kentucky Legislature.

On the 16th of June, General Peter Dudley died at his home in the city of Frankfort. He was First Lieutenant in Capt. Hickman's company, and was with him at the River Raisen, but he escaped capture and returned to Frankfort and raised another company. Gen. Peter Dudley held many positions of honor and trust, both civil and military. He was one of the very strong characters of the day in which he lived. He was eighty years of age at the time of his death. He was buried in the Frankfort cemetery with military honors. The funeral discourse was delivered by Rev. L. W. Seeley; the procession was in charge of Col. J. Stoddard Johnston, with Gen.

D. W. Lindsey and Major John B. Castleman as assistants. The military was composed of soldiers of the rebellion, irrespective of the armies in which they served. Federal and Confederate soldiers marched side by side, without uniforms, but equipped with muskets and other accoutrements.

Capt. John W. Russell died August 1st. He was born in Virginia in 1794 and brought to Kentucky while an infant. He was apprenticed to a blacksmith, but before his time expired he became a soldier in the War of 1812 and gained distinction before he became of age. After the war he was employed in the transportation of products to New Orleans. The unsettled and unsafe condition of the Western Country was such that no man without great physical courage would engage in that business. When steamboats were placed in the trade Captain Russell was given command of one of the first boats. His adventures on the river and in the river towns, which were overrun with gamblers and robbers, sounds like fiction. When the steamer "General Brown" was lost by an explosion in 1838, Capt. Russell's presence of mind and heroism saved the lives of six men. His fight with the robber band of Lafitte in New Orleans, established his reputation as a man of courage.

President Harrison appointed him commander of a fleet of "snag boats" and he remained in the service of the United States for several years and accumulated considerable property. Later he became a successful farmer. He built a steam flour mill, the first of the kind ever built in the county. This mill was located on Benson Creek. He was a member of the State Senate in 1850 and was largely instrumental in building the State Arsenal, which was erected in that year. Capt. Russell was the father of Mrs. Mary Brown Russell Day, who was elected and served two terms as State Librarian for the Commonwealth of Kentucky.

A total eclipse of the sun took place August 7th. At the time there was not a cloud to be seen and the atmospherical conditions for accurate and satisfactory observations were perfect. The stars were as clear and bright as they are at night. The chickens went, hurriedly, to roost, and about the time they got well settled the sun came out clear and bright. Some people through the county who were not informed in reference to the event, thought that the judgment day had come.

The Frankfort Cotton Mills had on exhibition at a fair for textile fabrics held at Cincinnati in 1869, some of its manufactured goods. The mill at Frankfort was awarded a premium for the best yarn. The specimen exhibited was taken from the stock made every day and competed successfully with yarns manufactured especially for exhibition. There were a great many competitors. These mills were successfully operated until about 1880.

Judge J. M. Hewitt died in November, 1869. He was born in Virginia in 1793. He was commissioned Lieutenant in the regular army in 1815. He was licensed to practice law in 1816. He was appointed Judge of 5th Judicial District of Kentucky in 1833. In 1836 he located in Frankfort and resumed the practice of law. Judge Hewitt was married twice; he was the father of twenty children, six by his first and fourteen by his last wife. He became identified with all the interests of Frankfort and Franklin County and was prominent in the political, business and social affairs of the city and county. He was prominent as one of the framers of the constitution of 1849. He represented Franklin County in the Kentucky Legislature in 1855.

The statistics of Franklin County for the fiscal year ending October 10, 1869, gives the following:

Total valuation of property	$4,829,693 00
State revenue at 30 cents on the $100	14,489 08
The total tax chargeable to the Sheriff was	15,517 30

The following is the valuation of each item of taxation:

119,634 acres of land, value	$2,401,588 00
557 town lots, value	1,118,030 00
3,668 horses, value	208,595 00
626 mules, value	35,815 00
Amount forward	$3,764,028 00

THE HISTORY OF FRANKLIN COUNTY.

Amount brought forward	$3,764,028 00
17 jennets, value	390 00
4,263 cattle, value	81,573 00
114 stores, value	220,550 00
Value under the equalization law	681,934 00
Value of pleasure carriages, barouches, buggies, stage coaches, gigs, omnibuses and other vehicles for passengers	27,739 00
Value of watches and clocks	25,892 00
Gold and silver plate	14,327 00
Pianos	18,260 00
Total	$4,829,693 00
White males over 21 years of age	2,081
Enrolled militia	1,494
Children between 6 and 20 years	2,504
Number of hogs over six months old	2,920
Pounds of tobacco	189,220
Pounds of hemp	77,980
Tons of hay	967
Bushels of corn	450,533
Bushels of wheat	32,298
Negroes over 18 years of age	730
Negro children between 6 and 18	418

Those who represented the county in the Kentucky Legislature from 1860 to 1912 are as follows: R. C. Anderson, 1861-63; H. M. Bedford, 1863-65; Jas. Harlan, Jr., 1865-67; Samuel I. M. Major, 1867-69; Daniel M. Bowen 1869-71; Harry I. Todd, 1871-73; Dr. Ben F. Duvall, 1873-75, Geo. W. Craddock, 1875-77; T. W. Scott, 1877-79; L. Hord, 1879-80; Ira Julian, 1881-2-3-4; J. A. Scott, 1885-6; Scott Brown, 1887-8; S. I. M. Major, 1889-90; E. H. Taylor, Jr., 1891-2; Len Cox, 1894-5; J. A. Violett, 1896-7; South Trimble, 1898-9-1900-1; Dr. Owen Robertson, 1902-3; L. F. Johnson, 1904-5-6-7; James T. Buford, 1908-9-10-11; Elwood Hamilton, 1912-13.

CHAPTER XII.

From 1870 to 1880.

The people of Franklin County were much excited over the assassination of Ben Farmer, which occurred at his home near Farmdale, about six miles from Frankfort. He was a citizen of the county and had been a resident of that neighborhood for many years. The assassination was on Saturday night, March 5th, 1870. Mr. Farmer was asleep on a sofa, his head being near a window which opened out on a porch. Thomas J. Mayhall and William Wright were in the room with him at the time the shot was fired; they went to the door but could see no one. When they attempted to awake him they found he was dead, with a wound in the head which had penetrated to the neck. A negro man named Charles Holmes was arrested on suspicion but the evidence at the examining trial was not sufficient to hold him. Some time after that circumstances led to the arrest of William Hawkins and Charles Polk. Hawkins was indicted and tried by a jury but he was acquitted. The impression has deepened as time passed, that the man who planned and possibly who carried into execution the assassination of Mart South, which occurred some years later, also had something to do with the death of Ben Farmer. Both of them were butchers by trade and the tragedies were so much alike in many respects that it seems probable that the same party planned both of them. It was on the morning of April 1st, 1876, that Martin V. South was assassinated at the market house in Frankfort. Walker Stephens, Robert G. Shields, Hick Kersey and Thos. H. Holder were charged with the murder. Great excitement prevailed, the court house was crowded during the examing trial. Walker Stephens was held without bail. He afterwards secured a change of venue and the final trial was held in Henry County, where he was acquitted.

At the election of county officers in 1870, R. A. Thompson was elected Judge, Ira Julian, Attorney; James G. Crockett, Clerk; Joseph Roberson, Sheriff; Robert Lawler, Jailer; J. C.

Coleman, Coroner; E. A. W. Roberts, Surveyor, and Peter Jett, Assessor. John B. Major was elected Police Judge of Frankfort, and H. H. Hyde, City Marshal. All the officers for both county and city were Democrats.

The bridge across Benson Creek, near its mouth, was completed in 1870, the Baldknob turnpike road was also built during that year and a floor was placed on the railroad bridge for the passage of vehicles and general travel. There was also a bridge built across Flat Creek near the mouth. These improvements were of great benefit and convenience to the people in the northwest section of the county. Prior to that time it was difficult and sometimes impossible for the citizens in that section of the county to reach the county seat for days and even weeks at a time on account of high water.

The aurora borealis of 1870 was the finest exhibition of that phenomena which had been seen from the location of Frankfort since 1837.

On the night of November the second there was a very destructive fire. It commenced on St. Clair street, and the half square bounded by St. Clair, Market and Lewis streets was consumed. The fires of 1853 and 1870 destroyed the entire square. The loss at this time was $113,150, with insurance amounting to $66,950. The Odd Fellows Hall valued at $11,500 and the Christian Church valued at $5,000 and several store rooms with stock, were consumed.

The kuklux became active in Franklin County during the year. Out of forty-five colored voters in the Baldknob precinct all of them were driven away except Abe Dodson. He was the only negro voter in that section of the county for more than a quarter of a century.

On December 6th, 1870, the kuklux visited the house of Harrison Blanton in search of a negro named Freeman Garrett, but failing to find him they shot two other negroes who were living on the Blanton place. They continued their raids in different sections of the county for several months. In 1872 they visited Mr. John R. Gay's place and whipped some of his servants. John Triplett, John Willson and Charles McDaniel

THE HISTORY OF FRANKLIN COUNTY.   177

were arrested and tried. McDaniel was convicted, the others were acquitted.

The bonded debt of the county in 1870 was $3,993; the floating debt was $75,500. The bonded debt of Frankfort was $123,000, the floating debt was $85,000. The amount of taxes collected for State purposes was $15,192; for county purposes was $20,000. The amount raised for city purposes was $23,000, exclusive of water and gas tax.

In that year the county took stock in the Kentucky River Navigation Company and issued bonds therefor. It also issued bonds to the amount of $10,000 for bridge purposes.

The number of white paupers supported by the county during that year was nineteen, and the number of colored paupers was sixteen. The cost of supporting them amounted to $1,750.00. At that time there were three Methodist Churches in the county with church property valued at $16,000; two Presbyterian Churches which were valued at $22,500; two Episcopal Churches which were valued at $42,000; one Catholic Church valued at $20,000; five Christian Churches which were valued at $17,000, and ten Baptist Churches which were valued at $39,500. Frankfort had five steam saw mills, two shingle factories, five large distilleries, one large cotton mill, a chair factory, tobacco factory and furniture factory. At that time Franklin County had 62,205 acres of improved land and 32,176 acres of woodland and 1,395 acres of unimproved land. The value of farm lands was placed at $2,651,192.

The amount of wages paid per year, $74,404. The amount of farm products, $633,214; orchard products, $4,047; forest products, $14,941; the home manufactures, $1,376; animals slaughtered were valued at $160,160; the live stock was valued at $450,251. The number of horses, 2,651; the number of mules and asses, 478; the number of milch cows, 1,642; working oxen, 242; other cattle, 2,146; sheep, 4,170; swine, 11,583. The number of bushels of wheat, 28,981; rye, 19,337 bushels; oats, 53,638 bushels; barley, 18 bushels.

The number of pounds of tobacco raised, 123,250; wool, 16,336 pounds; irish potatoes, 16,472 bushels; sweet potatoes, 1,407 bushels. The amount of wine made was 572 gallons;

butter, 82,429 pounds; the amount of milk sold, 20,000 gallons; the amount of hay raised was 1,430 tons; grass seed, 110 bushels; hemp, 238 tons; flax, 75 pounds; the amount of maple sugar made was 530 pounds; the sorghum molasses amounted to 18,452 gallons; wax, 180 pounds, and honey, 2,460 pounds.

At the city election in 1871 there was a small riot which came near being a race war. The trouble commenced at the court house. Mr. William Newman, a grocer on Market street, was killed; Capt. W. G. Thompson was wounded in the arm; James Winter and Winston Coleman, of color, were seriously wounded, and several other parties, both white and colored, were slightly wounded.

It was during this year that P. and D. Swigert had imported to them from the Isle of Jersey twenty-one head of Jersey cattle, all of which arrived in fine condition. They were exhibited in the State House yard. The Swigerts, at that time, had the largest herd of Jersey cattle in the United States. On January 14th Thompson Scroggans and a colored man by the name of Strother Trumbo had a difficulty near the south end of the tunnel and as a result Scroggans killed him. At that time the United States district court had jurisdiction to try the case where a negro was killed by a white man. Scroggans was arrested and committed to jail without bail. On the 27th of the following February the jail was broken open by an armed band, estimated at a hundred and fifty men. Scroggans was taken from jail and released. He had been a rebel soldier and it was supposed that they had something to do with his release. Scroggans remained out of the county for several years and in the meantime he became an officeholder in another county. After an absence of about forty years he visited Frankfort and he was requested to tell about his release. He said: "It was about twelve o'clock at night when someone took me roughly by the arm and said, 'get up from there we want you.' Some fifteen or twenty men were in the jail, they did not permit me to put my clothes on and I was hurried away without any clothes except my night shirt. I thought at that time it meant death at the end of the rope. I was carried across the St. Clair street bridge and down near the city school where a large number of men were congregated. They gave me a new suit of clothes, a hundred dollars in money, a good horse, saddle and bridle and some good advice, all of which I appreciated. It took me a very short time to get out of the county."

A "birds-eye view" of Frankfort was made by Prof. Ruger in 1871. The view is from a point above the city and presents the entire town and suburbs in picturesque style; the work was exceedingly well done; the map makes a handsome ornament for the library or office. Several of them have survived the ravages of forty years' time, perhaps a dozen of them are still extant.

At the August election there was another negro riot in Frankfort at which two white men were killed and several wounded. Capt. William Gilmore and Silas N. Bishop were killed, Policeman Jerry Lee and Dick Leonard were wounded, and several other citizens were injured by stones which were thrown by the negroes. Henry Washington was the only negro who was wounded during the fight. The Mayor, Col. E. H. Taylor, Jr., called out the militia and quelled the disturbance. The trouble at this time occurred on Broadway near the market house. When the polls were closed the negroes were on the north side of the railroad track and the whites were on the south side. Immediately after the train from Louisville passed them the firing commenced. This disturbance greatly increased the bitter feeling which had existed between the white and colored people for some time and a race war in Frankfort had seemed probable for several months. A few days prior to this trouble a negro named Harrison Johnson was charged with criminally assaulting a white woman of good character. He had been arrested and lodged in jail. The night of the riot Henry Washington, though wounded, had also been placed in jail charged with having killed Capt. Gilmore. Within a few hours after that a mob took both negroes from the jail, carried them across the river and hung them to a tree near the city school building. Following the hanging of the negroes James Alley, Richard Crittenden and D. Howard Smith, Jr., son of the State Auditor, were arrested charged with being implicated in the hanging. They were taken to Louisville and tried before the United States Commissioner and held, bail being denied them. All of them were finally released. The veterans of 1812 who were living in Franklin County in 1871, were John B. Bibb, Major of 4th brigade; Thomas Theobald, Captain in Moders' company of mounted riflemen, Moses Hawkins, Alexander Crockett, William Nelson, John Cardwell, Joseph Clark and A. H. Rennick.

A. H. Rennick died at the residence of his son-in-law, James M. Todd, on the 18th of December at 80 years of age. He had been a resident of Frankfort for seventy-eight years. He was Clerk of the Franklin County Court for sixty-one years, forty-six of which he was chief Clerk. He was with Captain Pascal Hickman at the battle of the River Raisen but was one of the few who escaped.

On December the 31st Philip Swigert, another one of Franklin County's distinguished citizens, died at the age of seventy-four years. He was born of poor but respectable parents in Fayette County in 1798. He came to Franklin County when he was twenty-four years of age. In 1830 he was appointed Circuit Court Clerk, and was elected to that office in 1850. He was a prominent Mason and he was a large importer and breeder of fine cattle. He left a handsome estate.

The east wing of the old capitol was built in 1871 at a cost of $155,000. It was occupied in the following year but the building has never been completed. The idea at that time was to complete the east wing in which was to be located the House of Representatives and a west wing was to be constructed on the same plan, and in which was to be located the Senate chamber.

In the year 1800 the population of Franklin County was 5,978; in 1810 it was 8,013; 1820, 10,950; 1830, 9,254; in 1840 it was 9,420; in 1850, 12,460; in 1870, 15,300.

On February 19th, 1872, Daniel Clark, the faithful old colored porter of the Governor's office, died. He was a native of Africa. He and his brother were stolen while playing on the beach, they were brought to Charleston and sold. Daniel afterwards became the servant of Governor Clark and came with him to Frankfort in 1836 and was employed as porter in the executive office. He remained in that capacity until the administration of Governor Leslie. During all of these years he sustained an unblemished reputation for honesty and faithfulness. When he grew too old and feeble for further labor the Legislature of Kentucky passed an act giving him a pension of $12.00 per month for the rest of his life. When Clark died the Governor caused that fact to be recorded upon the executive journal, with an appropriate tribute to his fidelity and long service. He was the only negro who was ever honored to that extent in Kentucky.

Jeremiah Tracy died at his home in the county on March 12, 1872. He was born in Culpepper County, Va., in 1774. He moved to this county in his early manhood and became one of the most sterling and substantial citizens of the county. He raised a family of ten children. At the time of his death he left surviving him nine of his children; more than one hundred of his descendants were living at the time of his death. He was the forbear of the numerous branches of the Tracy family in Franklin County and other sections of Kentucky.

The Christian Church, located on Ann street, was built during this year, through the munificence of Mrs. Emily Tubman, a sister of Mr. Landon A. Thomas. Mrs. Tubman was a devout member of that church. She had been born and raised in Frankfort and she desired to show the Frankfort people, in some substantial way, her appreciation of them. The building cost $26,000. It was dedicated on August 11. Mrs. Tubman endowed a chair in Betheny College. She materially assisted the Kentucky University and the orphan school at Midway and did many other charitable acts which endeared her to the people of this county.

The penitentiary was considerably improved during the year. The arched gate was raised five feet. The prison grounds were enlarged by inclosing within the walls one acre immediately north of the cell house, this was designed for women. There were several brick buildings erected within the walls which have been used for kitchen, dining room, cells, hospital, etc.

There was a jail delivery on December 30. The jail had been newly constructed and it was thought to be secure. Six negroes made their escape, all of whom were charged with grand larceny. Only two of them were ever recaptured.

More than a quarter of a million dollars was spent in buildings during the year. Some of the improvements were as follows:

The Christian Church, $26,000; the Swigert block on St. Clair opposite Odd Fellows building at a cost of $25,000; improving the malt house on Mero street, $20,000; improvements on cotton factory, $28,000; improvement on the Valley Merchant Flouring Mill, $6,000; a wholesale liquor house on Ann street at a cost of $8,000; the Capital Livery Stable on Ann street, Church Bros., $8,000; Alley & Mahoney Stable in front of Capital Hotel, $3,000; B. B. Sayre residence on hill, $15,000; H. H. Johnston cottage, corner Second and Main, South Frankfort, $3,000; R. H. Lawler cottage near State prison, $3,000; Col. Orlando Brown house on Owenton road, $6,000; Sanford Goins, near Capitol square, $4,000; Frank Short, on Upper Main street, $2,500; Con Newman cottage near cemetery gate, $3,000; J. W. Gault residence on Steel street, $2,000; Landon A. Thomas, improvement on his residence, $10,000; William Saffell, near depot, $5,000; Mrs. William A. Sneed, near Mr. Saffell, $4,000; Warden South, a brick stable near prison, $2,500. Improvements in Bellepoint amounted to more than $15,000. Col. E. H. Taylor, at O. F. C. distillery, $9,000, and a great many smaller improvements amounting in the aggregate to more than $30,000. A new fire bell was purchased in 1873 to take the place of the old cracked bell. The new one weighed 830 pounds and it cost the city $365.

In the year 1873 W. J. Chinn was elected Sheriff; in 1875 H. I. Morris was elected; in 1877 M. H. P. Williams was elected and in 1879 he was re-elected Sheriff of the county.

In the year 1874 the county officers elected were as follows: R. A. Thompson, Judge; James G. Crockett, Clerk; Thomas B. Ford, County Attorney; Robert W. Lawler, Jailer; John M. Quarles, Assessor; John R. Graham, Coroner; Richard Crittenden, Surveyor; Pat McDonald, Magistrate in the city precinct, and Robert R. Parsons was elected Police Judge of the city of Frankfort.

Mardi Gras was celebrated in Frankfort on the 17th of February. The procession through the streets in the afternoon was of great interest to the thousands of people from Franklin and surrounding counties. The streets of the city were densely lined with spectators during the passage of the masqueraders. It was estimated that ten thousand people witnessed the parade. The celebration of the carnival was concluded by a grand masquerade ball at the Capital Hotel, which was largely attended.

The Grangers became very prominent in Franklin County during the year 1874. This was a farmer organization which had in view the betterment of the farming interest of the county. There were several Granges organized in different sections of the county and doubtless they would have been productive of great good to the farmers had not a few designing politicians become leaders of the organization with the idea of advancing their political interests and in that way demoralized the organization and in the course of time destroyed it.

The Pigeon Tournament was held in Frankfort on February the 7th and 8th. A number of the most famous "shots" of America were present. Capt. A. H. Bogardus, the champion of America, and L. C. South, of Franklin County, scored the same number during the meeting and they agreed to divide the prize between them, but in order to gratify their friends they decided the championship by another contest which resulted in the defeat of South by one point in thirty-three. South killing thirty-two of his and Bogardus all of the thirty-three birds.

The Baptist Association of Kentucky held its thirty-eighth annual session at Frankfort. It was the largest and the ablest representative body of that church which had ever been held in the State. The lay delegates as well as the ministers were representative Kentuckians of the highest and most intellectual class.

A blacksmith by the name of George W. Hitzelberger was murdered on June 13th. Jim and Dave Kelley and John

Graham went to his home and called him out. While John Graham and Dave Kelley held him, Jim Kelley inflicted five or six wounds with a knife from the effects of which he died. John Graham had stolen Jim Kelley's saddle and charged the theft to Hitzelberger, the outcome of which was the killing. John Graham and Dave Kelley were arrested but Jim Kelley made his escape and has never since been heard from.

Mrs. Mary Freese, who died in Frankfort on August 23, 1874, was a very eccentric person. She was a native of Ireland who became a resident of Frankfort about thirty years prior to her death. For several years after she moved to Frankfort she was regarded as an object of charity. After she had lived in Frankfort for about ten years she spent a whole summer and winter in a stable without lights or fire. At the time she was receiving $75 per year from the Ladies' Aid Society of the Presbyterian Church, she was erecting a comfortable dwelling house of six rooms. When she completed the house she moved in the small rear room and rented out the rest of the house. She subsequently purchased a considerable quantity of land near the penitentiary upon which she built a number of tenement houses. Since which time that section of the city has been known as "Freesetown." Her annual rental for several years prior to her death was supposed to be about three thousand dollars. She was buried in the Frankfort cemetery, where a handsome marble monument marks her last resting place.

The 15th of September, 1874, was the day set apart by Governor Leslie for the re-interment of the remains of Governor Greenup, Governor Madison, Adjt. George N. Cardwell, Hon. John C. Mason, Gen. Carey, H. Fry and Col. Theodore O.'Hara. The remains of Governor Christopher Greenup and Governor George Madison were originally buried on the hill north of Frankfort in the old burying ground which was used until about 1843, when the Frankfort Cemetery Company was organized and a burying ground east of Frankfort was purchased, a part of which was set aside by the State for her illustrious dead. On the morning above referred to, at an early hour, the streets of Frankfort were crowded with people from all sections of the State who were drawn to the Capital City by

THE HISTORY OF FRANKLIN COUNTY. 185

a patriotic desire to honor the memory of Kentucky's noble dead. The business houses of the city and all the public offices of the State, county and city were closed in order that all might unite in a fitting testimonial to the great men whose bones were brought from other states to find a final resting place in their own mother soil.

Three companies of the State guard and a large number of Mexican soldiers came from Louisville and other parts of the State were well represented. Gen. Thomas Taylor, of Louisville, acted as Chief Marshal. There were several thousand people in the procession which included nearly all of the prominent men of the State.

Hon. R. J. Jacob and Gen. William Preston were the speakers of the occasion. Governor Christopher Greenup was born in 1750 in the colony of Virginia. He was a Revolutionary soldier and gained distinction as such. He came to Kentucky in March 1783. In 1792 he removed from Danville to Frankfort and was elected that year to Congress and was twice re-elected. He was one of the three chief judges under the new Constitution. He was elected Governor in 1804 and discharged the duties with high honor and credit as well to the State as to himself. During his term as Governor he also served as chairman of the Board of Trustees of the town of Frankfort. After his term as Governor he made the race to represent Franklin County in the Kentucky Legislature, but he was defeated by Humphrey Marshall, Sr., the historian. In 1812 Governor Greenup was appointed justice of the peace for Franklin County. He owned a large amount of property both in the city and in adjacent sections of the county.

Governor George Madison was born in Virginia in 1763. Before he was grown he distinguished himself in the Revolutionary war. He was wounded at St. Clair's defeat in 1791, and was again wounded by the Indians in 1792. He became State Auditor in 1792, and held that position for twenty years. He was a major in Col. John Allen's regiment in the war of 1812, and he was largely instrumental in saving the remnant of the American forces from massacre after the fatal battle of the River Raisen. He was elected Governor in 1816, but died in a short time after he was inaugurated. He was at one time Clerk of the city of Frankfort and at another time Treasurer. He lived at the Heffner property near the southwest corner of the old State house square. Theodore O'Hara studied law in the office of Gov. Owsley and was a fellow student of John C. Breckenridge.

In the year 1875 the Frankfort and Benson Turnpike Company was organized and the road was built in a short time thereafter.

On June the 7th John W. Jackson, B. F. Head, G. C. Hughes, F. Satterwhite, Milton Wiggington, Jas. Harrod, William A. Smoot, G. W. Gwinn and Pat McDonald qualified as Magistrates. The county court subscribed $5,000 to the Glenn's Creek turnpike and $3,000 to the Lewis Ferry turnpike at their first meeting after they took the oath of office.

The Kentucky Mineral Paint Company was organized by James L. Sneed and John E. Kirtley, of Frankfort, and they procured a patent for manufacturing mineral paint out of a soft grayish stone, to be found in certain portions of Franklin county, and especially in the Bridgeport section. A company was chartered under the Kentucky Statutes for manufacturing this paint at Frankfort. At that time the paint industry promised to be a very lucrative one, the mineral rights on thousands of acres were leased for a period of twenty years. From analysis of the rocks made by Prof. Shaler and Prof. Peter, it was thought that the cheapest and best paint ever made in the United States could be made of this material. It has never been fully explained just why this industry was not a financial success. The people of Bridgeport were satisfied that the precious metals existed in several localities in that section of the county. A man by the name of William Fields came from Wisconsin and leased several tracts of land; from one of these farms he took a thousand pounds of rock which he sent to New York for a test. The ore was reduced and it yielded at the rate of $12.60 in gold and $10.12 in silver or $22.72 per ton. It was thought at that time that the ore could be worked for five dollars per ton, making a clear profit of over $17 per ton. No one has explained why this venture was not a financial success.

Judge G. W. Craddock was elected to represent the county in 1875 and Judge W. L. Jett was elected Police Judge of the city of Frankfort.

Joseph Clark died at his residence near the city on November 10th in his 83rd year. He was one of the most substantial citizens of the county. He was a member of Pascal Hickman's company in the war of 1812, and was wounded at the battle of River Raisen. He was one of the thirteen members of that noted company who returned to Frankfort after that defeat and slaughter by the Indians.

The law establishing a workhouse went into effect in 1876; for a few weeks there were fifteen or twenty and sometimes as many as twenty-five inmates, but after it got into good working order the number was reduced to five or six. Prior to the institution of the workhouse system the prisoners were sent to jail without labor where they had plenty to eat at the expense of the county and a white man to wait on them.

On the 25th of June Gen. Custer with sixteen officers and three hundred enlisted men were massacred by the Indians. Among the officers was Lieut. John J. Crittenden, of Frankfort, who was on the staff of Gen. Custer. He was twenty-two years of age at the time of his death. He was buried in the Frankfort cemetery.

During this year Capt. Thomas J. South became the champion bird shooter of the world by defeating the champion, Bogardus, first at a tournament near Philadelphia and later at a tournament near St. Louis. By these two victories he won an international reputation.

Judge Franklin Chinn died at his home near the Forks of Elkhorn on August the 10th, in his seventy-sixth year. In 1827 he removed to Henry County and during the ten years he lived there he represented that county twice in the Kentucky Legislature. He was for many years a magistrate of Franklin County and in 1861 he was elected County Judge of the county. He was universally esteemed and honored by the people of Franklin County.

THE HISTORY OF FRANKLIN COUNTY.

During the year 1876 the Franklin County Court issued bonds to the amount of $35,000, the proceeds of which were used in paying off the outstanding floating debts of the county; $15,000 of which was for building a new jail and $20,000 was for turnpike purposes.

Col. R. T. P. Allen was a graduate of West Point and for many years was superintendent of the Kentucky Military Institute, which was located on the Lawrenceburg road about six miles from Frankfort. He was a man of great intellectual endowment. When quite a young man he built the first concrete house ever built in Franklin County. This house is located on the south side of the Kentucky river about three miles above the city of Frankfort, and it is in as good condition as it was when first constructed over sixty years ago and it looks like it might stand for a thousand years without any deteoriation in the foundation or walls. Col. Allen also invented a type-writing machine which was a fore-runner of the type-writing machine industry, but he received neither credit nor money from the invention. He also invented a steam wagon which originated the idea of the automobile of later date. He drove his machine from the Kentucky Military Institute to Louisville, but on his return he ran it into a stone fence and made a complete wreck of it. At a later date, about the year 1876, he invented the type distributing machine which has since become almost indispensible to the large printing houses of the country. He claimed that this machine could distribute accurately, as many as twenty thousand type in one hour. The Kentucky Military Institute was established by Col. R. T. P. Allen and it was run on the same plan as West Point.

In the early part of the last century a man by the name of Oliver Perry Scanlan owned the land on which the Scanlan Springs were located and which afterwards became famous as the Franklin Springs. This was the first health and pleasure resort west of the Alleghanies and it was largely patronized for many years. When General Jackson was President of the United States, Col. R. T. P. Allen, then a boy sixteen years of age, conspired with other and older boys, at West Point, to rid the campus of a nuisance on the grounds and one night they set fire to the building. An inquiry was at once made and young Allen was the only one who was man enough to admit that he was connected with the offense. On account of the admission and on the charge of insubordination in refusing to divulge the names of his accomplices he was expelled. He took his case to the President, but still refused to betray his friends. His manly conduct made such an impression on the President that he restored him to the institution. After he graduated he was commissioned Captain and soon thereafter he was promoted to Colonel and placed in charge of the engineering of the harbor on lake Michigan. While making a visit at the White House, he met the President's niece, Miss Julia Bond, who afterwards became his wife and who in later life was known as "Old Miss" by the hundreds of "her boys" as she always called the cadets of the K. M. I. A visit of this couple in 1843 to the then famous watering place led to the purchase of the grounds and the charter was granted to the Kentucky Military Institute by the Legislature of Kentucky, and this became the first military school of the South and West.

The contractor who erected the buildings was George Vest, the father of United States Senator Vest of Missouri. The main building was burned in 1854 and it was rebuilt by Hiram Berry, contractor.

Prior to the war the K. M. I. was patronized almost exclusively by the South. Many noted men were educated there. This statement applies especially to the officers of the Southern Confederacy. Senator John Sharp Williams and other United States Congressmen were educated there.

After Col. R. T. P. Allen grew too old to manage the school, his son, Col. R. D. Allen, took charge and successfully conducted it for about fifteen years, after which a joint stock company purchased the property and attempted to continue the school, but after a few years gave up the effort and it was discontinued. The K. M. I. charter has since gone into the hands of Col. C. W. Fowler at Lyndon, Kentucky, who having been educated at the old K. M. I. is an excellent man to have charge of the new. The real estate of the old K. M. I. was purchased by Dr. J. Q. A. Stewart and since that time has been known as The Stewart Home. It has become one of the most prosperous institutions for the training of children of backward mental development in the West or South.

In 1877 there were several hundred hogs running at large on the streets of Frankfort. This had been the custom from the earliest history of the town. When the City Council passed an ordinance prohibiting the further use of the streets for that purpose, a great protest was made by many good citizens who thought their personal rights had been invaded.

At the city election of this year, Col. E. H. Taylor, Jr., was elected mayor of Frankfort by a majority of one vote. Col. S. I. M. Major was the contending candidate. In June of the same year Col. Taylor resigned and Col. S. I. M. Major was elected.

Thomas W. Scott was elected to represent the county at the August election of that year and Judge Lysander Hord was elected Representative in 1879.

For several years boat racing was one of the favorite sports of the young men in Frankfort. A great contest was to be decided in the month of September. The railroad bridge and the banks of the river were lined to see the race. It was supposed that there were more than three thousand people present. Col. J. Stoddard Johnston and Mr. J. L. Waggoner were the judges; Judge W. L. Jett, umpire, and J. W. Pruett, starter; the distance was one mile and five-eighths and the time twelve minutes. The race was between the Zozma, manned by George L. Payne and Dr. J. Lampton Price, and the Undine, manned by Clarence Drane and Howard Jett. The Zozma won the blue silk pennant which was presented by Col. J. Stoddard Johnston in an appropriate address.

Thomas N. Lindsey died Nov. 22, 1877. He was the father of Gen. D. W. Lindsey and John B. Lindsey. He was one of the leading lawyers of the Frankfort bar and a writer of considerable note. For a period of thirty or forty years he was a constant contributor to the press, under the *non de plume* of Black Jack. He was a strong writer and he discussed a great many different subjects. If his articles were collected and put in a bound volume, it would make a very material addition to the literary productions of the county. At a bar meeting held at the court house Judge Craddock said that "Thomas N. Lindsey was a good story teller, industrious, kind, affectionate, temperate, even tempered, faithful and most agreeable." After several other lawyers had made appropriate remarks Col. S. F. J. Trabue arose and attempted to speak but his emotions overcome him. He spoke not a word and resumed his seat. Judge G. C. Drane said, "Gentlemen that is the most eloquent speech made today."

On December 7th John Julian, the father of Judge Ira Julian, died. He studied law under John J. Crittenden and entered the practice of his profession with bright prospects of success, but on account of bad health he had to give up his profession. He was known as a man of superior mind and culture.

The election for county officers in the year 1878 resulted as follows: R. A. Thompson re-elected Judge; R. W. Lawler, Jailer; William Julian, Attorney; James G. Crockett, Clerk; D. M. Woodson, Surveyor; John R. Graham, Coroner; Robert Sanford, Assessor, and Thomas B. Ford, School Commissioner. The following year John R. Graham died and Alexander McEwan was appointed Coroner.

Frankfort owned a lottery franchise which had been granted by the Kentucky Legislature and which the city continued to lease as late as 1879. The lessees executed a bond in the sum of $100,000 for a faithful preformance of their contract.

A statement was made by the Franklin County Fiscal Court that more than four hundred ex-convicts had settled in and around Frankfort and the Legislature was requested to pass an act requiring all convicts to be returned to the county from which they had been sent when their terms of service expired. The fact that for nearly a century the ex-convicts and their descendants were permitted to remain in Franklin County explains, to some extent, the great amount of lawlessness and crime which has marked the progress of the city and county. For several months prior to October the city of Frankfort and its vicinity was flooded with counterfeit silver coin of various denominations. On investigation it was found that the inmates of the penitentiary had started up a mint of their own. The moulds from which the counterfeit coins were cast were of plaster paris, but they served the purpose of turning out a very passable article. A large number of home-made dimes, quarters and half dollars were found, together with the metal from which they were made and the crucible in which the metal was melted.

On Monday, March 26th, 1879, Hon. John M. Eliott, Judge of the Court of Appeals, was shot and killed near the ladies' entrance to the Capital Hotel, by Thomas Buford, of Henry County. The weapon used was a double barrelled shot gun loaded with buck shot. Judge Eliott and his associate, Judge T. H. Hines, were at the point designated when Buford approached Judge Eliott with the gun in his hand and said, "Judge, I believe I will go snipe hunting, won't you go along?" The Judge refused and Buford then said, "Won't you take a drink," and before any further conversation ensued the gun was discharged and Judge Eliott fell. Buford lowered his gun and said, "I am sorry I did it." He then knelt down and placed his hand upon the Judge's brow and his hat under his head. The shot entered the right side about the lower ribs, passing through to the opposite side. After Buford was placed in jail he said that he killed Judge Eliott because of the decision which the Judge had rendered against him on the Saturday preceding wherein $20,000 were involved. He said that he had made up his mind to kill both Judge Eliott and Judge W. S. Pryor, but he thought of Judge Pryor's children and let him off on that account. Buford had also threatened the life of General D. W. Lindsey, who as special Judge had decided the case against him in the circuit court. Buford was removed to Louisville in order to prevent a mob from hanging him. On his application for a change of venue, Judge O. D. McManama granted his petition and the case was tried in Owen County. Buford plead insanity and the jury acquitted him.

The residence of Pascal Hickman, who was killed at the River Raisen, was torn down and the warehouse of Col. J. W. South near the mouth of the tunnel was built on the site. The house was occupied by Pascal Hickman and family in 1812-13, but it was built several years prior to that time. The nails which joined the wood work were made of wrought iron and the window and door frames were fastened together by locust pins.

John Cardwell died at the home of his daughter, Mrs. William P. Johnson, on September 17th, 1879, at the age of ninety-three years. He was born in Culpepper County, Virginia, in the year 1786. His father, William Cardwell, was a native of Virginia, from which State he moved to Kentucky and settled in Mercer County in 1796. John Cardwell lived there until 1813 when he enlisted in Capt. Terrell's company, Col. Bate's regiment of Kentucky volunteers in war of 1812. He participated in the battle of New Orleans, January 8th, 1815. After the close of the war he returned to Kentucky and married Margaret Arnold, daughter of James Arnold. To them were born a large family of children. Some of their numerous progeny have settled in Kentucky, Indiana, Illinois and Missouri.

In the month of November the citizens of Frankfort and Franklin County were much excited over the disappearance of Hezekiah Gardner, a farmer and merchant who lived near the mouth of Gleen's Creek; about the same time a blacksmith shop near the State arsenel was burnt and with it a small child, the grandson of M. H. P. Williams, at that time Sheriff of the county.

Three men, Wilson, Dougherty and Lacy, were arrested on suspicion and the excitement became so great that the County Judge placed guards at the jail to prevent the men from being hung by a mob. On the examining trial Lacy and Dougherty were released and Wilson was held to the grand jury.

On Thanksgiving Day Gardner's body was found floating in the river, only a few hundred yards below his home. It was generally supposed that after he got home from Frankfort he went down to the river to see about a small boat and it being dark, he fell in the river and was drowned. It was never determined how the shop was fired or how it happened that the child was burnt in it.

Theodore O'Hara, poet, journalist and soldier, was born in Danville, Kentucky, on February 11th, 1820, but while he was a small boy his father came to Franklin County and located a short distance from Frankfort on the Peak's Mill road where Theodore grew to manhood. He died in Alabama, June 6th, 1867. He was educated at St. Joseph's Academy at Bardstown. He read law and was admitted to the bar and in 1845 was appointed to a position in the Treasury Department at Washington. He was a captain of volunteers in the army against Mexico and on August 20th, 1847, was breveted Major for gallant conduct in the battle of Contreras. At the close of the war he returned to Washington where he practiced his profession. He afterwards went with a filibustering expedition to Cuba where he commanded a regiment. He became editor of the Mobile Register and was afterwards connected with the Louisville Sun and Frankfort Yeoman. He performed several diplomatic missions for the Government and was prominent in the negotiations regarding the Tehuantepec grant.

At the beginning of the Civil War he cast his fortunes with the confederacy and was made Colonel of the twelfth Alabama regiment and subsequently served on the staff of Gen. John C. Breckenridge and Gen. Albert Sidney Johnson. He died in Alabama, June 6th, 1867, and his remains were brought to Kentucky by special act of the Legislature and interred at Frankfort in the State cemetery.

When the remains of the Kentucky soldiers, who fell at Buena Vista, were brought to their native State, Maj. O'Hara wrote for that occasion the immortal poem by which his fame is established, "The Bivouac of the Dead."

CHAPTER XIII.

From 1880 *to* 1890.

In the year 1880 Judge Lysander Hord's river bill passed the House without a dissenting vote. This bill authorizing the United States Government to improve the Kentucky river was passed by the Senate and became a law at this session of the Legislature. Judge Hord deserved credit for passing this bill. As a result he has been called the father of the Kentucky river navigation, but the actual truth is, there was more business done on the Kentucky river before the United States took charge of it than there has been since, but the decrease in river trafic was caused more by the increased railroad facilities than from any other cause.

During the decade, 1870 to 1880, tobacco grown on Franklin County land brought a higher price on the market than that grown in any other county in the State and since that time it has been known as one of the very best white burley tobacco growing counties in the State.

Charles Stewart Parnell, a leader in the British Parliament, visited Frankfort in February of 1880. A committee of prominent citizens went from Frankfort to Lexington to meet him. He addressed the Kentucky Legislature which was in session at that time.

The veterans of the Mexican war met in Frankfort in February of that year. Those who were living in Franklin County at that time were Capt. B. C. Milam, Lieut. W. P. D. Bush and musician Thomas Heffner. The privates were Robt. Sheridan, S. P. Montague, Ben Utterback, L. Mangan, Daniel Hancock, Monroe McDowell, Landon Montague, George W. Daniels, Lafayette Martin, A. B. Reed, Lieut. Col. Green Clay Smith, J. H. Redish, E. T. Parrent, Walker Stephens, H. S. Mayhall, R. A. Hawkins, Wm. Morrison, Samuel H. Bradley, C. Featherston, A. W. Polsgrove, D. O. Morris, A. W. Hampton, G. W. Chambers, Alex. Moss, John E. Miles, Cyrus Calvert, A. A. Gordon, Wm. Manly, Alex Mitchell, Newt Dean and

William Phillips. Out of the thirty-four named only two are now living (1912), to-wit: A. W. Polsgrove and Ben Utterback.

North Frankfort and South Frankfort were united and made one corporation in 1880. A joint committee composed of D. W. Lindsey, B. F. Meek and Green Clay Smith were appointed to represent South Frankfort and W. P. B. Bush, J. W. Pruett and W. T. Reading, to represent North Frankfort in the settlement of the accounts between the two corporations, and to determine what part of the existing debts each corporation should pay. It was determined by this committee that it was to the best interest of both North and South Frankfort to cancel and relinquish all accounts between them and to make all the property of every kind and description belonging to North Frankfort, the common property of the city of Frankfort and all the debts of both corporations were assumed as liabilities of the city embracing both North and South Frankfort, and it was so reported to the council and the two towns were consolidated on that basis, by an act of the General Assembly which was in session at that time.

In 1850 the two towns were consolidated and were run under the same government, but their property rights were not fully settled until the act of 1880.

Col. J. W. South died suddenly in the Senate chamber on April the 15th. He was warden of the State penitentiary and had held that position for ten years prior to his death. Both Houses of the Kentucky Legislature adjourned and all the public offices were closed by order of the Governor. The remains were followed to the cemetery by many of his friends, by the Governor and staff, public officers, members of the Senate and House of Representatives, and a large concourse of citizens. He was a man of strong personality and he left numerous progeny, some of whom have become prominent in the affairs of State and nation.

On the 15th of May there was a destructive fire in Bridgeport. The Odd Fellows building and Dr. Williams' and J. B. Russell's residences were totally destroyed. The fire engine from Frankfort went to the scene in charge of convicts and did effective service. Hon. S. I. M. Major, Mayor, also went and remained with the fire company until danger of further loss was over.

At the meeting of the fiscal court of the county in May, the county purchased one-third interest in the St. Clair street bridge and made it free to the people of the county.

In June the inventer, Col. T. L. Rankin, put up an ice machine for Mr. Sigmund Luscher, which had a capacity for producing 20,000 pounds daily. The cost of the machine was about $10,000. At the time this first ice factory was built in Frankfort it was considered one of the greatest inventions of that day. About the same date M. H. P. Williams, Jr., Wiley and John Williams, known as The Williams Bros., placed the telephone exchange in Frankfort.

During this year bicycles came into use. About the 1st of September the people of Frankfort were much interested in two young men who went through the city on bicycles, going from Lexington to Louisville. These machines had very large front wheels and the seats were so high that it was difficult and dangerous to ride on them.

On September 22nd Col. J. W. Hunt Reynolds died, possessed of a large estate. He was a noted breeder of thoroughbred horses and he succeeded in producing several of the most noted running horses known to the turf. He was only thirty-five years old at the time of his death, but his uniformly gentle and courteous bearing endeared him to all who knew him.

Gen. George Bibb Crittenden died in November, 1880. He was a son of Hon. John J. Crittenden, and began the practice of law with his distinguished father. He served as an officer in the war between Texas and Mexico. He was captured by the Mexicans and was in a Mexican prison for nearly a year. This story has been told about him: "The Mexicans having determined upon a retaliatory measure declared that a certain number of the prisoners should be shot and to that end designated which should be the victims by requiring that lots should be drawn. A box containing a certain number of white and black beans was produced, those who drew the white beans were to be spared, and those who drew the black were to be shot.

Gen. Crittenden, being an officer, was among the first to draw and he got a white bean, one of his intimate friends, who came later, was a man of family having a wife and several children. Gen. Crittenden gave him the white bean and risked his life by another draw, which fortunately resulted in his drawing another white bean." After his release from the Mexican prison a friend of his father, who resided in that city, gave him a horse, saddle, bridle, some blankets and money for his return home. One of his countrymen, who had been released with him, was sick and Gen. Crittenden gave the horse and blankets to him and made his way back home with his other companions. In the war between the United States and Mexico he was an officer and served through the war. In the war between the states he served on the side of the South with the rank of Brigadier General. During this war he borrowed $200 in gold from a member of the Confederate Congress and though there was no written obligation on his part, in 1871 he sent this money by Judge William Lindsay to the widow of the man from whom he borrowed it. He came back to Frankfort after the war and in 1867 was elected State Librarian which position he held until 1871. He was buried in the Frankfort cemetery.

On December 6th, 1880, the iron work of the Benson bridge gave way and fell into the creek. It had just been placed in position and was thought to be self-sustaining. Eight men were on it at the time, but none of them were seriously hurt and the abutments were not damaged.

During this year Marshall J. Allen and William E. Bradley, of the W. A. Gaines & Co. Distillery, secured a patent which created a revolution in whiskey making. The new process made an increase of half a gallon of whiskey to the bushel of grain and it also made a remarkable improvement in the quality of the goods.

George W. Gwinn died of pneumonia January 27th, 1881. He had been, successively, Deputy Clerk of the Court of Appeals, Councilman and Mayor of Frankfort, Master Commissioner of the Franklin Circuit Court and Magistrate. He held the latter position for about thirty years. He was a man of strong character and was an efficient officer.

Albert G. Hodges died the following March at the age of seventy-nine years. For half a century he was identified with the history of Kentucky. He commenced his newspaper career in Lexington, but he moved to Frankfort in 1826. He married a Frankfort woman and went into partnership with James G. Dana in the publication of the "Commentator." In 1833 he began the publication of the Commonwealth and was elected public printer which position he held for a quarter of a century. He was buried in the Frankfort cemetery.

On the 18th day of March a sad accident occurred near the mouth of Flat Creek. The boiler of the circular sawmill belonging to Tyler & Harrod burst and killed John Harrod, one of the owners, Lawrence Harrod, his brother, and Frank Graham. William Arnold had his jaw bone broken. James Redding, William Whalen, Lewis Harrod and Hugh Tyler were more or less injured. Everyone in the mill at that time was hurt except William Skeggs. The boiler was a portable one that had been used for a threshing machine. The boiler was torn into two large pieces, one piece weighing 2,500 pounds was thrown one hundred feet one way and the other part was thrown 261 feet another way. The parts of the house and machinery were torn and scattered in every direction.

The rooms of the Kentucky Historical Society, located on the third floor of the old State house, were opened and dedicated June 7th, 1881. This being the anniversary of the discovery by Daniel Boone of the beautiful plateau of Kentucky. The chief address was made by Prof. Jos. D. Pickett, and some remarks were made by Governor Luke P. Blackburn and ex-Governor J. B. McCreary. During this year the county voted $100,000 for the Kentucky Midland R. R., and the city of Frankfort voted $150,000 for the same purpose.

One of the most exciting, but bloodless, episodes in the history of Frankfort occurred on September 16th. Adam Forepaugh's circus was advertised to be in Frankfort on that day. The city council by ordinance undertook to prohibit it from being unloaded in the city. Col. E. H. Taylor, Jr., Mayor of Frankfort, ordered the police not to permit the unloading of the effects of the circus within the limits of the city. The railroad company thereupon secured an injunction from the Franklin Circuit Court restraining the Mayor and council from interfering with the unloading. After the service of this order upon the Mayor, he went in person to the train and assumed command of the police force and notified all parties concerned that any attempt to unload the cars would be at the peril of those who did it—that he would shoot down any man who made the effort.

There was an immense crowd at the station. Several thousand people were packed in the street and the whole city was in a state of excitement. It was announced that the city authorities had openly defied the law and had arrayed the police force of the city against the authority of the State. This being made known to Judge Thompson (County Judge) he immediately ordered the Sheriff to proceed to the train and see to the execution of his order of injunction. The Sheriff, E. O. Hawkins, believing that there was an armed resistance, and that he was without sufficient force to enable him to carry out the order of the court, went to the Governor and asked that the McCreary Guards be directed to report to him. The Governor having a personal knowledge of the trouble and knowing that great excitement prevailed in the city, promptly complied with the request and the troops were ordered out. At a quarter past four o'clock they appeared and went in double quick to the train where they, under the directions of the Sheriff, dispersed the police force and saw that the cars were unloaded without further molestation. The whole trouble arose from the fact that the circus company proposed to set up its tents beyond the city limits and thereby escape payment of the tax which the city had imposed upon it.

E. O. Hawkins was elected Sheriff in 1880. In the month of June, 1882, it was discovered that he was short in his accounts with the State, in the sum of $3,859.43 and thereupon J. W. Gaines was placed in charge of the Sheriff's office. In 1883 E. O. Hawkins was re-elected Sheriff notwithstanding his shortage but he was not able to execute the required bond and J. W. Gaines was again appointed until the next election, when W. L. Collins was elected. The election for county officers for the year 1882, was as follows: R. A. Thompson, Judge; James A. Violett, Attorney; James G. Crockett, Clerk; Dan Shehan, Jailer; Robert Sanford, Assessor; Alexander McEwan, Coroner, and D. M. Woodson, Surveyor.

The Mayor and Board of Councilmen of the city of Frankfort sold the city gas works to the Southern Gas Co. The company was to pay $40,000 for the gas works property and franchise, and for which the city accepted bonds payable in forty years with interest at 6 per cent. per annum. The purchaser engaged to furnish the city and private individual consumers with gas of the best quality at $2.00 per one thousand cubic feet and to light the street lamps on all nights when there was no moon for the sum of $24 per annum per lamp. The city agreed to use not less than one hundred lamps.

Following the sale of the gas works there were several public meetings of the citizens of Frankfort wherein they condemned in unmeasured terms the Mayor and councilmen for making the sale and especially for the private way in which it was made and also for the terms of the contract.

During the month of June Rev. George O. Barnes conducted a revival service in Frankfort. The court house was crowded to overflowing each evening and great interest was exhibited. During the meeting there were 1,253 who made confessions. He was a most eloquent and learned man. The singing and playing by his daughter, Miss Marie, was a great feature of the service. No man ever visited Frankfort who left a stronger impression upon the citizens of the city.

On July 7th Charles Penn was assassinated, near his home, while taking his horse to the pasture. In a few moments after he left his house two shots were fired. Upon investigation the body of Penn was found not far from the bars leading to the pasture. He received the contents of a double barreled shot gun which was loaded with buck shot. The condition of the ground and weeds at the place of the murder disclosed the fact that the assassin had been lying in wait for his victim for some time and that the assassination had been well planned. Suspicion soon rested on a man by the name of George Gaines, who was arrested in a short time afterwards and in due course of time was tried and convicted and sent to the penitentiary for life. The general supposition was that the wife of Penn was indirectly the cause of his death.

On Sunday night, September 10th, an affray occurred in front of the Frankfort Hotel from the effects of which Jerry Lee, Chief of Police, received a mortal wound. In the early part of the night there had been a difficulty, the participants being Jerry Lee, Adam Kahr and Frank Egbert. Later in the night another trouble arose between Frank Egbert and Stephen Scarce. It was not known whether Egbert was shooting at Scarce or Lee when Lee received a wound in the left side from the effects of which he died. Jerry Lee had served as city Marshal and as Chief of Police. He was a man of marked personal courage and was regarded as an efficient officer. He was a generous, impulsive man, always ready to aid a friend or fight a foe.

On November 11th the City Hall, Buhr's Hotel, the postoffice and several private offices and residences were destroyed by fire. The money loss was seventy or eighty thousand dollars. Dr. Hatchitt, the postmaster, succeeded in removing, practically, everything from the postoffice. Several people were injured during the progress of the fire. Everybody fought fires in those days.

Not in the recollection of the oldest inhabitant of Frankfort nor in either history or tradition was there any account of the waters of the Kentucky river ever having been so high as in February, 1883. Nearly all the families in the lower part of the city were moved out. All of the section known as "Craw" was completely covered. On Sunday night the 11th of February, a great many Frankfort people remained up all night, expecting to see the St. Clair street bridge washed away. A heavy drift was running and it began to accumulate above the piers. An immense log lodged against the middle pier and there was a rapid accumulation of drift upon it. Houses began to come down, nearly all of which struck the bridge and were broken to pieces. A large new tobacco barn struck the middle pier and its timbers were scattered in every direction. The upper sidewalk of the bridge was greatly damaged, the sides and floor for some distance were completely destroyed and much of the sheeting under the roof was torn away.

More than half of the city was under water. All of the prison yard was covered from two to three feet. The back water extended back of the penitentiary to and beyond Woodland Park so that the water which backed up the Cove Spring or Leestown branch to the same point made an island of Fort Hill. At one point the Owenton road was more than ten feet under water. Every road except the Versailles, which lead to the city, was covered from two to ten feet. The floor of the city school building was reached. Traffic across the St. Clair street bridge was stopped, ropes were stretched across the ends of the bridge. The railroad bridge was considerably damaged by the drift and for some time it looked like it would be impossible to save it. A long freight train heavily loaded was left standing on it to help hold it. All the houses on Broadway and High streets from the Farmers Hotel, east, were completely surrounded. More than a hundred houses passed under the St. Clair street bridge, nearly all of which were torn to pieces.

The Farmers, or Merriwether, Hotel had about three feet of water in it and all the people who lived on that square had to move upstairs. The O. F. C., Carlisle, Hermitage and Saffell distilleries all had water on the first floor from two to ten feet deep.

The street in front of the court house lacked only two feet of being covered. The gas works were under water and the city was in total darkness. More than two hundred families were without homes. The public buildings of the city, county and State were used for temporary homes and the people were fed at the expense of the city. Many acts of heroic conduct were reported, and those who were charitably inclined had all the work they could do.

W. J. Chinn's sale of registered Jersey cattle was made in July. The vacant lots where Sam Shackleford and Judge T. H. Paynter's residences now stand were used for display of stock. The sale was attended by representative Jersey breeders throughout the United States and Canada; it was the largest and most successful sale of that kind ever held in Kentucky. The herd was a most excellent one, perhaps the best that was ever offered for sale. A large crowd was present. There were purchasers from Canada and nineteen different states of the Union. The proceeds of the sale amounted to over $36,000. The average price paid was $812.

Capt. D. A. Murphy arrived in Frankfort August 2nd, and in a few days thereafter he commenced work on the custom house and postoffice. The corner stone of this building was laid December 15th, 1883. Governor J. Proctor Knott officiated at the ceremonies.

Judge Ira Julian was re-elected to represent the county in the Legislature in 1883.

The dam at lock number four was completed October 6th, 1883. It is 528 feet long at the crown; 21 1-2 feet high and 34 feet wide and it contains about 40,000 lineal feet of timber 12x12 inches, 160,000 feet of sheathing; 5,984 cubic yards of rip-rap stone and about 16,000 pounds of iron spikes and it cost the Government $18,500.

The Kentucky River Mills were burnt October 6th. The loss was $80,000, the insurance was $40,000. These mills were built in 1877-8, the building cost $12,000, the machinery $50,000 and the stock was valued at $25,000.

In the early morning of August 15th, a trusty convict from the penitentiary rode hastily through the streets of Frankfort, proclaiming that an outbreak had been made at the penitentiary. John R. Wolf, a desperate young man, who had been sent from Scott County for forgery, led the attempted delivery. He had a package which he requested to have sent to Georgetown and when he came in he struck the guard, Ed Johnson, with a stick on the back of the head and knocked him insensible and thereupon eight other convicts made a rush through the open gate and into the room set apart for arms and ammunition. A trusty named Cunningham saved the life of Johnson, but was himself severely stabbed. The convicts secured all the fire arms they wanted and one of them leveled his pistol at Clerk S. D. Holloway who, unhesitatingly, jumped through the window.

Jerry South, Clay Payne, D. O. Robinson and others took part in the shooting which followed. D. O. Robinson was shot through the leg and was made a cripple for life. A convict named Alsop was shot through the shoulder and Wolf had his thigh shattered. Three of them went out the Owenton road. They met a man in a buggy and made him get out and all three of them got in and drove as fast as they could for several miles when they abandoned the buggy and took to the hills.

A few days afterwards Governor Knott pardoned Cunningham for his timely assistance to Johnson.

Col. Ambrose W. Dudley died at his home in Frankfort in September, 1884. He was one of the oldest and most distinguished citizens of Frankfort. For fifteen years he was quartermaster general of the United States and for thirty-seven years was president of the Branch Bank of Kentucky located at Frankfort.

For more than half a century he was identified with the business and social interest of Frankfort and was regarded as one of the most useful and valuable citizens in promoting the general welfare of the city, county and State. In 1824 he married Miss Eliza Talbott, daughter of Hon. Isham Talbott, and granddaughter of Governor James Garrard.

On May 21st, 1885, Napoleon B. Smith was appointed Clerk of the Franklin County Court to take the place of James G. Crockett, deceased, and who had been Clerk for a number of years prior to that time. At the following August election Napoleon B. Smith was elected to fill out the unexpired term and Col. S. I. M. Major was elected to represent the county in the Legislature.

E. H. Steadman, an old and honorable citizen of Franklin County, died in April, 1885. He came to the county in 1835 and he and his brother Samuel built the village known as Steadmantown. For more than thirty years they furnished the State with all the paper used in printing the laws of the State, besides supplying most of the newspapers of the State. In 1852 Samuel Steadman retired from the firm and after that the paper mills were burnt three times and each time without any insurance. In 1861 he filled an order from the Confederate Government for paper on which to print the notes which were to give life and credit to the South in her struggle for independence. He was a man of superior ability. No man in the State knew more of the general incidents of Kentucky history or could relate them more entertainingly.

On August 10th a destructive fire occurred on the corner of Main and St. Clair streets. The property of P. C. Sower and the building of Sol Harris adjoining it, and the elegant office of Col. E. H. Taylor, Jr., were destroyed. The loss amounted to about sixty thousand dollars. On December 7th the Frankfort public school building was destroyed by fire, entailing a loss of about $30,000. The building was erected in 1868. It was insured for $16,000.

President Cleveland appointed Judge W. L. Jett postoffice inspector, July 23rd, 1886, and Capt. T. C. Jones consul at the port of Funchal, Madeira Island, in April of same year.

Col. S. I. M. Major died on June 21st. He was born in Franklin County, September 14th, 1830, and was educated by B. B. Sayre. He was regarded as one of the best educated men in Frankfort. In 1853 he became the editor of the Yeoman which was considered the leading Democratic paper of the State during the time he was editor. An incident in his editorial life was a challenge to fight a duel in 1857 sent by Thomas M. Green. Col. Major was public printer for twenty-five years. In 1867 he was elected to the Legislature and in the following year was elected Mayor of Frankfort which position he held for four succeeding terms. In 1885 he was again elected to the Legislature.

James Francis Leonard, the first practical sound reader of the Morse alphabet, was born in Frankfort, September 18th, 1854, in the old Pascal Hickman house, located near the mouth of the tunnel where the South warehouse is located. He entered the telegraph office as messenger boy in 1844, and he learned the art of telegraphy in a short time. He received messages by sound in the Frankfort office in the summer of 1848. He died of typhoid fever in Columbus, Miss., July 29th, 1862.

The old time telegraphers, at their annual meeting in

New York in 1885, appropriated funds and appointed a committee to bring his remains back to Frankfort and to erect a monument suitably inscribed over them in the Frankfort cemetery.

The county election for the year 1886 resulted as follows: R. A. Thompson, Judge; B. G. Williams, Attorney; N. B. Smith, Clerk; Thomas Hunter, School Commissioner; Lewis Harrod, Assessor; Minus Williams, Jailer; John W. Gaines, Sheriff, and M. H. Phythian, Coroner.

The first meeting, at which initiatory steps were taken for the celebration of the centennial anniversary of Frankfort, was held in the office of Col. John L. Scott on June 10th, 1886. Col. Scott was elected chairman and L. F. Johnson, secretary. At this meeting was inaugurated the work of gathering up and presenting such statistical facts in regard to the origin, growth and standing of all the departments, business interests, churches, societies, courts and other specific interests and features of Frankfort.

From the start the plan to hold a centennial celebration was a popular one, the subject soon became too large for the few who had it in charge to handle, and thereupon a mass meeting of the citizens was called for the 23rd of August. At which a committee of eight prominent citizens were appointed for the purpose of organizing the "Frankfort Centennial Association." On the 28th of the month the committee reported to an adjourned meeting and in the report it was recommended that Gen. D. W. Lindsey be permanent president and Judge W. H. Sneed, S. C. Sayre and H. B. Ware, secretaries. Seventy-two vice presidents were named. This list included some of the most prominent citizens of the city. Col. J. Stoddard Johnston was at the head of the list. There was also appointed a general committee on arrangements and supervision and also the following committees: Invitation, reception, finance, entertainment, decorations, procession, music, relics and curiosities. By resolution the citizens of Franklin County were invited to co-operate with the citizens of Frankfort.

The centennial celebration was held on October 6th, 1886. One hundred years having passed since the city was established.

It was doubtless the greatest day in the history of the city. There was a record breaking crowd on the streets, estimated at 25,000. The street parade was divided into five divisions and it was the longest ever seen in Frankfort. It consisted of secret and benevolent orders, Christian organizations, etc. A large part of the State guard, in fact nearly every military company of the State, was present. Knights Templar and other secret orders from all sections of the State and every drum corps and band in the State were in the parade. All the benevolent societies and Christian organizations of Frankfort and the public schools of the city participated. Thirty-six business houses in Frankfort had floats in the parade, advertising their various business interests. The ceremonies took place on the Capitol (old Capitol) square. The speaker's platform was between the two front gates, facing the Capitol grounds with seats extending nearly to the Capitol building. The stand was decorated with evergreens, flags and flowers.

The exercises were opened by Mayor E. H. Taylor, Jr., who introduced to the assembled thousands, Judge William Lindsay, who made the welcoming address. Mrs. Eudora South and Mrs. Jennie C. Morton were on the programme, each of whom read an original poem. Major Henry T. Stanton, the poet laureate of Kentucky, read a centennial poem which he had prepared for the occasion. Col. W. C. P. Breckenridge delivered a short address and John Mason Brown, the chief orator of the day, discussed "The Political Beginnings of Kentucky."

The ceremonies of the day were closed with a fine display of fireworks on the river front. A large number of papers giving an historical account of many interesting things connected with a history of the city were contributed. Mr. Landon A. Thomas, Mrs. T. J. Mayhall and Rev. Philip S. Fall, three of the oldest citizens of Frankfort at that time, each contributed an article. Scores of other valuable articles giving a history of the different churches, secret orders, courts, and in fact, almost everything that had happened in Frankfort during the century were prepared and sent in to be filed as a part of the archives of the city, but on account of the gross and almost criminal negligence of the city authorities, nearly all of these records were destroyed, about the only thing left was the centennial register which was turned over to the Historical Society and filed with the archives of the society. The loss by the city and county by reason of the destruction of these papers is inestimable.

The corner stone of the new city school building was laid July 17th. The Mayor and city council were assisted in the ceremonies by the other city officials, Masons, Odd Fellows, Knights of Honor, Knights Templar, Good Templars, Blue Ribbon Club and a great concourse of citizens. The principal addresses of the day were delivered by the Mayor, E. H. Taylor, Jr., and Rev. George Darsie, pastor of the Christian Church. Major H. T. Stanton read a poem which he had written for the occasion.

This new structure was opened for occupancy in March, 1887, it cost over $30,000 and it was considered a very handsome building.

Gen. John Rodman died at his home in Frankfort, October 29th. He was about sixty years of age. When he was a young man he tried merchandising but soon gave it up and read law in the office of Judge Nuttell. He commenced the practice at LaGrange, Kentucky. In 1853 he moved to Frankfort and soon became one of the leading lawyers of Frankfort and for years he was regarded as one of the ablest lawyers of the State. In 1859 he represented Franklin County in the Kentucky Legislature. In 1867 he was elected Attorney General of the State and was re-elected in 1871. In 1879 he was elected reporter of the Court of Appeals, which position he held at the time of his death. During his term as reporter he published 78-79-80-81 and 82 Kentucky Reports.

Gen. Rodman was not only a good lawyer but he was also a good politician and a fine speaker. He was quick, aggressive, positive, tactful, sarcastic and humorous, he was especially strong as a jury lawyer.

The 2nd day of May, 1886, was the 55th birthday of James W. Tate. At that time he had been nearly eighteen years State Treasurer. State officials and friends made him a present of a cane. In the following January Governor S. B. Buckner sent the Legislature the following: "Gentlemen of the Senate and House of Representatives: It is my painful duty to announce to you the fact that for reasons which appear in the accompanying act of the Governor, Auditor and Attorney General, the State Treasurer of the State has been suspended from the exercises of his official duties. The hasty examination which has been made of his books induces the belief that there is a large deficit in his accounts. This examination was made yesterday and the action reported to you was taken last evening as soon as the deficit appeared. The fact is communicated to you at the earliest moment for your information and action. It is believed that the bond of the Treasurer will fully cover any possible deficit that a more complete investigation may reveal. In the meantime the Auditor and Secretary of State have been directed to take temporary charge of the Treasury.

"Respectfully,
"S. B. BUCKNER."

The defalcation of James W. Tate was not a complete surprise, rumors of trouble along that line had found their way into the newspapers and the approaching catastrophe had been privately discussed by a few Frankfort citizens for several weeks.

For several days following the flight of Treasurer Tate, all kinds of wild rumors were heard on the streets of Frankfort. It was generally understood that his defalcation would cause a large deficit and the Legislature thought it best not to make any further appropriations until the matter could be thoroughly investigated. A special committee was appointed to consider the subject of removing him from office and the committee recommended "That James W. Tate, Treasurer of the Commonwealth of Kentucky, be impeached for high crimes and misdemeanors in office," and a committee was appointed to prepare articles of impeachment. The articles of impeachment were presented to the Senate by the House of Representatives on the 24th of March and a committee from the House was appointed to conduct the prosecution before the Senate. At twelve o'clock on March 29th the Senate of Kentucky resolved itself into a high court to consider the articles of impeachment. The unusual and novel scene was witnessed by a large concourse of people.

Judge W. S. Pryor, Chief Justice of the Court of Appeals, administered the oath required by the Constitution. After the oath was administered to the Senators the sergent at arms made proclamation that the Senate sitting as a high court was then ready to consider the articles of impeachment against James W. Tate, Treasurer of Kentucky, charging him with high crimes and misdemeanors in office. After the testimony of several witnesses had been heard a vote was taken and thirty-three Senators voted in the affirmative and only one in the negative. The President of the Senate thereupon declared that the Senate of Kentucky sitting as a high court for trial of impeachment had found James W. Tate, Treasurer of Kentucky, guilty of high crimes and misdemeanors in office, being convicted thereof by concurrence of two-thirds of the members present and the judgment of the court was "That said James W. Tate be, and he is hereby, removed from the office of Treasurer of Kentucky and disqualified to hold any office of honor, trust or profit under this Commonwealth."

James W. Tate was a native of Franklin County. He served nearly five terms as Treasurer. He was known throughout the State as "Honest Dick Tate." It was never determined the amount of money which he took with him but the supposition was that he only carried with him a small amount.

Several years after he left, his daughter brought suit in the Franklin Circuit Court against a life insurance company for the amount of a policy on her father's life, alleging in the petition that more than seven years had elapsed since he had been heard from. On the witness stand she testified that he had gone to South America and after visiting several sections of that country he went to California and that the last time she heard from him he was arranging to start, that day, to a small mining town in the interior of the State.

On June the 18th, 1887, the remains of Joel T. Hart, Kentucky's greatest sculptor, were buried in the Frankfort cemetery. A large number of prominent citizens from all sections of the State were present. The remains were taken from a vault in the cemetery where they had been for two years and were taken to their last resting place about one hundred feet south of the Richard M. Johnson monument. The services were opened with prayer by Rev. G. F. Bagby, after which the choir sang "My Country 'Tis of Thee." Gov. Knott then introduced Robert Burns Wilson, who delivered an oration. After which he introduced the orator of the day, Judge Wm. M. Beckner, who delivered a most excellent eulogy. The crowd present was estimated at 2,500.

The election on the proposition of Franklin County subscribing $150,000 to the capital stock of the Frankfort, Georgetown and Paris Railroad was taken in July, 1887, and was carried by a large majority. Great interest was manifested in the election. Bands of music paraded the streets and a large vote was polled. The city voted almost unanimously for the appropriation and the county outside of the city was almost solid against it, except the Forks of Elkhorn, which gave a good majority for the proposition. There were 2,838 for the proposition and 1,208 against it.

Ex-Governor Luke P. Blackburn died at his residence in Frankfort, September 14th, and was buried in the Frankfort cemetery. He was born in Woodford County in 1816. He was elected Governor in 1879. He was a man of strong character and tender heart, his kindness of heart and sympathy for the suffering led him to pardon more men from the penitentiary than perhaps any other man who was ever Governor. He practiced medicine in Frankfort for many years. He and Dr. Churchill Blackburn were partners and they had an office in the old mansion house upon the site where the McClure building was afterwards erected.

The monument in the Frankfort cemetery, erected by order of the State in memory of Gov. Blackburn, was unveiled on May 27th, 1891. The Masons conducted the ceremony. Addresses were delivered by Hon. William M. Beckner, of Winchester, and Gen. Basil W. Duke, of Louisville.

The fire alarm system was adopted in Frankfort in November, 1887.

J. C. Noel was elected Sheriff in 1888.

CHAPTER XIV.

From 1890 *to* 1900.

Gen. Scott Brown represented the county in the Kentucky Legislature in 1890-1.

The county election for the year 1890 resulted in the election of B. G. Williams, Judge; L. F. Johnson, County Attorney; N. B. Smith, Clerk; Thomas Hunter, School Commissioner; Thomas K. Jett, Surveyor, and O. B. Polsgrove, Assessor.

Mrs. Mary Brown Day became State Librarian March 26, 1890. Ed Porter Thompson resigned.

Judge T. H. Hines was elected to represent Franklin County in the Constitutional Convention of 1891.

Dr. Ben. F. Duvall died at his residence in Frankfort in May, 1890. He served as a surgeon in the Confederate army during the rebellion. He represented Franklin County in the Lower House for one term.

Judge R. A. Thompson died October 23rd of the same year, in his sixty-third year. For twenty years he was County Judge of Franklin County. He was a Confederate soldier for four years, a part of which time he was Quartermaster, with the rank of Captain. In 1869 he was elected door-keeper of the House of Representatives and in 1871 he was Sergeant-at-Arms of the State Senate.

On county court day, the 2nd of November, 1891, Ambrose Polsgrove shot and killed Jerry Williamson, his brother-in-law, and at the same time he wounded three other men. The shooting took place on the corner of Main and St. Clair streets, while the streets were crowded. Williamson was shot three times, but one of the bullets made six holes. It went through the flesh of his left arm and through the left breast passing above the skin on the breast bone and on through his right breast. The shot which killed him struck him in the back. Polsgrove was a member of a strong family and was at one time deputy sheriff. The jury found him not guilty.

Judge Alvin Duvall died at his home November 17th. He was one of the most prominent lawyers of Kentucky. He was born in Scott County, March 20, 1913. His father was an officer in the war of 1812 and was afterwards a member of the Kentucky Legislature. Judge Duvall graduated from the Georgetown College in 1833. He studied law under Jas. F. Robinson, and afterwards graduated from Transylvania University. He too represented his county in the Kentucky Legislature. He was Circuit Judge and Judge of the Court of Appeals. He was afterwards elected Clerk of the Court of Appeals. When he became a member of the Court of Appeals he also became a citizen of Frankfort. At one time he made the race for Mayor but was defeated by a few votes.

Rev. H. H. Kavanaugh, chaplain of the State Penitentiary died January 18, 1892. He was born at Mt. Sterling in 1836. He spent several years on the frontier with his father, who was an Indian teacher. In early manhood he became a traveling preacher of the Methodist Church. He was a chaplain in Gen. Morgan's command, and was exposed to the dangers which were incurred by that intrepid leader, and as a result he brought home with him the scars of three federal bullets. He was known as "the fighting parson." At the close of the war he returned to the ministry and about ten years prior to his death he became the chaplain of the Penitentiary, where his faithful service was productive of much good among the unfortunates confined there. He was the father of F. K. Kavanaugh, State Librarian, (1912).

On the 22nd of January, 1892, it was discovered that Hugh Gaines, City Treasurer of Frankfort, was short in his accounts in the sum of about $3,000. He left for parts unknown and his bondsmen, Gen. Fayette Hewitt, Col. C. E. Hoge and J. W. Gaines, made good the shortage.

Col. E. H. Taylor, Jr., represented the county in the House of the Kentucky Legislature in 1892-3.

Mrs. Mary B. Day was elected State Librarian for the second time in 1893.

An explosion occurred about two miles from the city, near the Louisville road. James Force and H. L. Sanders were engaged in taking powder from some old shells which had been at the State Arsenal since the war. They had agreed to do the work for one third of the powder; the state authorities had contracted to purchase their part. They had gotten 2,600 pounds and on the Saturday previous had delivered 1,000 pounds, and they had arranged to deliver the balance on the day of the accident. The cause of the accident was unknown. There was no one present at the time except the two men who were killed. Their bodies were so mangled and charred, when found, that they were almost beyond recognition. Mr. Force's house was about forty yards from where the explosion occurred. It was badly damaged, a number of holes were shot through the roof and weather-boarding, and all the glass in the house were broken. The shock from the explosion very much startled the people of Frankfort.

A society of The King's Daughters was organized in Franklin County in January, 1893. The object of the society was to extend charity where it was needed and to do good generally. In the two decades of its existence it has been productive of much good in the city and county. The organization has erected a large building known as the King's Daughters Hospital, located on East Main Street. The city and county have given material assistance in maintaining the institution.

State Senator William Lindsay, who was representing, in the State Senate, the district of which Franklin County was a part, was elected to the United States Senate in 1893, and Col. E. H. Taylor, Jr., who was representing Franklin County, was elected to the State Senate, and Mr. L. J. Cox was elected to fill out the unexpired term of Col. Taylor, in the House.

In July, 1893, the city and county made a contract with the King Bridge Company of Cleveland, Ohio, to build a new bridge across the Kentucky river at St. Clair street. The original contract price was $62,500. This amount was increased on account of changes made in the plans, to the sum of $65,700. The committee which had active control of the work was Esq. Pat McDonald, and the County Attorney. There was a contest, at that time, over the city offices, which was not settled until the bridge was practically completed. There was considerable dissatisfaction about the work; this was especially so in reference to the south abutment. Threats were made that the work would not be received and the bridge was closed for several weeks and work was discontinued on account of these threats. The bridge was finally opened to foot passengers in February, and to the general traveling public on March 24, 1894. The work was commenced on Thursday the 3rd day of August, 1893, which was the same day that work was commenced on the new electric railway for the city.

The State Press Association convened in Frankfort on June 7, the chief features of which were the boat excursion up the Kentucky river and the Governor's reception. On the evening of the last day of their stay, there was a banquet and ball at the Capital Hotel. Many noted newspaper men were present. Following this meeting the press of the State said many nice things about Frankfort and her people.

While moving a threshing machine and traction engine near the Forks of Elkhorn on July 27th, Mr. Lee Triplett fell from the engine and in falling he reversed the leever and before he could get out of the way the engine backed over him and crushed him to death. Norman Wilkerson, who was also on the machine was thrown off, his right arm was broken and he received other severe bruises

The remains of Chief Justice Caswell Bennett, who died in Hopkinsville were brought to Frankfort on August 11th. They were taken direct to the State House where they lay in state during the day. A special military guard was detailed to watch over them. The public buildings were closed and no business transacted.

Bellepoint was, by ordinance, annexed to Frankfort in 1894. There was considerable contest over the annexation, which continued through several months. At that time there was about $125,000 of taxable property situated in Bellepoint. The ordinance took effect January 1st, 1895.

The 73d Annual Kentucky Conference of the Methodist Episcopal Church, South, was held in Frankfort on September 13th. It was presided over by Bishop W. W. Duncan. There were many ministers of high character and intellectual endowment who spoke during the conference. Rev. S. F. Pollett was sent to the Frankfort station.

On August 14th, 1894, Mrs. Martin Nolan was criminally assaulted by a negro, known as Marshall Boston, while on her way to Frankfort, she being at the time, on the Devil's Hollow road, about a mile from the city. When the news of the assault reached the city it created a great deal of excitement and in a very short time nearly half of the male citizens of Frankfort were in search of him. In the afternoon he was arrested and carried before Mrs. Nolan, who identified him. That night, about twelve o'clock he was taken from the jail by a mob and carried to the new St. Clair street bridge and hung. Only a few members of the mob were masked, but no one seemed to be interested in trying to identify any of them, the general impression seeming to be that a merited punishment was speedily though unlawfully inflicted. After he was hung more than a hundred shots were fired into his body.

On November 12th, the State's large warehouse, filled with chairs, belonging to the Chair Company, was burned. About $16,000 worth of chairs and the building, valued at $8,000, were a total loss, but most of the loss was covered by insurance.

In compliance with the order of the Secretary of War, the Louisville and Nashville Railroad Company raised the bridge across the Kentucky river at Frankfort, about 8 feet above the old bridge. This order was given with the idea of preventing any further obstruction to the steam boat navigation. The work was completed August 16th.

An explosion occurred at Tom Pence's saw mill in Bellepoint, October 19th. A can about half full of powder was in a shed near where Joe Downey and Howard Masters were at work filing a saw. A spark from which fell in the can; both of the men were badly burnt and several bones were broken.

On the 13th of January John W. Payne died. He was proofreader for the Frankfort Yoeman for a number of years. In 1877 he was elected City Treasurer and was afterwards elected a member of the City Council. For several terms he was elected a Clerk of the State Board of Equalization and he was also the collaborator of tables in the office of the Superintendent of Public Instruction. At the time of his death he was forty-five years of age.

Dick Suter shot Urban Stephens in Luscher's saloon, February 6, 1893. Some papers in Stephen's pocket saved his life. On August 5, 1895, Suter shot and killed Harry Kelley at Porter's saloon in Craw. The trouble came up over the testimony of Suter against Kelley in the police court. Kelley was shot twice; either wound would have killed him. Suter was convicted on the charge of murder and sent to the penitentiary for life, but through the influence of his brother, Lee Suter of Louisville, Governor Brown pardoned him.

On March 19th, 1893, Mr. George A. Robertson died at the age of 86 years. He was a nephew of Chief Justice George Robertson. In 1827 he came to Frankfort and became a clerk in the State Treasurer's office and was afterwards a clerk in the Auditor's office. When the Legislature established the office of State Librarian in 1832, he was elected to that office, which position he held for seventeen years. In 1862 he was again elected to the office of State Librarian which he held for six years, and after that he was elected sergeant-at-arms of the Court of Appeals, which position he continued to hold until his death. His long tenure in office enabled him to become acquainted with all the public men of the State.

The following month Esq. John W. Bohannan died. By a special act of the Legislature he was granted license to practice law when he was only eighteen years of age. He had a most excellent memory. He knew the Code of Practice so well that he could give the number and repeat almost any section of it. He was twice elected magistrate for the Frankfort magisterial district. He was serving his second term at the time of his death.

The thirty-eighth annual session of the State Medical Association was held in Frankfort in May, 1893. The attendance was large, nearly every county and town in the State was represented. All the prominent physicians of the State were present.

Prof. E. A. Fellmer died at his home in Frankfort, September 5th, 1895. He was a German by birth but he lived in Frankfort for about thirty years. He was a music teacher by profession; he was a polished scholar and a gentleman of stainless honor. For several years prior to his death he was connected with the State Geological Bureau. His especial duty was to look after the emigration of foreigners and to see that the better class of emigrants had proper inducements to settle in the State. He succeeded in establishing several colonies.

On January 5th, 1895, Jeff Lucas was fatally stabbed by Joe Newton in a fight near the Forks of Elkhorn. The trouble came up over a stove which Lucas had left with Newton for repairs. Jeff Lucas was a bright young man who had selected the law as his profession. Joe Newton was a brother of Cal Newton, who in August, 1905, shot and killed two of his neighbors, George Smith and James D. Smith, his son, who lived on an adjoining farm. The Smiths were out repairing a fence which joined their division fence; Newton took his double-barreled shot gun and cut the shells so that the shot would not scatter and walked over to where the men were at work and killed both of them. Newton was a school teacher and up to that time had borne a good reputation. He was convicted of murder and sent to the penitentiary for life.

On Friday, February 29, 1895, George Magee, a negro convict from the local penitentiary was hung by Sheriff R. D. Armstrong and his deputies, for having murdered another convict at the State penitentiary. The hanging of Magee was the first legal execution in Franklin County since the slave woman of Mr. Hiram Berry was hung in 1860 for trying to poison the Berry family.

In September, 1894, the public schools of the city were closed for several weeks on account of the numerous cases of diphtheria. A number of cases in both the city and county proved fatal.

The county election for 1894 resulted as follows: B. G. Williams, County Judge; N. B. Smith, Clerk; R. D. Armstrong, Sheriff; Minus Williams, Jailer; Jas. H. Polsgrove, County Attorney; W. S. Dehoney, Coroner; T. K. Jett, Surveyor, and M. B. Dorton, Assessor.

Section one of the penitentiary warehouse, filled with chairs, was burned on Monday night, November 12, 1894. The loss to the State was about $20,000 which was, only in part, covered by insurance.

The Woman's Club of Frankfort was organized on September 22, 1894, with forty members, which was afterwards increased to fifty, the limit fixed by the constitution. This organization has been productive of much good to the members of the society and to the general public.

On April the 25th, 1905, a fire occurred on Bridge street, in what was known as the Fincel Block, wherein three people were burned to death, and the whole block of buildings swept away. Five families occupied the rooms over the several stores. The flames spread so rapidly that those who escaped did so in their night clothes. James Yager and two small children who were sleeping in a back room could not be aroused in time and all of them perished.

Judge Ruben Brown, one of the most prominent men of the county died at his home near Bridgeport on May 24th, 1895. He was a son of Scott Brown, a pioneer, who came to Kentucky about 1782, and who was at one time a Magistrate and later was Sheriff of the county. Judge Brown was a brother of Gen. Scott Brown, who represented Franklin County in both the House and Senate, and who was Adjutant General under Governor Magoffin. Judge Brown was twice elected County Judge of the county. He was a plain honest gentleman of the old school and he held the respect and esteem of all who knew him.

On January 1st, 1896, County Judge Williams appointed his brother, Wiley C. Williams, jailer of the county to take the place of Minus Williams, deceased.

Attorney James A. Violett represented the county in 1896. On the 14th of February of this year, Officer Henry Brown was shot and killed in U. Kagin's saloon on Broadway street, by a man named Lucien Hawkins, and immediately thereafter Hawkins was shot and killed by Police Officer Will Gordon. Hawkins had come to the city from Shelby County, and was drunk and disorderly. The officers had been sent for and in the attempt to arrest him, he shot Capt. Brown five times and in turn was shot three times by Officer Gordon; both men died within two minutes after the shooting. Capt. Brown was an excellent officer and a good detective. He was 64 years old and for 38 years had been on the police force of Frankfort.

On Sunday night, March 15th, Governor W. O. Bradley ordered the "riot call" to be rung, and in a few moments the greatest excitement prevailed in all sections of the city. Men who lived in the outskirts of the town hurriedly armed themselves and went to the court house to find the cause of the alarm. Various reasons were assigned for the call. Every one was excited but no one could tell why it was made. No good reason was ever assigned for it. The people of Frankfort were very indignant by reason of the Governor's conduct. The Mayor of Frankfort, Hon. Ira Julian, issued a proclamation calling a meeting of the citizens of Frankfort and strong resolutions condemning the conduct of the Governor were passed.

There was a negro riot in Frankfort on Sunday, June 8th. The societies of the negro hod-carriers and teamsters of Louisville came to Frankfort on a crowded train. Two of the visiting negroes were fighting when they reached Frankfort; the police officers of the city undertook to arrest them, other negroes undertook to prevent the arrest and two or three hundred of them were making it warm work for the officers and they were getting the worst of it when several white men went to their assistance. The riot continued for a considerable time; several white men and a large number of negroes were injured but no fatalities resulted.

On the night of July the 21st, 1896, a disastrous flood occurred in Benson Creek which arose very suddenly in the night time and washed away several houses, a large amount of fencing, stables and other outbuildings, farming products, and in some places the soil, leaving nothing but bare rocks where there had been fertile fields. The daughter of Judge J. D. Moore and two of her children were drowned. Many other people in that section had almost miraculous escapes. About one and a half miles of the L. & N. Railroad was washed away, entailing a great loss upon the company. The work of reconstruction was more difficult than was the original construction. Gainey's bridge, which consisted of three steel spans, was entirely swept away, the two piers were taken out to bed rock. The length of the new bridge is 122 feet. The oldest inhabitants in that section say that the volume of water was at least four feet higher than the previous highest water.

On Tuesday, the second day of September, 1896, the Institution for Feeble Minded Children was burned. The loss to the State was about $65,000. On the 3rd of May a like fire occurred in which the building used at that time was destroyed entailing a further loss of more than $50,000. On September the 18th, the frame buildings located on the State ground, and which were temporarily used after the fire of September 2nd, were also consumed. The children were then moved to Frankfort for a few days, and until the Commissioners rented the Walcutt farm, where the children remained until the buildings could be reconstructed. The last new building was completed in 1897. It is a more handsome building than were either of those which burned.

During the year 1896 the night riders destroyed nearly all of the toll gates in the county and practically forced the Fiscal Court to purchase all of the turnpikes and make them free. On October 24th, they visited the toll houses on the Louisville and Lawrenceburg roads and destroyed the gates. On November 13th the toll house on the Owenton road was burned and the toll gate was taken down and cut to pieces. This destruction of property with threats and intimidation continued until the roads were made free.

Dr. James Russell Hawkins died at his home near Bridgeport on February 1st, 1897, at the age of 92 years. He was a man of strong personality. He moved to Boone County in his early manhood and represented that senatorial district in the Kentucky Legislature. After his term of office expired he removed to Franklin County where he resided the remainder of his life. He was a practicing physician and became prominent in his profession. He was also a licensed preacher. For 29 years he was the chief clerk of the Senate. He had a fine voice, was a good reader and was very popular as an officer and citizen.

On the 9th of February, 1897, the boiler which was used at the jail for heating purposes and which was located under the jail office, exploded with disastrous effects. Cabell Hardin, Dr. Alvin Duvall, Capt. Lew Hill, Emmett Triplett, Jay Robinson and James C. Rogers were all injured, some of them very severely. James C. Rogers was so seriously hurt that he died from the effects of the wounds on the next day.

Hon. Ed. Porter Thompson published his "Young People's History of Kentucky" during the year 1897. This work was prepared for the public schools of the State. It is a good work and is well suited to the purpose for which it was written.

The State Bankers' Association was convened in Frankfort in September, 1897. About one hundred delegates from different sections of the State were present. Governor Bradley delivered the address of welcome in behalf of the State, and General D. W. Lindsey on behalf of the local banks. This meeting was of interest not only to the bankers but also to the general public.

An election riot took place in Frankfort on Monday night, November 1st, 1897. Some of the Democratic politicians and workers undertook to collect a boat load of negroes and carry them up the river and in that way prevent them from voting the next day in the city election. The Republicans found out what was being done and they very promptly stopped further proceedings along that line. The Democrats then undertook to corrall the negroes at Dailey's barn which was located on the Georgetown road about one mile from Frankfort. The Republicans, white and colored, led by Frank Egbert and Howard Glore, all of them well armed, started out to release the negroes who had been collected at the barn. When they reached a point on the road near the colored Normal School, they met one of the wagons which had been used in carrying the negroes to the barn; a man by the name of John Smith and known as "Sweet Thing" was driving, and several white men were in the wagon. The Republicans undertook to stop the wagon and the shooting commenced. Howard Glore was killed, John Smith was shot through the knee and lost a leg as the result, and a negro by the name of Charles Graham was shot through the breast and was seriously but not fatally wounded. The Democrats came on to Frankfort and had a warrant issued against Frank Egbert and placed in the hands of Tes Deakins, a fearless Deputy Sheriff of the county. Later in the night when Deakins undertook to execute the warrant of arrest on Egbert, at the corner of Main and St. Clair streets, Egbert and his friends commenced firing at Deakins and the Democrats who were located at the four corners of the street, commenced shooting at Egbert. As a result Deakins was shot twice and instantly killed and Egbert was shot five times and he, too, then and there died from the wounds. Walter Goins, an uncle of Egbert, was shot in the foot. Several men were arrested and lodged in jail but none of them were ever tried. Deakins left a wife and three small children, and Egbert also left a wife and three small children. Glore was not married.

Judge George C. Drane died on the first day of the new year, seventy-one years of age. He was elected Circuit Judge in 1862 and was re-elected. He served fourteen years on the bench.

On January 15th Dewitt Clinton Barrett died in his 75th year. He came to Frankfort from Pennsylvania in 1858, and commenced work on the Kentucky Yeoman. In 1875 he purchased an interest in the Yeoman which was run under the firm name of Major, Johnston & Barrett. He was modest, unassuming, true, upright and honorable.

The election for county officers in 1898 resulted as follows: J. D. Moore, Judge; J. H. Polsgrove, Attorney; Ben Suter, Sheriff; W. H. Hawkins, Assessor; James Alley, Jailer, and Miss Lucy Pattie, Superintendent of Schools.

Judge Thomas H. Hines died at his home in Frankfort, January 24th, 1898. He was born in Butler County, October 8th, 1838. He was well educated and was employed as a professor in Funk Masonic Seminary at LaGrange, Kentucky. He was Captain in General Morgan's command during the Civil War and was captured with him during the raid through

Ohio and was confined with him in the Columbus penitentiary. It was Judge Hines who planned and carried into execution their escape from the penitentiary. Afterwards he went to Canada to cooperate with Jacob Thompson in the attempt to liberate the prisoners in northern prisons. At the close of the war he studied law and was editor of a newspaper. In 1878 he was elected Judge of the Court of Appeals, and at the expiration of his term of office retained his citizenship at Frankfort. In 1891 he represented Franklin County in the Constitutional Convention. He was tall, slim and delicate. He had the moral courage to express his opinion and the physical courage to carry them into execution.

On the 8th of the following May Maj. H. T. Stanton died, in his 64th year. He, too, was a Confederate soldier, and was promoted for gallantry to the position of Major. He was a genial, companionable man and he was a poet of high order. His "Jacob Brown" and "The Moneyless Man" gained for him a national reputation as a man of letters. He assisted Col. J. S. Johnston in writing the History of Louisville. For many years he was assistant editor of the Frankfort Yeoman. A small stone giving his name, birth and death marks his last resting place in the Frankfort cemetery.

Walter R. Franklin died on the 19th of July, 1899, in his 76th year. He spent fifty years of his life in the Franklin Circuit Court Clerk's office. He was deputy clerk for fifteen years and chief clerk for thirty-five years. He was very careful and accurate. Every one had implicit confidence in his word and no lawyer thought about examining the order book to see whether or not an order was properly entered. He was always ready to advise and help a young lawyer. There was not a lawyer at the Frankfort bar who was better informed as to the general practice.

Frankfort's first street fair was opened with due and imposing ceremonies on the 3rd of September, in the presence of a large assembly of people. The procession was led by the News Boys' Band of Louisville. Governor Bradley formally opened the exercises with an eloquent address. The fair was a great success. Thousands of out of town visitors were present during the week.

The Kentucky Historical Society re-established the original corner stone of Frankfort. On October 6th the unveiling occurred. The Governor and other state officials, the Mayor and other city officials and a large number of people took part in the ceremony. The stone is located on the east side of Ann street, near the south end. The chief address of the day was delivered by Judge Lysander Hord.

A roster of the soldiers in the Spanish-American war from Franklin County is as follows: Adjutant of 1st Batallion, H. T. Gaines; Chief Surgeon, W. H. Dade; Chaplain, Rev. W. L. Waits; Hospital Stewart, Howard H. Farmer; Dr. Nevill Garrett was Assistant Surgeon. Company "E" Second Regiment, Kentucky Volunteers, known as Bradley Guards—Captain, Julian Kersey; 1st Lieutenant, W. N. Bridgeford; 2nd Lieutenant, Estin Hieatt; Sergeant, Robert Semones; Corporal, J. W. Gilpin. Privates—Augustus Baker, Chas. Berry, B. D. Betts, R. L. Bentley, E. F. Brown, ——— Brown, Sam Carr, Albert Chilson, Henry Chilson, Rudolph Childer, Wm. Choate, Wm. Crane, John P. Cox, Dudley Cohn, Chas. Collins, R. S. Croggin, J. E. Cleveland, W. M. Cleveland, David Howard, Jeff Davis, Cad Davis, Geo. M. Egbert, W. J. Ellard, Otis Evans, H. H. Farmer, J. T. Fitzgerald, Lee R. Foster, G. F. Gayhart, Carlton Gaines, Arthur Glore, J. E. Graves, J. D. Holmes, Wallace Hunter, F. C. Hutchinson, W. W. Huss, James Johnson, William Kavanaugh, Taylor Kinkade, John B. Kingkade, John W. Lawson, William McClure, Henry B. Kinkade, John W. Lawson, William McClure, Henry Mitchell, J. S. Moore, Nerly Moore, Charles Netherton, Harry Nichols, R. L. Nixon, Chas. Orine, Dan Owens, Lawrence Owens, Sidney Parker, Arthur Ponder, John Richards, Charles Schuyler, George Semones, Albert Seibert, James Sharp, Claude Smith, J. F. Smither, W. F. Staples, W. R. Steffey, P. D. Stevenson, Patrick Haly, Geo. Hays, Herndon Hill, David Howard, Geo. L. Horine, Duncan C. Holmes, John E. Triplett, Emmett C. Triplett, John Tobin, Morris Updike and C. M.

Walcutt. Stewart Farmer and Charles Ahler were members of the band.

The men from Franklin County in the Georgetown Company were W. C. Jones, Herbert Morrison, Thomas R. Markham, Allen W. Travel, Robert R. Craik and Ralph W. Jones.

Capt. Noel Gaines, U. S. V. of Gen. Ludlow's staff was Provost Marshal of Havana; promoted to rank of Major.

CHAPTER XV.

Course of Events From 1900 to 1910.

On January the 18th, 1900, Col. D. G. Colston of Middlesboro, came to Frankfort as a witness before the Contest Board. He had gone to the Capital Hotel and was sitting near the front window in the office of the hotel, talking to some friends, when Lieutenant E. D. Scott came into the office through the west entrance leading from the dining room. As soon as Scott saw Col. Colston he drew his pistol and commenced firing at him. Col. Colston immediately drew his pistol and commenced firing at Scott. A young lawyer from Shelbyville by the name of L. D. Demaree was standing close and Scott immediately made a breastwork of him by throwing one arm around him and holding him in front and firing from behind him; while in that position Colston put three bullets through Demaree's heart. When each of the combatants had exhausted the contents of his pistol, Col. Colston very deliberately drew another pistol, and Scott, seeing no other way of escape, attempted to run down the steps to the basement but fell dead from Colston's firing when he reached the bottom step. After the duel was ended, it was found that Lieutenant Scott, L. W. Demaree and Charles H. Julian, a wealthy citizen from Franklin County were dead and that Harry McEwing, O. D. Redpath, Capt. B. B. Golden and Col. Colston were all seriously wounded. The cause of the trouble dated back several months, when the two army officers had a shooting scrape at Anniston, Alabama.

Great excitement prevailed, and an immense crowd soon gathered at the hotel. The tragedy was in no way connected with the political contest which was at that time being tried for the state officers.

Col. Colston was indicted by a Franklin County Grand Jury but on the trial of the case he claimed that Scott brought on the trouble by following him and by commencing the fight. The Jury found him "not guilty."

A traveling salesman representing a house in an eastern state had heard the reputation of Kentucky and Kentuckians discussed and he had no desire to form any acquaintances in the state. In the year 1894 his firm prevailed on him to come to Frankfort and he reached the city about an hour before Polsgrove shot and killed Williamson and wounded several other men, on the corner of Main and St. Clair streets, and he witnessed the tragedy. On his return he told his firm that he would resign rather than make another trip to Kentucky. In 1900, after much persuasion and some threats of discharging him, his firm again prevailed on him to come to Frankfort and he landed at the Capitol Hotel about thirty minutes before the Colston-Scott tragedy. He was seated in the lobby near the railing which protected the entrance to the basement having his shoes shined. When the shooting commenced he jumped over the railing and fell to the bottom of the steps and broke both legs. Immediately after his fall Lieutenant Scott fell across him and was found to be dead when taken up.

The election of state officers in 1899 was close and exciting. The chief interest was centered in the race for Governor, the contest being between Attorney General W. S. Taylor, the Republican candidate, and Senator William Goebel, the Democratic candidate. Senator Goebel's course in the State Senate had arrayed certain interests against him and the fight against him was very bitter. The face of the returns disclosed the fact that Gen. Taylor was elected by a small majority. Senator Goebel's friends prevailed on him to make a contest and in due course of time the contest was filed. During the contest in the month of January, 1900, thousands of people from all sections of the State visited Frankfort. The State was stirred from center to circumference. Threats were indulged in and it was openly stated that if the contest was decided in favor of the Democrats that Senator Goebel would be assassinated. All kinds of rumors were floating around. Senator Goebel was repeatedly warned of his danger, notwithstanding which he attended all the sittings of the Senate. Some of his personal friends constituted themselves a body guard and went to and from the State House with him. On the morning of January the 30th, Col. Jack Chinn from Mercer County, and Col. Eph Lillard from Franklin County were with him. When they reached the front gate of the old capital grounds, it was remarked that the usual crowd was not in front of the capital building. When they reached a point about fifty feet from the steps leading to the main building a shot was fired from the window in the Secretary of State's office which struck Senator Goebel in the right side, and went entirely through him and lodged in a hackberry tree near the west entrance to the grounds. Senator Goebel was immediately taken to the Capital Hotel where he lingered until the 3rd day of February; in the meantime he had been declared elected and had taken the oath of office. For several weeks after his death the conditions at Frankfort were dreadful. Governor Taylor still claimed that he was Governor and Lieutenant Governor J. C. W. Beckham, who had taken the oath of office on the death of Governor Goebel claimed that he, too, was Governor, and he assumed the duties as such with his office in the Capital Hotel. Each of them had several companies of the State Guard under arms and a conflict between them was almost hourly expected. The citizens of Frankfort had also taken sides, and each side had armed themselves. The Republicans generally claimed that it was a just retribution summarily inflicted, and the Democrats claimed that it was the greatest outrage ever perpetrated in a free country. After the flight of Governor Taylor and peace had, in a measure, been restored, the grand jury was convened and indictments were returned against Caleb Powers, who was the Republican Secretary of State, and W. S. Taylor, who was the Republican Governor, and W. H. Culton, F. W. Golden, Green Golden, John L. Powers, John Davis, Chas. Finley, Henry Youtsey, James Howard, Berry Howard, Garnett D. Ripley, Harland Whittaker, Richard Combs, Zack Steele and Frank Cecil, charging that all of them were implicated in the murder. The Republicans openly charged that the defendants could not get a fair trial in Franklin County. Caleb Powers and Henry Youtsey were granted a change of venue to Scott County. Capt. Garnett D. Ripley was tried at the April term, 1901. He was the first one of the defendants to stand trial. He was prosecuted by the able Commonwealth Attorney, Robert B. Franklin, assisted by Thomas Campbell, of Cincinnati and Judge Benjamin G. Williams, of Frankfort. He was defended by Judge J. T. O'Neal, of Louisville, Col. William Cravens of New Castle, Judge P. U. Major and L. F. Johnson of the local bar. Judge James E. Cantrill was the presiding judge. The jury was composed of the most intelligent and best educated men in the county who could be secured. The court house was crowded almost to suffocation, during the whole time. After a long and intensely interesting trial the jury brought in a verdict of "not guilty."

Henry Youtsey was convicted and sent to the penitentiary for life, and in the year 1912, is still serving his sentence. After his conviction Youtsey made a confession in which he claimed that Jim Howard fired the shot which killed Governor Goebel, and that the other above named defendants were in the conspiracy. Jim Howard was tried three times and convicted. The Court of Appeals reversed the lower court twice, but he was finally sent to the penitentiary for life, but was pardoned by Governor A. E. Willson. Caleb Powers also had three convictions and he, too, with several other of the most prominent defendants, were pardoned by Governor Willson. The trial of these cases, known as the "Goebel cases," continued through a period of about eight years. The defendants made a strong fight for life and liberty and only two of them were ever placed behind prison walls. On April 23, 1909, Gov. Willson pardoned W. S. Taylor, Chas. Finley, John L. Powers, Harland Whittaker, John W. Davis and Zack Steele.

The County Assessor for the year 1901, returned the following assessments: Number of acres of land, 123,831, with improvements valued at $2,410,130; number of town lots, 1,563; improvements, $2,149,563; number of horses, 4,428, valued at $100,519; number of hogs, 3,831, valued at $17,325. The total assessment amounted to $6,192,020. Number of legal voters, 2,398.

Pat McDonald, lawyer, editor and Democratic politician died on March 14, 1901. He was a Magistrate of the county, and was the best informed man on county affairs in the county.

For many years he was editor and publisher of The Western Argus. He displayed marked ability as an editor and as a business man.

The corner stone of the Elk's Lodge, located on Lewis street, was laid May 27, 1902. Hon. G. Allison Holland was the orator of the occasion.

The election of county officers in 1902 resulted as follows: J. H. Polsgrove, Judge; James Buford, Attorney; A. G. Jeffers, Sheriff; Brose Quarles, Assessor, who died in office and R. C. Hieatt was elected to fill out his term; M. L. Lawrence was elected Jailer, and Miss Lucy Pattie Superintendent Schools. South Trimble was elected to represent the county in 1898, and re-elected in 1900. He was speaker of the House during his second term. Dr. Owen Robinson represented the county in 1902. Col. E. H. Taylor, Jr., was elected State Senator for his district in 1901, for a term of four years. L. F. Johnson was elected in 1903 to represent the county, and re-elected in 1905.

Judge Patrick U. Major died in July, 1903. He was born in Frankfort in the year 1822, and was educated by B. B. Sayre and at Union College. He studied law under the instruction of Judge T. B. Monroe and Gov. Chas. S. Morehead, and was admitted to the bar in 1844. In 1852 he was elected County Attorney. In 1856 he was elected Commonwealth's Attorney, and in 1870 he was elected Circuit Judge, and was re-elected to succeed himself. He was a Judge of pure heart and strong intellect. He was faithful, kind and efficient. On retiring from the bench he resumed the active practice of law and was connected with some of the most important litigations in the State. He was an excellent judge of human nature and a "reader of men." He was doubtless the strongest criminal lawyer who ever engaged in the practice at Frankfort.

In 1903 the citizens of Frankfort commenced the final contest for an adequate appropriation for a new capital building and which meant a permanent location of the capital at Frankfort.

For more than a hundred years Lexington and Louisville had desired to remove the capital but neither of them would

234   THE HISTORY OF FRANKLIN COUNTY.

agree for the other to have it. The Senator from the Frankfort senatorial district and the Representative-elect with sixteen prominent citizens of the city and county composed a committee which took charge of the contest. Under the supervision of this committee a booklet was prepared setting forth the history of "The Capital Question," and the necessity for the new building. A copy of this booklet was sent to every member of the Legislature, and the Representative-elect of Franklin County visited different sections of the State and made an especial effort to interest the newspapers and prominent citizens from all parts of the State in "The Capital Question."

The Legislature convened January 5th, 1904, and on January the 12th the Representative from Franklin County introduced House Bill No. 69 which provided for the appropriation of one million of dollars with which to erect and complete a new capitol and other necessary buildings at the seat of government. When the measure came up for passage there was only one dissenting vote in the House and with like unanimity the bill passed the Senate. An amendment tacked to the bill in the House which named the old capitol grounds as the site for the new building caused Governor J. C. W. Beckham to call an extra session of the Legislature in 1905 in order that the site might be changed.

On November 15, 1904 a primary election for county officers was held. A nomination at that time was equivalent to an election. The nominations resulted as follows: J. H. Polsgrove, County Judge; F. M. Dailey, Attorney; R. C. Hieatt, Sheriff; W. H. Hawkins, Assessor; E. R. Jones, School Commissioner; J. W. Bridges, Jailer and L. F. Johnson, for Representative. The contest for Representative was probably the fiercest struggle ever had for any position in Franklin County. The successful candidate won by only four votes from his competitor, Col. E. H. Taylor, Jr. Col. Taylor contested the nomination and took the case to the Court of Appeals twice before the final settlement. Col. Taylor had been Mayor of Frankfort for several terms; Representative of his county twice and State Senator twice. He was known as "The veteran war horse of local politics." Doubtless the cause of his defeat was his announcement in the papers that he would not make the race for Representative and was afterwards induced by his friends to change his mind. The officers nominated in November, 1904, were elected in 1905 and commenced their terms of office in January, 1906.

During the Legislative sessions of 1904 and 1906 there was appropriated more money for the permanent improvement of public buildings at Frankfort than was spent by the State for that purpose during its whole history prior to that time. The million and a half dollars for the capitol building was supplemented by eighty-six thousand for the State penitentiary at Frankfort; twenty thousand for the Colored Normal School; twenty thousand for the Feeble Minded Institute; twenty thousand for the William Goebel monument; two thousand for repairs on the Boone monument, and five thousand per year for the collection of relics for the Historical Society.

The corner stone of the new capitol building was laid by Gov. J. C. W. Beckham on June 16th, 1906, in the presence of a crowd of people estimated at from twenty to twenty-five thousand.

John W. Milam was chief marshal of the parade and Gen. D. W. Lindsey was master of ceremonies. Hon. H. V. McChesney, one of the capitol commissioners, and as the representative of the commission, delivered an able address. The chief address of the occasion was delivered by Hon. William Lindsay, which was able, scholarly and eloquent.

John B. Dryden died August 6, 1906, in the 64th year of his age. He was Commissary Sergeant in the 9th Kentucky Cavalry, U. S. A., commanded by Col. R. T. Jacobs, in the Civil War. Several years prior to his death he became the editor and publisher of the "Sunday Call," which paper he afterwards enlarged and made an afternoon daily. He was a genial, clever gentleman who was esteemed by the people of Frankfort, and through his paper did much good for Frankfort by advocating certain improvements. His persistent efforts along that line resulted in many permanent improvements in the city.

The contest between ex-Governor J. C. W. Beckham and ex-Governor W. O. Bradley for the position of United States Senator was the main feature of Legislative session of 1908. On February 29 Governor Bradley was elected amidst great confusion.

The last issue of The Frankfort Roundabout was on February 29, and the first issue of the Frankfort Weekly News was on March 7, 1908.

One of the most delightful banquets ever enjoyed by the people of Frankfort was given by the Young Men's Democratic Club on March 12th in honor of Governor J. C. W. Beckham. The toasts responded to were as follows: "The Public Servant," by Judge William Rogers Clay; "My Old Kentucky Home," by Hon. Harry Schobert; "Keep It Sweet," by Judge J. M. Benton; "The House," by Representative W. A. Shanks; "The Senate," by Senator Frank Reeves; "Party Honor," by Representative George S. Willson. Governor Beckham made the closing address which was well received.

On March 16th John N. Crutcher passed way in his 78th year. He was a man of strong character and he contributed many articles to the papers. He was a practical jober. When he was a young man he and Dick Tate were frequently associated in playing jokes on some one.

For many years prior to 1908 the White Burley Tobacco growers had been trying to secure a better price for their product. The American Tobacco Company had succeeded to a great extent in defeating them in their efforts. As a last resort the tobacco men agreed to "cut out" the 1908 crop and in their attempt to do so, some of their irresponsible followers took the law in their own hands and sent out some threatening letters, destroyed tobacco beds, burned barns and did other things of a lawless nature. In a short time they were known as "The Night Riders." Governor Willson undertook to suppress them by patroling the militia through the county for several months. This increased rather than allayed the disorder and on the night of May 22nd N. B. Hazelett was killed near the Shelby County line. A military company was in that neighborhood at the time and a large number of night riders were also out and terror reigned in the western section of the county. Walker Duncan, Riley Harrod and Hubert Kessler were charged with the killing and after the Governor had pardoned the defendants before the trial, the widow of Hazelett brought a suit for damages against the parties. Scott & Hamilton and the County Attorney of Shelby County represented the plaintiff and Willis & Todd of Shelby County, and L. F. Johnson of the local bar, represented the defendants. When the case was called for trial the defendants by their attorneys filed an affidavit and made a motion for Judge R. L. Stout to vacate the bench and as a result of which the attorneys for the defense were ruled by the court to show cause why they should not be punished for contempt of court. When the response to same was filed the court held it was not sufficient and entered a fine of $30.00 against each of the three attorneys and ordered them to jail for thirty hours, but he afterwards set aside the jail part of the sentence. The fines were promptly paid. The Judge vacated the bench and the defendants escaped from the payment of any judgment against them.

The new capitol was completed October 30th, 1908, and occupied in September, 1909.

In the month of November Capt. L. H. Finnell, a veteran of the Union Army, shot himself through the head, causing instant death. On the same day Mrs. John Leitner, who lived at Thorn Hill, murdered her two little children, aged eight and six years, and then killed herself. Her husband had been drinking for some time and hopeless poverty seemed to have prompted the killing.

A persistent rumor of graft in county affairs prompted an investigation. A committee of citizens composed of Gen. D. W. Lindsey, Geo. B. Harper, Sidney Bedford, R. C. Hieatt and Rev. C. R. Hudson selected the expert accountant to investigate the county books. On September 29th, 1909, the report was made showing the financial condition of the county, in which report it was stated that $7,507.82 had been paid into the county treasury by reason of the investigation and that there still remained due and unpaid a balance of $4,276.71 from former officials of the county.

The county officials elected in the year 1908 were as follows: R. C. Hieatt, County Judge; Ben Marshall, Circuit Clerk, Crawford Lee, County Clerk; Wiley Marshall, County Attorney; M. B. Lucas, Jailer; Lee Buckley, Sheriff, and Harrison Lee, Assessor. The Magistrates elected for the county were Hiram Stafford, George W. Johnson, Nick Sullivan, R. L. Wiley and James Waldner.

On April 30th, 1909, great damage was done by a storm of wind and rain, fences were blown down, outhouses and stables were destroyed, the roofs on several warehouses of the O. F. C. Distillery were blown off and property in all sections of the county greatly damaged. The government gauge at the Custom House showed that in seven hours two and sixty-two one hundredths inches of rain fell. Elkhorn Creek rose about fourteen feet and the Kentucky river about five feet in that time.

On June 2nd Howe's Show was exhibited in Frankfort and during the evening exhibition a negro by the name of John Maxey, shot and dangerously wounded Bert Bowers, who was in some way connected with the show. About two o'clock the next morning Maxey was taken from the jail to the St. Clair street bridge and hung by a mob. During the promiscuous shooting which followed the hanging a young man by the name of R. J. Weindel was dangerously but not fatally wounded.

During this year the Louisville & Nashville Railroad Company purchased the Highland Road and extended the line to Versailles and there connected with the L. & E. which runs to the mountains of Eastern Kentucky.

On September 4th, during the military encampment at Lake Park, there was a battle between some soldiers and citizens, in the lower part of the city known as "Craw," in which two men were killed and three others wounded. Sergeant Ingram Tate and Jeff Cook, a civilian, were killed and Wm. Nickles, Alex McNally and Ed Miller were wounded. The fight took place at Howser's saloon. It commenced in the house but the soldiers left the saloon and about fifty of them congregated on the outside, some had revolvers and others rifles. The citizens took refuge in the upstairs rooms and a great many shots were fired by each side; the building and the furniture were almost completely demolished. This battle brought on a crusade against allowing saloons in Craw. The ultimate outcome of which was the discontinuing of saloons in that section of the city.

Senator William Lindsay died at his home in Frankfort on October 15, 1909. He was born in Virginia on the 4th of September, 1835, and was educated in the common schools of Virginia. At the age of eighteen he began the study of law and in 1854 he moved to Hickman County, Kentucky, and taught school for several years. In 1858 he was admitted to the bar and commenced the practice of law at Clinton. In the Civil War he enlisted as a private but he soon became Captain of his company and later in the service became a member of General Forrest's staff. After the war he came back to Hickman and was elected to represent his district in the State Senate in 1867, and in 1870 he was elected a member of the Court of Appeals. He served eight years on the Court of Appeals bench. The last two he was chief justice. In 1877 he resumed the practice of law at Frankfort. In 1890 he was sent to the State Senate from Franklin County and in 1893 he was elected United States Senator to fill out the unexpired term of John G. Carlisle and in 1894 was re-elected for a full term. He filled various positions by appointment from the President of the United States. Judge Lindsay was a leader of men and he was considered one of the greatest of men. He was one of the greatest lawyers this republic has produced. He was broad shouldered and broad minded. He was almost a giant in statue and he was full grown giant in intellect. He was remarkable for his simplicity and directness. He was round-headed, smooth-shaved, awkward in gesture, talked very loud when making a public speech; he lost some of his teeth during the latter part of his life which caused a considerable impediment in his speech; he was a portly, handsome man with brown eyes and dark hair. He was a great Judge, a statesman and a patriot.

On December the 18th William Cromwell died. He was

a practitioner at the Frankfort bar for about thirty-five years, about twenty years of which he was chief clerk of the State Senate. He was a true friend and a good lawyer. His memory and power of endurance were marvelous.

The body of Arthur Goebel, who died in Phoenix, Arizona, arrived at Frankfort, January 31st, 1910, and was laid to rest by the side of his distinguished brother, in the Frankfort cemetery. On the tenth anniversary of William Goebel's death a handsome monument of marble and bronze typifying him as the orator defending the rights of the great common people, was unveiled in the presence of a large crowd. Senator James B. McCreary and Justus Goebel, brother of the dead Governor, were the orators of the occasion. Ex-Governor J. C. W. Beckham, as master of ceremonies, made some appropriate remarks and introduced the speakers. The statue is of bronze and it is a good likeness of the dead statesman; it was paid for by popular subscription.

On February the 21st, one of the city street cars collided with an interurban car. The wreck was caused by a dense fog; the result was that several people were severely injured. The motorman, Owen Graves, was so severely injured that he died from the effects of the injuries.

On March the 21st, Roger Warren, a negro convict in the Frankfort penitentiary, sent from Louisville for murder, cut the throat of Melvin Ratcliff, another convict, and from the effects of which Ratcliff died. Warren was tried in the Franklin Circuit Court and convicted of murder and the punishment fixed at death. The case was appealed and the highest court affirmed the decision. The Governor fixed the 25th of May, 1911, as the day for execution. On that day the Sheriff, Lee Buckley, and his deputies promptly executed the judgment.

Warren was the last man hung under the old law and Charles Howard, convicted in Franklin County for the murder of Ed Rice was the first man sent to the Eddyville penitentiary for electrocution, under the new law.

Thursday, May 26, 1910, the restored Daniel Boone monument was formally unveiled. The women of the Rebecca Bryan Boone Chapter of the D. A. R. started a movement to raise sufficient funds to restore the monument to its original beauty and after many years they raised seven hundred dollars, and the State Legislature appropriated two thousand dollars. A large crowd was present and participated in the ceremonies. The new panels were made by Leopold Fettroheirs, of Cincinnati; the material used was Italian marble. The panels were an exact reproduction of the old panels.

On June the 2nd the new State capitol was dedicated. A number of distinguished people were present. Gilbert White, the artist who painted the lunettes in the capitol, with his attractive young wife was there. United States Senator, W. O. Bradley, was chief orator of the day. There was some political bickerings and much dissatisfaction. A change in the State administration had placed the Republicans in office. The general idea prevailed that the programme had been arranged and the ceremonies controlled by a few Frankfort sycophants and parasites who had nothing to do with the erection of the building and who were not in sympathy with those who did. One enjoyable part of the day's proceedings was the reunion of the Kentucky Military Institute Cadets at the old K. M. I., six miles from Frankfort. Addresses were made by Dr. William Bailey, Judge W. G. Deering and Col. W. B. Haldeman of Louisville, and Col. C. W. Fowler from the new K. M. I. Dr. U. V. Williams and other Franklin County citizens, who had been students there, responded to toasts on that occasion.

The Governors of twenty-three states met in conference at the new State capitol on the 29th of November; most of them brought their wives with them. The names of the executives who were present are as follows: Gov.-elect Emmett O'Neal, of Alabama; Richard E. Sloan, of Arizona, John F. Shafroth, of Colorado; Frank R. Weeks, of Connecticut; Joseph M. Brown, of Georgia; Charles S. Dineen, of Illinois; Thomas R. Marshall, of Indiana, Augustus E. Willson, of Kentucky; Frederick W. Plaisted, of Maine, Eben S. Draper, of Massachusetts; Edmond F. Noel, of Mississippi; Herbert S. Hadley, of Missouri; Edwin L. Norris, of Montana; John Franklin Fort, of New Jersey; Woodrow Wilson, Gov-elect of New Jersey; W. W. Kitchin, of North Carolina; Judson Harmon, of Ohio; Lee

Cruce, of Oklahoma; Abraham J. Prather, of Rhode Island; M. F. Ansel, of South Carolina; R. S. Veesey, of South Dakota; William Spry, of Utah; William Hodges Mann, of Virginia, and Francis E. McGovern, of Wisconsin.

The meeting of the Governors was of great interest to the general public and many people from all sections of the State were in Frankfort to see them.

The population of Franklin County in 1910 was less than it was twenty years prior to that time. The population in 1890 was 21,267; in 1900 it was 20,852, and in 1910 was 21,135.

The white population in 1900 was 16,501; colored was 4,343. The white population in 1910 was 17,389; colored was 3,746. The increase in white population in ten years was 888 and the decrease in colored population same time was 597.

CHAPTER XVI.

The Organization and Growth of the Churches in Franklin County.

A few records of the early churches in Franklin County have been preserved, and the records of the county court give additional information on the subject.

There is a well founded tradition that the first sermon preached in Frankfort was by Rev. John Gano in 1786. It was during this year that General Wilkinson prevailed on him to locate in Frankfort. He purchased a lot on the corner of Broadway and High Streets and erected a log house thereon, and lived there until his death, August 10, 1804.

The Baptists have been the strongest denomination, in the county, during its whole history. In the very early history of the country, there were four Baptist preachers who were intimately connected with the growth and development of the county and who have left the impress of their personality upon the succeeding generations. These four men were John Gano, John Taylor, William Hickman and Silas M. Noel. Since their day there have been but few, if any, who could equal them.

Perhaps the greatest Baptist preacher who ever lived in Frankfort was the Rev. John Gano. He was educated at Princeton College and he was recognized as being the most learned and eloquent preacher in the western country. So great was his fame that people would travel for miles to hear him preach. He was the first chaplain of the Kentucky Legislature. There is a tradition of the Baptist Church that General George Washington was immersed by him, but there is no documentary evidence to that effect.

In the memoirs of Rev. John Gano, is given a very interesting account of the Revolutionary War. Of his first battle, the writer says: "We next fell back to White Plains where Gen. Washington had his main army; here a severe but indecisive battle was fought by about one-third of the armies on either side. Rev. Gano was found in the hottest of the fight, leading and rallying the men like an officer. When it was suggested that the place for the chaplain was in the rear with the surgeon's staff he said 'I durst not quit my place for fear of damping the spirit of the soldiers by setting a bad example.' So frequently was he found in the van, in time of danger and so seldom in the rear that he was known as 'the fighting chaplain of the army.' "

In reference to his preaching in Frankfort, he said, "Church meetings were frequently held at Frankfort, though there was no settled church there of any denomination. Mr. Hickman had at times held services in the assembly room at the State House and Mr. Shannon of the Presbyterian church had consented to preach there part of his time. I agreed to supply them every first and third Sabbath in the month, and did so."

In Smith's History of Kentucky is the following: "John Gano was a great man—great as a busy toiler in the building of our nation, in the building of our Commonwealth, in the building of our civilization, in the building of religion the better life of it all."

There is some question as to where this Christian patriot was buried, but his remains should rest with his compatriots in the State cemetery, with a monument suitably inscribed, erected to his memory.

Rev. John Taylor, who did the first preaching for the Frankfort Church, as its regular pastor, was a man of limited education, but was of a remarkably strong, clear intellect and of a calm, sound judgment. He was a plain, practical and very successful man. He wrote a history of "The Ten Churches," which includes the Frankfort and Buck Run churches.

William Hickman was fifty-one years old when he first came to Kentucky. He was tall and gaunt; his deportment solemn and grave. "He was justly recognized as the first Baptist preacher of Kentucky. He preached at Harrodsburg in 1776 and returning later to give forty years in this State, and in this church to the service of his Master."

William Hickman preached throughout Kentucky. In

activity, courage and usefulness he was the peer of any man of his day. He baptized more than one thousand converts, five hundred of whom became members of his church. He said of the Fork's of Elkhorn Church, "This church I hope to serve until I am laid in the grave, for they have ever manifested their love and esteem to me."

Dr. Silas M. Noel was the son of Theoderick Noel, a Baptist preacher, who lived and died in Virginia. Dr. Noel was educated for the law and he practiced his profession for some time, but feeling that he was called to the ministry he came to Kentucky and was ordained as a preacher. His first charge was the church at Big Spring, in Woodford County. At that time he was a young man. Some time after that he resigned the pastorate to accept the position of Associate Circuit Judge with Judge Henry Davridge and Nathaniel Richardson. He afterwards became a member of the Frankfort bar and practiced law for some time with success. After two or three years he returned to the ministry, where he became one of the strongest and most successful preachers the Baptists ever had in the State.

In Taylor's History of The Ten Churches, he said, "Mr. Noel's literary accomplishments, together with his zeal in the gospel with his great success therein, has procured him the high appellation of double D. D."

Dr. Silas M. Noel and his descendants have been prominent people in the county for more than a century. He was the third pastor of the Frankfort church. During the troublous times of 1824-1825 politics became rampant in the Frankfort congregation and for a while it seemed as though the church would be torn asunder, and a few years later when Alexander Campbell, with his new doctrine, divided almost every Baptist congregation in the western country, Dr. Noel was thought to be the only man who could hold the Frankfort congregation together and refute the arguments of Mr. Campbell.

The church government of the Baptist Church is the nearest approach to a pure democracy that has been known in the history of any organization. This Democratic idea, intensified to the last degree is an element of weakness to the separate churches, but it is an element of strength to the denomination as a whole. Whenever there has been a faction or division in a church the seceding element has withdrawn from the mother church and formed a new organization and built another meeting house. There has never been a time in the history of the county when the number of Baptists, outside of the city, did not exceed the number of members in all the other churches combined.

The churches which composed the Franklin Association in 1911-12, with date of organization, number of members and name of pastor were as follows:

Name.	Date of Organization	Membership	Pastor
Bethel	1802	293	L. D. Stucker
Buck Run	1818	77	Rev. Mr. Hill
Cedar Grove	1882	170	
Evergreen	1883	100	F. F. Brown
Forks of Elkhorn	1777	131	J. R. Sampey
Frankfort	1816	1030	F. W. Eberhardt
Lebanon	1825	262	J. A. Davis
Mt. Carmel	1824	240	J. A. Davis
Mt. Pleasant	1790	111	T. J. Singleton
Mt. Vernon	1872	150	E. R. Sams
North Benson	1825	185	W. D. Ogletree
North Fork	1801	252	W. D. Ogletree
Pleasant Ridge	1856	250	
Swallowfield	1891	72	J. A. Davis
Union	1810	163	

The Mt. Pleasant church was first known as Mt. Gomer. The first church meeting was held in the house of Bledsoe Hayden, on September 25, 1790. This private residence continued to be the place of worship until the church was built in 1791. In 1801 the name was changed to Mt. Pleasant. Frank H. Hodges was pastor of this church for about thirty years.

The North Fork church, located at Switzer, has been remarkably free from divisions and dissensions; the only one of any note was about 1830 when the Alexander Campbell reform movement led off a large number of its members.

The South Benson church had a long and useful life. It was organized in 1801, and it continued to prosper until the Alexander Campbell agitation in 1824-1825 when its membership was divided. A number of them went to Bridgeport and organized the Christian Church at that place and some went to the Buck Lick church in Anderson County; but in a few years it recovered from this division and it continued in a prosperous condition for more than half a century. Another discussion arose in 1883 and the split which followed caused the erection of the Evergreen Baptist Church which was organized by the dissenting members. The old South Benson church was sold in 1911 and converted into a tobacco barn.

Bethel Church is the largest Christian organization in the county outside of Frankfort. It has never had any dissension of any note. The Rev. Frank H. Hodges, who was one of the strongest preachers ever located in the county, was pastor of this church for more than fifty years.

The Buck Run church was organized on January 31, 1818. The meeting was held at "Bro. Wilson's." William Hickman was moderator; Silas M. Noel was clerk; John Taylor, James Suggett, John H. Ficklin, Mordica Boulware and Theodorick Boulware were the other ministers who were present. There were twenty-one present who agreed to become members of the new organization. Rev. John Taylor was called for their first pastor. He continued to preach there once a month for about five years and during that time, "a snug little brick meeting house, forty feet long by thirty wide" was built. In a short time after that Rev. William Hickman was called to preach once a month. In 1888 the church building was removed to Woodlake, and later it was removed to the Forks of Elkhorn.

The North Benson church was organized in 1825 and the meeting house erected in a short time thereafter. Several years afterwards this house was razed and another built; which has also been torn down, and during the present decade an up-to-date church has been built on the old site. A number of noted preachers have been called to that station, among them were William Hickman, Jr., W. C. Blanton, Frank H. Hodges and others.

The first pastor called to the Evergreen Baptist Church after its organization in 1883 was Rev. Frank Hungerford, who has been and is an exceptionally strong preacher. It is worthy of note that four of the strongest Baptist preachers who ever had charge of churches in Franklin County were educated for the law, towit: Silas M. Noel, F. H. Hodges, Green Clay Smith and B. F. Hungerford.

The Frankfort church was organized in 1816 with thirteen charter members. The first meetings were held in the church building, which was erected in 1812, on the southwest corner of the old capitol square. This building was erected by act of the Kentucky Legislature. The money with which it was built was the proceeds of a lottery. The trustees of the building were appointed by the Governor. It was intended to be non-sectarian. There was considerable controversy and contention among the Presbyterians, Baptists and Methodists over the use of this building which continued from about 1817 to December 1825 when the house burned.

The first Baptist Church was built about 1827 or 1828. This house was burned about 1867.

In 1868 a new building was erected on St. Clair street, which has since been remodeled several times.

The most noted Baptist preachers in Kentucky have been in charge of the Frankfort church, among them are named John Taylor, Silas M. Noel, Porter Clay, the brother of Henry Clay. The controversy between Porter Clay and Peter Dudley shook the church to its foundation. The pastor preferred three charges against Col. Dudley, and he in turn made thirty-one charges against the preacher and later added one other, that of insanity. The trials of these charges took up several weeks and they resulted in no good to the church.

The Rev. A. Goodell was a talented man, finely educated and a pleasant speaker, but his usefulness as a christian minister became very much impaired on account of some idle talk which connected his name with that of a young married woman, a member of his congregation and with whom gossip said he was very much in love. After some time this lady withdrew from his church and became a regular attendant and an earnest worker in the Methodist Church where she continued the rest of a long and useful life. She was known as an earnest, faithful worker in the Methodist Church, and at the time of her death only a few of her intimate friends knew that she was not a member of that church.

General Green Clay Smith was the pastor in charge of the Frankfort church for several years prior to 1878. He graduated at Transylvania University in 1850. He represented his county in the Kentucky Legislature and his district for two terms in Congress. He volunteered as a private in the 4th Kentucky Federal Cavalry; was promoted to Major General for meritorious conduct in the engagement with Gen. Morgan at Lebanon, Tenn., May 5, 1862.

He was Governor of Montana, and nominee for President of the United States on the prohibition ticket. He practiced law for several years before he entered the ministry.

Dr. J. M. Lewis was a man of recognized ability and a most eloquent speaker.

Rev. W. C. Taylor was a strong, eloquent preacher who was greatly loved by all the people of Frankfort, irrespective of religious tenets.

F. W. Eberhardt, the pastor in charge (1912), is regarded as one of the strongest preachers of that denomination in the State. The Frankfort church is in a flourishing condition. Its membership is larger than ever before. The meeting house is crowded at every service.

The first Presbyterian Church organized in the county was in 1795. It was located near what is now the Anderson County line. It was known as the Upper Benson or Little Benson Church. Rev. Samuel Shannon was the first preacher in charge. The church building, erected about 1796, was 28x40 feet. It was built of hewed logs and chinked with an excellent quality of mortar. The work was done by the friends of the organization, and the material used was taken from the adjoining woods. The roof was made of clabboards and fastened on with hand-made wooden pegs. The building has stood for more than a century. It has outlived the church organization. Many noted pioneer preachers visited it, and regular preachers were in charge of it for more than half a century.

The next church of this denomination was organized near Bridgeport in 1805 and was known as the Lower Benson or Franklin Church. The Rev. Samuel Shannon was one of the chief organizers, and in a short time after the house was built he moved into the neighborhood and divided his time between the two churches. This church came under the supervision of the Frankfort church in 1834. The preacher in charge at Frankfort preached there in the afternoon of each Sunday. This arrangement continued until the close of Rev. John R. Hendricks' ministry, since which time the church has accomplished but little.

The people in Frankfort were slow about organizing churches and erecting church buildings.

In 1808 there was an act passed by the Kentucky Legislature granting a lottery franchise, with the object of raising $4,000 for the purpose of building a church; which was built in 1812. The building was used harmoniously for a few years and no efforts were made to organize a church, but as soon as the Baptists, Presbyterians and Methodists commenced quarreling about who should have the right to use the building each of them commenced a church organization. As the outcome of this religious controversy the Presbyterians were the first to withdraw from the contest and they commenced holding their church meetings at the Love House, at that time the chief hotel in Frankfort. And in a short time (1815) the first church organization was effected, but there was no regular pastor called until 1817, when Rev. Eli Smith began a service which continued for about ten years. After he resigned the church was without a pastor for some time; the Ruling Elder also resigned and the church organization came very near being destroyed. John J. Crittenden, John H. Hanna, Mason Brown and other public spirited men, who were not members of that denomination took the matter in hand and prevented the dissolution.

Some time after that Rev. John T. Edgar was prevailed on to accept the charge and in a short time thereafter there were sixty persons added to the church membership. His pastorate ceased in 1833 and in 1834 Rev. Daniel Baker was in charge for two years and the church continued to prosper under his ministry.

In 1837 Rev. Joseph J. Bullock became the pastor and he remained until 1846.

In 1847 Rev. Stewart Robinson commenced service and he resigned in 1853. From that time until 1854 the pulpit was supplied by Rev. John R. Hendrick. In 1855 Rev. J. P. Safford accepted the charge for two years. He was succeeded in 1858 by Rev. B. F. Lacy, who continued in charge until 1861, when he accepted the position of chaplain in the Confederate Army, and the church thereupon dissolved the relationship existing between him and the church. In 1862 Rev. John S. Hays accepted the position which he held until 1867.

In 1867 Dr. J. McClusky Blayney commenced a service which lasted two years and Rev. J. H. Nesbitt succeeded him in 1870 and remained for six years.

In 1877 Rev. J. W. Pugh accepted the call and remained until 1882. After he resigned the church was without a pastor for two years. Dr. Blayney returned in 1884; his pastorate was a long and useful one. He was broad minded and liberal in his views and he did a great deal for the betterment of the city and citizens of Frankfort. He was one of the leaders in securing the capital appropriation of a million dollars in 1904. Dr. Blayney resigned in 1906 and Dr. Jesse R. Zeigler accepted the charge in 1907. He, too, is a broad minded and philanthropic christian gentleman who is calculated to do much good in the work which he has undertaken.

In 1823 a lot was purchased on Wapping street, fronting 100 feet and extending back 200 feet. On this lot the first church was built in 1829. In 1849 this property was sold to the Catholic Church and other property bought, located on

Main street. A handsome building was erected. It is one of the largest auditoriums in the city.

The earliest Catholic Church station in Frankfort was the house of Mrs. Ellen Barstow. This building stood opposite the Capitol. It is not known who said the first mass, but it is supposed, however, that it was Father Badin.

In 1826 Rev. Francis P. Kenrick preached occasionally in Frankfort. Rev. George A. M. Elder, who was located in Scott County, also preached occasionally. A dwelling house near the entrance of the tunnel was the first property purchased by the Catholics. This dwelling house, known as "the tunnel house" was fitted up for a church. This was afterwards sold for two thousand dollars and the sum expended in the purchase of a church building, which was erected some years before by the Presbyterians and used by them for their Sunday service. This property is located on Wapping street, near the Custom House and is still in use by the Catholics. The purchase was made by Rev. James Madison Lancaster, who was the first resident pastor of the church. Prior to this time the Catholics at Frankfort had been served by the pastors stationed at the church, St. Pius, in Scott County. This property was purchased in 1849 and in 1850 Father Lancaster commenced the erection of the new church. The old church was very much smaller than the new, and it was left standing, and was used by the congregation while the new one was being built. The new one was built around and over the old one. When the new church was nearly completed the old one was razed. This church is still standing and it is known as the "Church of the Good Shepherd." Since it was first built it has been enlarged and improved and it is now considered the handsomest church edifice in the diocese.

Rev. James M. Lancaster was born in Kentucky in 1810. He was also educated in Kentucky, but he was ordained to the priesthood in Rome in 1836. In 1848 he was appointed by Bishop Spalding, pastor at Frankfort. He was an earnest, honest worker at the Frankfort station. For seventeen years he did much good and many were added to the church during his ministry. In 1867 he was called to Covington and in 1868 he was transferred to that point. Father Lancaster was a man of more than ordinary talents. He had excellent conversational powers and was greatly loved by his people. He was succeeded by Rev. Lambert Young who remained at the Frankfort station until 1897, when he resigned and returned to his home in Ireland. Very few pastors of any church were ever regarded so highly by all the people of Frankfort as was Father Lambert Young. His refusal to testify in the United States District Court at Louisville, concerning information which he had obtained by reason of the fact that he was a christian minister, and on account of which he was sent to jail for several months for contempt of court, only increased the love and admiration of his people for him. The card which he issued at the time of his release from jail explaining why he had taken the course he did was almost universally commended, not only by the members of the Catholic Church but also by all other well informed people throughout the country.

The next minister in charge of the Frankfort station was Rev. James L. Gorey, who died in a short time, and was succeeded by his brother, Rev. William E. Gorey, and in a few months he was succeeded by Rev. Edward Donley, who only served the Frankfort station a short time when he was succeeded by Rev. William Cassander, who did not like Frankfort, and in a few months he abandoned the position without leave of the Bishop. He was willing to accept such punishment as might be inflicted on him rather than to return to a position he did not like. In 1902 Rev. Thomas Major was sent to the Frankfort station where he remained until his death in 1911. Father Major was converted to the Catholic faith during the Civil War. He was a Confederate soldier. He was captured and sent to a jail in Chicago where he fell sick and was ministered to by some nuns. These sisters of charity converted him to their religion. He was not as well educated as the priests in the Catholic church ordinarily are but he was well thought of by both Catholics and protestants. Some of his warmest friends in Frankfort were not members of his church. The Rev. J. A. Flynn succeeded to the Frankfort station in 1911. He seems to be well equipped for the position. He is regarded as an intelligent, well educated christian gentleman, less friendly, perhaps, than his predecessors, but fully awake to the needs of the church. There are about two hundred families, which average about four members to the family, under the watch-care of the Frankfort pastor.

The Episcopal Church in Frankfort was organized about 1835. Bishop B. B. Smith, then Bishop of the Diocese of Kentucky, commenced work creating interest in a church building at Frankfort. Some one in New York sent him a thousand dollars to be used for that purpose. In the following year a lot on Washington street was purchased for $200; at that time it was a crab orchard with a lawyer's office near the center of the lot. B. B. Sayre had formerly taught school in the building and it was used for a church building for some time after Bishop Smith purchased it. The parish was organized with eight communicants. The Rev. Mr. Purviance was in charge until 1841, when he was succeeded by Rev. A. F. Dobbs. In 1842 the corner stone of the church was laid. The building was thirty by sixty feet and it was patterned after the "Grecian Church of the Ascension," in Canal street, New York City. In the fall of 1842 the church was consecrated and the Rev. Mr. Presby was installed as rector. He was succeeded by Rev. Moses H. Hunter, and in 1846 the Rev. John N. Norton became rector. During the 23 years of his rectorate the parish enjoyed the most prosperous years of its existance. In 1850 the church was enlarged. On the 8th day of August the corner stone of the present building was laid. On the 12th day of August, 1852, the new church was consecrated by the Bishop, who was assisted by Rev. James Craik, of Louisville; Rev. Dr. Claxton, of Madison, Indiana; Rev. Thos. I. Trader, of Danville; Dr. Norton and Rev. Mr. Venable, of Frankfort, in the presence of a large congregation. The church and furnishings cost twenty thousand dollars, all of which was presented by Mr. John H. Hanna, a lawyer who was located at Frankfort. Mr. Hanna and his wife also endowed the parish school.

In 1864 the Ladies' Guild of Ascension Church was organized for the purpose of building a rectory. They purchased a lot for a thousand dollars and built the rectory and furnished it. In 1867 the church was enlarged by building a transept and a new chancel, and the Diocese purchased a house and lot adjoining the church, on the opposite side from the rectory, as a home for the Bishop. In 1870 Dr. Norton resigned. He was a thoroughly educated man who did a great deal of good while in Frankfort. He not only looked after his church work but he also wrote several books and almost an endless amount of tracts which he distributed throughout the county. Rev. Lucien Lance was the succeeding rector. He remained two years and was succeeded by Rev. Henry T. Sharp. He remained six years, when he resigned, and for ten months there was no rector but services were held by Wm. H. Hampton, who was afterwards ordained.

In April, 1880, Rev. E. A. Penick was installed and he remained for thirteen years. The Rev. R. L. McCready succeeded him. Rev. A. B. Chinn succeeded Rev. McCready in 1904, and Bishop C. C. Penick became rector November 9, 1908, and resigned November 9, 1912.

Under the administration of Rev. R. L. McCready the old mission of "St. John's in the Wilderness" was revived and the Bishop's residence purchased from the diocese and converted into a parish house, which was made a home for the parish school and orphanage. On Nov. 1st, 1906, the church was badly damaged by fire, but it has since been refitted, and as a memorial there were erected a handsome pulpit and altar, with its furnishings. A legacy of $5,000 was left to the church by John and Lewis Harvie. Miss Fannie Wilhams also left some money with which to build an orphanage. There are at present (December, 1912) about three hundred members of the church in good standing.

The Disciples' or Christian Church of Frankfort was organized December 2, 1832, by Elder P. S. Fall, assisted by Elder John T. Johnson. The charter members were P. S. Fall, Nancy Fall, Ambrose W. Dudley, Eliza G. Dudley, Elizabeth Bacon, Elias B. Myers and O. L. Leonard.

Rev. Mr. Fall came to Frankfort from Nashville, Tenn.,

where he had been preaching for five years, and established a young ladies' seminary at Poplar Hill, three miles northeast of Frankfort. Prior to that time only a few preachers of that denomination had preached in Frankfort. John Smith, who was known in that day as "Raccoon John Smith," had preached at Frankfort some years before that. He was a very rough and uneducated man but he had a great deal of natural ability and shrewdness, and he was a good debater. His reputation had preceded him and all the churches were closed against him, but he secured the court house, which was packed with legislators, lawyers and other professional and business men. His text was, "And when John came to Frankfort his spirit was stirred within him when he saw the city wholly given up to sectarianism." The church was organized in the court house and for some time their meetings were held there; afterwards John L. Moore's residence was used as a meeting place. Their first church was built in 1842 on the present site at a cost of $4,531.31. It was burned November 2, 1870, after which there was no preacher or church building for two years.

In 1872 the church was re-built at a cost of $26,000. Mrs. Emily Tubman, who had been raised in Frankfort, furnished the necessary means with which to build and furnish it. It was dedicated August 11, the Rev. Isaac Everett preached the dedicatory sermon. From the organization of the church to 1857, a period of twenty-five years, Mr. P. S. Fall was the only regular preacher. Several other preachers occupied the pulpit for one or two Sundays in the month during a part of this time. Among these were Enos Campbell in 1845, L. L. Pinkerton in 1846, Samuel Pinkerton, 1848, Carroll Kendrick, 1850, and John G. Thompkins in 1851, but Mr. Fall did most of the preaching and he did it without any compensation. He returned to Nashville in 1857. At that time the membership of the church numbered 221, of this number 83 of them were received by baptism.

Rev. W. T. Moore succeeded Mr. Fall as pastor. He commenced his service on October 1, 1858, and continued for about five years. During his ministry ninety-six members were received into the church, forty-four of whom were by baptism.

Rev. W. S. Crutcher became pastor in 1865 and remained for only one year, but during the year there were twenty-five additions to the church membership.

Rev. T. N. Arnold was the pastor in charge for about eighteen months, when he was succeeded by Rev. Aylett Rains for a period of one year. During his service there were thirty additions to the church.

Rev. J. L. T. Holland then preached for about seven months; his service ended June 30, 1869.

Rev. T. N. Arnold returned in 1870, and he was in charge when the church was burned. Perhaps the stormiest period of the church was during the ministration of Mr. Arnold. The question of whether or not the organ or other musical instrument should be used in the church was the one on which the congregation divided. Mr. Arnold took the position that no music, except that of the human voice, should be used in the worship of God. Many of his congregation differed with him and for some time a split in the church seemed impending. On January 5, 1873, Rev. B. B. Tyler became the pastor and remained for three years. During his time there were one hundred and one additions. Rev. L. H. Early succeeded him, but he remained for only a few months.

Rev. George Darsie was called to this station in 1879 and remained until his death, June 4, 1904. He went to Boston during this time but he was not satisfied there and he came back as soon as he could make his arrangements to do so.

Rev. C. R. Hudson became the pastor in 1905 and resigned in 1911, when he was succeeded by the Rev. Roger T. Nooe, the present pastor.

From the organization of the church to 1882 there were received into the church 640, and there was lost by death, removal, etc., 390. At the present time (1912) there are about nine hundred members.

Rev. George Darsie was greatly loved, not only by the members of his own church, but also by the people of Frankfort generally. At the time of his death it was thought that no one could acceptably supply the vacancy, but the ability and christian spirit of his successor endeared him to his people to such an extent that they felt they had sustained an irreparable loss when he resigned. The present incumbent seems endowed with the same christian graces of his predecessors and in a short time will doubtless be regarded as highly as were those who preceded him.

Protracted meetings have been held in this church by several noted preachers, among whom can be named, John Smith, Curtis J. Smith, Barton W. Stone, John T. Johnson, John Rogers, D. S. Barnett, Jacob Creath, Sr., William Morton and Alexander Campbell. The Rev. Alexander Campbell was at Frankfort on three different occasions, to-wit: 1835, 1836 and 1842. When he first came to Frankfort all of the churches were closed against him except the Methodist, who offered him the use of the church building, which he accepted. The doctrines preached by him were bitterly opposed by the other denominations and his followers were called in derision, Reformers or Campbellites. The Baptists were especially bitter against him, as well they might be, for he split nearly every Baptist Church in the county. The prejudice engendered against him did him a great injustice. His book, titled "Alexander Campbell's Christian Preacher's Companion," or "The Gospel Facts Sustained," stamps him a great man. Succeeding generations will and should rank him with Martin Luther, John Wesley and other great reformers. He was Irish by birth and was educated for the Presbyterian ministry. He withdrew from the Presbyterian Church and joined the Baptist. In 1823, during a debate in Mason County, Kentucky, he avowed the doctrine of "Baptism for the remission of sins." This doctrine separated him from the Baptist Church. The Baptist Churches in every section of the State became disrupted, in some instances whole congregations followed him and for a while the very existence of the Baptist Churches in the State seemed imperiled, and the other churches throughout Kentucky were, more or less, affected by the spirit of "heresy" so termed by the other denominations.

When the Methodist Episcopal Church, in America, was organized in 1784, the Episcopal Church had been in existence, in this country, one hundred and seventy-seven years. The Baptist Church for one hundred and forty-five years and the Presbyterian Church seventy-nine years.

At a conference held in the city of Baltimore in 1786, Bishop Asbury sent James Haw and Benjamin Ogden to the Kentucky Circuit; they reached the territory of Kentucky in the latter part of the summer of 1786. In 1787 the work in the west was divided into two circuits, one of which was known as Kentucky and the other was called the Cumberland. In that year James Haw was returned to the Kentucky Circuit, and Thomas Williams and Wilson Lee were appointed his colleagues. A report of the conference of 1787 showed a membership of ninety in Kentucky. In 1788 the conference was again held at Baltimore. Thomas Williamson, Peter Massie and Benjamin Snelling were sent to the Lexington Circuit, with Francis Poythress as the Presiding Elder. At that time there were no stationed Methodist preachers in the western country. The Lexington Circuit embraced the section of the country afterwards known as the counties of Fayette, Jessamine, Woodford, Franklin, Scott and Harrison. The first conference held in Kentucky was at Masterson's Station, five miles from Lexington, in the year 1790. There were only six members of the conference present. Henry Burchett was sent to the Lexington Circuit, where he remained until 1793, when John Ball and Gabriel Woodside were sent for two years. In 1796 Aquilla Sugg was in charge, but in the latter part of that year his health failed so that Thomas Scott was sent to take his place. The circuit at that time included Lexington, Versailles, Frankfort and sixteen other stations. Organizations or societies had been previously formed at each of these points and the Rev. Mr. Scott reported that most of them were in a healthy condition. Thomas Scott afterwards left the ministry and practiced law and held political positions for the remainder of his life.

John Buxton was sent to the Lexington Circuit in 1798. In 1800 James Haw, one of the first Methodist preachers in the western country, had some trouble with Bishop Asbury and on that account withdrew from the Methodist Church and became a preacher in the Presbyterian Church.

The preachers who were sent to the Lexington Circuit while Frankfort was in the circuit from 1800 to 1820, were as follows: Thomas Wilkinson, 1800; Lewis Hunt, 1801-2; Miles Harper, 1803; John Sale, 1804-5-6; Joseph Hays, 1807; Caleb W. Cloud, 1808-9-10; Nathan Stamper, 1811; Thomas D. Porter, 1812, William Patterson, 1813-14; Thomas D. Porter, 1815-16-17; William Adams, 1818; Josiah Whittiker, 1819. David Gray became the last circuit rider in 1820. The first pastor stationed at Frankfort was Nathaniel Harris, 1821. William Holman, 1822-3-4-5; B. T. Crouch, 1826-7; George C. Light, 1828-9; B. T. Crouch, 1830; Henry S. Duke, 1831; H. H. Kavanaugh, 1832; Thomas W. Chandler, 1833; Thomas C. Cropper, 1834; George W. Kelso, 1835-6; Henry N. Vandike, 1837; A. D. Fox, 1838, died while at Frankfort that year; Peter Taylor, 1839-40; W. Atherton, 1841; James D. Holding, 1842; C. P. Parsons, 1843; W. H. Anderson, 1844; Drummond Welburn, 1845; Joseph A. Waterman, 1846-7; George W. Brush, 1848-9; George W. Smiley, 1850-1; George W. Brush, 1852; John H. Linn, 1853-4; John M. Bonnell, 1855; John C. Harrison, 1856-7-8; Joseph Rand, 1859; William McD. Abbett, 1860-61; Daniel E. Stevenson, 1862; S. R. Robertson, 1863-4-5-6; H. A. M. Henderson, 1867-8-9; T. J. Dodd, 1870-1-2; D. A. Beardsley, 1873; Robert Hiner, 1874-5; J. W. Mitchell, 1876; C. W. Miller, 1877-8-9-80; E. L. Southgate, 1881; Morris Evans, 1882-3; Gilby C. Kelly, 1884-5-6-7; H. C. Morrison, 1888-9; H. G. Henderson, 1890-1-2-3; S. F. Pollett, 1894-5; George H. Means, 1896-7; T. F. Taliaferro, 1898-9; J. R. Savage, 1900-1; J. O. A. Vaught, 1902-3-4; C. J. Nugent, 1905-6; J. S. Sims, 1907-8-9-10; H. G. Turner, 1911-12.

Thomas Wilkinson was one of the greatest preachers of that day. He dressed in plain homespun clothes, and could not be induced to wear black. He would often have his whole audience in tears.

Caleb W. Cloud left the ministry and practiced medicine in Lexington, Kentucky, for many years.

William Holman found no church building in Frankfort when he came in 1822. In the following year, April 15, 1823, Benjamin Hickman transferred to the trustees of the Methodist Church a lot fronting 50 feet on Ann street and extending back the same width one hundred feet. On this lot was built a small frame church which remained there until 1849, when it was torn down and a brick church was built. In the year 1854 this structure was destroyed by fire. In that year the lot on Washington street was purchased and the present church was built. During the pastorate of Gilby C. Kelley in 1886, this building was improved by the erection of the stone front and other improvements. The evangelist Sam Jones preached the sermon re-dedicating the church. An immense crowd was present.

The greatest preacher who was ever stationed at Frankfort was H. H. Kavanaugh (1832). He was afterwards a bishop of the Methodist Episcopal Church.

William McD. Abbett was a strong union sympathizer. While stationed at Frankfort in 1861, took occasion one Sunday morning to pray very earnestly for the success of the Union Army. To his great surprise more than half of his congregation arose from their knees and left the church.

There have been several able preachers located at the Frankfort station during the past quarter of a century, but for some reason the church has not flourished to any great extent. In 1912 there are only about three hundred members, the most of whom are poor. The minister in charge is an able, earnest man who is calculated to do much good, but the church organization does not have that aggressiveness which brings success.

On May 27, 1884, the South Frankfort Presbyterian Church, South, was organized by a commission from West Lexington Presbytery. There were thirty-one members enrolled, all of whom had signed the petition for the organization of the church. Joseph Robinson, Thomas G. Poore and Peter Jett were installed as the first elders. The church building had been erected on the same lot where the present building is located. It was a frame structure and fronted on Third street. On June 1, 1884, the church was dedicated, Rev. E. O. Guerrant preached the dedicating sermon. In a short time after the church was organized it was transferred from West Lexington to Louisville Presbytery. On September 8, 1886, union was effected with the old Franklin Church near Bridgeport. Dr. E. O. Guerrant and others preached during the summer of 1884. On October 31, 1884, Rev. Robert E. Caldwell was called and he became the first regular pastor.

During the twenty-eight years since its organization, nine ministers have served either as stated, supply or pastor, towit: Robert E. Caldwell, 1884 to 1886; Dr. J. T. Hendricks (supply) 1886 to 1887; B. M. Farris, 1887 to 1888; C. R. Jones, 1888 to 1890, died in office; W. G. Neville, 1890 to 1893. D. Clay Lilly, 1893 to 1895; William Crowe, 1896 to 1908; W. Monroe Clark, 1908 to 1909; Robert L. Cowan, 1909 to 1912.

Mr. Cowan has lately resigned his charge to become secretary of the local Young Men's Christian Association.

On November 6, 1904, the present church building was dedicated. It was completed at a cost of twelve thousand dollars. The old building was given to the Salvation Army, whose officers removed it to the army headquarters on Clinton street, North Frankfort.

During the twenty-eight years there have been five hundred and fifty members enrolled. The church has contributed to all causes $60,000.

The First Baptist Church (colored) was organized in 1833. Prior to that time the white and colored people worshiped together. A colored man by the name of John Ward donated the ground where the church stands. The deed was made to the First Baptist Church in 1844.

The first regular preacher was Henderson Williams, who began his service in 1838 and served five years. The preachers who succeeded him whose names have been preserved were James Monroe, 1845; Robert Martin, who remained for twenty years and who baptized hundreds of converts; George W. Patterson, Eugene Evans, (1887). J. W. Hawkins left one thousand dollars in the treasury with which to purchase ground for a new church. Robert Mitchell, A. M., D. D., purchased the lot on the corner across from the Governor's mansion on High street, at the price of $4,000, and petitioned the City Council for the right to build the church. The city refused to grant the right and a long legal fight ensued. The Court of Appeals passed on the case in 1904 and sustained the church, and the building was erected at a cost of twenty-five thousand dollars. It is the handsomest building for colored people in the State. C. C. Wakefield succeeded Dr. Mitchell in 1903, and W. R. Payne became pastor in 1904; Dr. W. T. Silvey in 1905, since which time he has performed an acceptable service for the church. During his eight years of service the church has prospered; the membership in 1912 numbered seven hundred and forty-two.

The Corinthian Baptist Church, located on Mero street, between St. Clair and Washington streets, was organized in 1876. James H. Parrish was the first regular pastor called. He was succeeded by C. C. Stumm in 1879. Rev. Reuben Strauss was called in 1882, and in a few months thereafter he was succeeded by James M. Mason, who continued in the work until 1884. The succeeding pastors are as follows: E. Richie, 1884; R. H. C. Mitchell, 1885; W. H. Craighead, called temporarily; Wm. A. Creditt, 1890; Benjamin W. Farris, 1892; W. E. Claybrook, 1896; D. S. Oner, 1897; E. T. Fishback, 1898; F. G. Brookins, 1909, and E. J. Jackson, the present pastor, was called in 1910. Rev. Jackson is highly regraded by both races. The church property is valued at $15,000. Membership number 105.

The St. John A. M. E. Church was established in 1839. The first building was erected in that year on the old site on Lewis street. The building and grounds were given by Mrs. Triplett, a white woman, to her servants, Benjamin Dunmore and Benjamin Hunley. It was afterwards deeded in trust to Harry Mordecai and George Harlan. The first pastor was George Harlan, who was in charge until 1840. Those who succeeded him were Moses Pitman, Aaron Green, Reuben Thomas, Henry Henderson (1850), Anderson Bryant, Jacob

Williams, Henry Hensley, William Brown, Henry J. Young, Ross Lee, Jilson Francis, Geo. H. Schaffer, Washington Hill, Grafton Graham, Alfred Newman, C. J. Waters, B. F. Lee, J. W. Riley, Chas. Herbert, Jessie Henderson, George Steamer, Levi Evans, D. S. Bentley, J. W. Asbury, J. F. Thomas, G. H. Burk, Geo. W. Bryant, Emanuel Wilson, J. M. Turner, J. W. Frazier, P. A. Nichols, G. F. David, J. M. Holt, D. D., 1906; J. Allen Viney, 1907-8-9; T. A. Thompson, 1910. During the pastorate of Rev. J. Allen Viney the mortgage debt of two thousand dollars was paid. The "mortgage burning" was the occasion of great rejoicing among the members.

D. C. Carter is the present pastor in charge. The membership numbers 235. In 1893 the present church was built.

CHAPTER XVII.

Present Time, November 1912.

The assessed valuation of land as returned by the Assessor of Franklin County for the year 1912 is	$3,004,646 00
Town lots assessed at	3,124,164 00
Personalty assessment	1,178,638 00
Total assessment	$7,307,448 00
Tax on 2,877 tithes at $1.50	$4,315 00
Tax on railroads	2,109 52
Tax on whiskey withdrawals	8,614 96
Tax on shares of bank stock	2,680 09
Tax on corporations and franchises	2,472 05
Revenue on storage accounts	8,420 31
The total gross revenue for the preceding fiscal year was	$79,140 98
The number of acres of land in the county as shown by the assessor's books is	131,799
The number of town lots	2,325
Pounds of hemp raised	1,851
Tons of hay	2,291
Bushels of corn	129,163
Bushels of wheat	26,001
The number of bushels of oats raised	2,110
The number of bushels of barley raised	4,020
Bushels of grass seed	1,327
The number of acres in wheat	1,667
The number of acres in corn	4,831
The number of acres in meadow	1,769
The number of acres in woodland	885
The number of acres in tobacco	1,204

A statement of the bonded indebtedness of Franklin County is as follows:

$62,000.00 at 4½ per cent issued July 1st, 1898, and due July 1st, 1918.

$57,000.00 at 5 per cent issued January 1st, 1904, first payment due January 1st, 1913; second and last payment due January 1st, 1918.

$23,000.00 at 5 per cent issued April 15th, 1904; first payment due April 15th, 1920; second and last payment due April 15th, 1924.

$19,000.00 at 5 per cent issued November the 1st, 1905, and will be due November the 1st, 1925.

$130,000.00 at 4 per cent Kentucky Midland Railroad bonds issued July 1st, 1899, and will be due July 1st, 1919.

The total amount of bonded indebtedness of the county is $291,000.00.

Poor House claims for fiscal year	$789 20
Pauper claims for year	646 70
Salaries and fees of county officers	8,380 83
Turnpikes and bridges	38,032 88
Promiscuous claims	14,964 75
Claims paid election officers	294 88
Amount of interest paid on bonds	7,765 00
Total amount paid out	70,870 00
The amount of net revenue for year	74,126 02

The assessed valuation of property for city purposes is generally higher than the assessment on the same property for State and county purposes. The assessed valuation of the real estate in the city of Frankfort for the preceeding year was $3,225,323.00, and the personal property was assessed at $1,640,630.00, making a total valuation of $4,865,961.00. The rate being $1.70 per hundred, the revenue would be $82,721.33.

The city spent during the year on the improvement of the streets the sum of $12,425.35, and on the sewers the sum of $3,070.00, and for cleaning the streets the sum of $1,298.42. The postoffice receipts for the fiscal year ending March, 1912, were $38,000.00.

James T. Buford represented the county in the House of

the Kentucky Legislature in the sessions of 1908 and 1910, and Elwood Hamilton in the session of 1912.

An appropriation of $75,000.00 was made at the legislative session of 1912 for the purpose of purchasing a site and erecting a mansion for the Governor. The commissioners selected a beautiful place adjoining the capitol grounds overlooking the Kentucky river and the Louisville and Nashville and the Kentucky Highland Railroads. If the plans for the new building are strictly carried out, it will be in keeping with the new State House and a credit to the State and to all who are connected with its construction.

The Legislature also appropriated $10,000.00 with which to make some needed improvements on the old State House and executive building, it being understood that several departments of the State government are to be removed to the old State building.

On the 13th of November, 1912, the Arboretum of Kentucky was established. Each of eighty-five counties in the State sent a tree to be planted on the new capitol grounds. An effort will be made to secure a tree from each of the remaining counties. Mr. H. F. Hillenmeyer, of Lexington, has agreed to complete the arboretum by furnishing such trees indigenous to Kentucky as have not been sent in by the counties.

During the present year the Frankfort Water Company has commenced the installation of a filter plant which will cost seventy-five thousand dollars.

The Young Men's Christian Association has just completed a fine building which is located at the South end of the St. Clair street bridge; the building cost about sixty thousand dollars.

Frankfort's seven-story building, erected by the McClure Realty Company, on the corner of Main and St. Clair streets, and which was known as "The McClure Building," has been purchased by The United American Insurance Company and its name has been changed to that of "The United American Building."

The United American Insurance Company has recently

been organized in the city of Frankfort with a capital of one million of dollars.

A secret benevolent organization known as the Modern Knights of the American Home has also been recently organized in Frankfort. The supreme council is composed entirely of Frankfort citizens. A Widows' and Orphans' Home is to be established at Frankfort. If the plans of these two organizations are carried out the city of Frankfort will be greatly benefited.

The State Journal has purchased a site on Main street and it now has under course of construction a large brick building. When completed it will be an ornament, and a great acquisition to the city.

The tobacco industry is one of the greatest in the county. The limestone soil seems especially adapted to the production of the white burley tobacco; more than twelve hundred acres of it were raised in the county in year 1912.

During the past few years Frankfort has built up a good loose leaf tobacco market. In the year 1909, the T. C. Geary Company sold about two millions of pounds. In 1910 The Farmers' Tobacco Warehouse Company built a large warehouse on Second street and during the year the two houses sold about eight and one-half millions pounds. In the year 1911, the two houses sold a little over five million pounds.

The Burley Tobacco Company is building a large warehouse on Holmes street, this building is now nearing completion and in a short time will be in competition with the other two houses. It appears now that the Frankfort market will go above the ten million mark, from the sales of the three houses during the year of 1912. The product has commanded good prices and the sales at this point have been more satisfactory than were those made in other sections of the State.

Some of the largest tobacco companies in the world have had their representatives at Frankfort, buying and shipping to all sections of the country. Among them were the American Tobacco Company of Richmond, Virginia; Liggett & Myers Tobacco Company, Louisville, Ky.; R. J. Reynolds, of Winston-Salem, N. C.; J. P. Taylor & Co., of Lexington, Ky.; W. L

THE HISTORY OF FRANKLIN COUNTY.   269

Petty Co., of Lexington, Ky.; Hancock Bros., of Lynchburg, Va.; G. O. Tuck & Co., of Louisville, Ky.; Brasswell & Levy (exporters), Rockymont, N. C.

In the amount of capital involved, as represented in the buildings, machinery, raw material and labor, combined with the vast stored products, the distillery interest of Franklin County is its largest and most conspicuous industry. The entire outlay embraced in this branch of manufacture, including the finished goods ripening for the markets of the world in storage barns, represents an investment and valuation of many millions of dollars.

The distinguishing character of the whiskey produced and shipped from the local distilleries are classed and recognized in all the markets of the commercial spirit trade, as a pure "straight whiskey" of the greatest excellence and highest value. It belongs exclusively to the sour mash method of distillation. It is boiled and vaporized in copper stills, condensed and received in copper worms and cisterns, and finally aged and ripened in wooden casks which are stored in large dry warehouses. In constituent elements and qualities, this whiskey is wholly unlike the fraudulent imitations or mixtures and compounds which the rectifiers so extensively advertise and sell to those who desire cheap goods regardless of quality. The superiority of Franklin County whiskey emanates not only from the character of grain used, the methods of manufacture and the essential elements of perfect maturation, but also from the constituent properties of the water which is used in the manufacture and which is found in the bird's eye limestone formation, peculiar to this region alone.

In fruitiness of flavor, richness of aroma, ripeness of maturity and delicacy of finish, the whiskey of the State Capital and its environs surpasses all other spirit products of grain as a table beverage.

There were some early attempts on Glenn's Creek and at Leestown to produce an acceptable article of whiskey, but the structures used were unsuited, the appliances crude, the methods imperfect and the output raw and unfinished as well as insignificant in quantity. It was not until after the close of the

Civil War, about the year 1868, that the growth and development of the distillery business in this county took an origin which has grown into its present magnitude and prosperity. It was then that the foresight, sagacity and energy of Col. Edmund H. Taylor brought him to the front and he became, and has continued to be, a recognized leader in distillery construction, development and improvement. It would be impossible to give an accurate history of the growth and expansion of this branch of county prosperity without mentioning him as a leader in the manufacture of pure whiskey. It was under his personal supervision that the Hermitage, The Old Oscar Pepper, O. F. C., Carlisle and Old Taylor distilleries were established and to him also was due the naming of the brands "Old Taylor," "Old Crow," "Old Oscar Pepper," "O. F. C.," and "Carlisle," which have since gained a celebrity, national and international. Col. Taylor was also the most noted advocate before Congress and in the public prints, of the spirit provisions of the pure food laws, and he was one of the first to erect in this locality an establishment for bottling whiskey in bond under that act.

Since 1868 the distillery growth and expansion have been steady and substantial, until today they represent vast plans, with an enormous area of distillery and storage structures filled with costly machinery. The Old Taylor distillery, located on Glenn's Creek, is owned and operated by E. H. Taylor, Jr. & Sons, Incorporated. Its medieval castle structure, colored tiled roofs, concrete bridges and avenues, its ornamental flower garden, fountain and gold fish basin attract visitors from all sections of the country. The Old Crow distillery plant, owned and operated by W. A. Gaines & Co., Incorporated, is located on the Woodford County line near the mouth of Glenn's Creek. The "Old Crow" brand of whiskey is one of the most noted in the world. A Scotchman, by the name of James Crow, came to Kentucky in 1835, and located on Glenn's Creek where he commenced making whiskey. He was a scientific distiller and he continued in the business until his death in 1856. To him is ascribed the first hand-made sour mash process with the use of spent beer or slop, which owing to its acidity caused the term "sour mash." The same method adopted by James Crow has been adhered to by the W. A. Gaines & Co., down to the present time. The popularity of James Crow has been perpetuated in the name "Old Crow." So popular has this whiskey become, that the company has concluded to withdraw the sale of it in cask and the entire output will now be bottled in bond. The Hermitage distillery on the banks of the Kentucky river in South Frankfort is owned and operated by the same firm; it has a capacity of one hundred barrels per day. On the opposite side of the river is the John Cochran or Spring Hill distillery which is operated by the Kentucky Distillers & Warehouse Co.

The O. F. C. and Kentucky River (formerly Carlisle) distilleries, located at Leestown on the Kentucky river one and a half miles below the city, are owned and operated by the Geo. T. Stagg Co. The Swastika or Frankfort distillery, on Elkhorn Creek, near Elkhorn Station on the F. & C R. R., is owned and operated by the Baker Bros. One mile west of Frankfort is the Old Judge distillery owned and operated by the S. C. Herbst Importing Company. The main offices of these distilleries are nearly all located in the city of Frankfort.

The distillery plants embrace an extensive, systematic arrangement of main manufacturing edifices, storage warehouses, grain elevators and cribs, slop drying houses or cattle pens, with establishments for bottling the product under the Pure Food Act of Congress.

The principal edifice enclosing distillery operations are, in most cases, substantially built of brick, stone or wood. The machinery employed in distillation is of modern type and in some cases of very costly construction. The processes vary according to the experience or skill of the operator or to the particular trade want that is sought to be filled. The product is either a high grade whiskey or it belongs to a cheaper variety, but in no case does it descend to the level in character or quality of the impure and unwholesome output from the neutral spirit factories' and rectifiers' tubs.

The bonded warehouses attached to the distilleries and held under government supervision are appropriated to the care and maturation for market of the barreled product of this large and valuable industry. They cover many acres of ground, are substantially built and have an estimated aggregate capacity for storage of nearly 600,000 barrels. Many of these warehouses are capable of holding from 10,000 to 40,000 barrels each. They are principally of the patent rick variety and arranged with a view to light, ventilation, dryness and facility in the handling of the whiskey stored. The barrels rest on dunnage in tiers, one above the other, each package unburdened by any weight except its own.

The leading feature of this warehouse storage is, that it ripens and perfects the whiskey for market, developing its essential oils and essences. In rectified whiskey these oils and essences are almost totally absent, so that age gives no improvement and storage is a waste.

The growth of the bottling in bond business, in the past few years, in this county, has been marvelous. Bottling houses are now attached to every distillery and the daily output during the operating season is about 3,000 cases or 36,000 bottles. The whiskey is bottled from bond under government supervision, not less than four years old, and is protected to the consumer in any part of the world, in its proof, age, quantity and genuineness by the unbroken green stamp over the cork of each bottle. This method of bottling in bond has had a depressing effect upon the bottling of impure free whiskies.

The whiskey industry of the county gives remunerative employment to hundreds of employees. It furnishes a home market for all surplus grain and it pays, probably, 85 per cent of the local taxes, State, county and municipal.

There are six banks located in Frankfort, the capital stock of which aggregate five hundred and fifty thousand dollars. At the end of the fiscal year, June 29th, 1912, the sworn statements made by the cashiers of the six banks, show that the deposits amounted to the sum of $1,748,454.78. The loans and discounts amounted to $1,983,402.70. The surplus and undivided profits amounted to $291,623.49. The real estate was valued at $73,328.29. The total assets amounted to $3,288,673.67.

A shoe factory of such magnitude as to be aptly classed one of Kentucky's important industries, has its home in Frankfort, and it is an enterprise of great benefit to the city and State by its extensive operations. The manufacturing concern of Hoge-Montgomery Company is maker of a superior product of all-solid leather shoes for women, girls and boys. This line of shoes is known far and near for its established values, and has become celebrated for its wearing qualities and the extremely reasonable price at which this dependable and staple footwear is sold. The official personnel of this company is as follows:

Chas. E. Hoge, President.
Jas. F. Montgomery, Vice-President and General Manager.
S. French Hoge, Treasurer.
H. H. Roberts, Secretary.
Chas. F. Straussner, Sales Manager.

The business was established in 1889 and was originally known as the Frankfort Shoe Manufacturing Co., but was changed in name in 1905. The capacity of the plant at the time of its inauguration in 1889 was about seven hundred pairs of shoes daily, but it flourished steadily and uninterruptedly, and the plant has been so successively enlarged and improved that at the present time there is a daily output of seven thousand two hundred pairs of well made shoes.

The factory operates every day in the year with the exception of Sundays and legal holidays. The machinery is of the most modern and improved type and the plant is larger than that of any other factory south of the Ohio river.

By contract with the State for a part of the prison labor, the company pays in to the State Treasury more than a quarter of a million dollars annually.

It is understood that this company pays a higher price than that obtained by any other State in the Union for similar labor, therefore, instead of this penal institution being a burden to the taxpayers it is more than self-sustaining, after a portion of the hire, as required by law, is set aside for the benefit of the prisoners or their dependent families. In the free labor factory of the company, pleasant and light employment, at good wages, is afforded to as many women and girls as can be secured. Although the company has never been able to obtain as much of this class of labor as it would like to employ, there are now over three hundred free operatives whose pay roll exceeds three thousand dollars per week.

To dispose of the large and steady output of shoes, the company employs a traveling force of thirty-five experienced shoe salesmen. The product of the factory is sold in every State in the Union, from the Atlantic to the Pacific. "Frankfort Shoes" are known and appreciated throughout the land, being everywhere handled by the largest dealers, and besides, a substantial export trade is being developed.

The ambition of the company is to furnish comfortable shoes, that wear longer and cost less than can be obtained from any other factory in existence, and, as a result of the impetus given by it to the manufacturing industry, Frankfort may in the days to come be known as a great factory city. The Hoge-Montgomery Company has done much to place Frankfort far on the road to such fame.

The Franklin County rural school system has been greatly improved during the past three years. According to the school census of 1912, Franklin County, outside of the corporate limits of the city of Frankfort, has three thousand and eighty-seven children between the ages of six and twenty years. Of these, two thousand eight hundred and seventy-three are white and two hundred and fourteen are colored.

The county is divided into four educational divisions, each division containing as nearly as possible the same number of pupils.

Educational Division number one (Forks of Elkhorn), contains nine sub-district schools; Educational District number two (Peak's Mill), contains fourteen; Division number three (Bridgeport), contains eleven, and Division number four (Bald Knob), contains fourteen.

The farmers of the county are interested in good schools as never before. They are beginning to realize that the money expended in the education of their children is not a cost, but a splendid investment. No part of the school system is more popular than that of the high school. Franklin County has developed this plan better, possibly, than any other county in the State, having five county high schools. One with a four years' course and four with a two years' course. The schools are so distributed over the county that no pupil will have a greater distance to travel in reaching school than six or seven miles.

The number of pupils matriculated in these high schools in the fall of 1912 is seventy-five, this is a marvelous record when it is considered that the system is only three years old. This shows that the rural population is very responsive to educational advantages.

The colored population of the county is so sparse that it is difficult to handle. The last statistical report shows that the average attendance, based on census, is nearly equal to that of the white children. Unless the tide of migration of this race from the country to the city be lessened, it will be difficult to find enough children in any community to support a school. The last census report shows less than half the number of colored pupil children in the county outside of the corporate limits of the city of Frankfort than there were six years prior thereto. At this ratio of decrease it will be but a few years when there will be no colored children in the county schools.

The city of Frankfort is now provided with six school buildings for white children and one for colored. The main building is a twenty-eight room structure with all modern conveniences, and is used for the high school and grammer grades. The new building located on the same lot west of the main building contains six rooms, and it is used as a primary building. There is a building in Bellepoint and one on Wilkinson street of four rooms. There was a lot purchased in the summer of 1912, and a nice primary building erected on Holmes street, at a cost of six thousand dollars. The Exum property on Murray street was purchased in 1912 and converted into a primary school and it is now taxed to its full capacity.

The colored school is located on Clinton street. The schools of Frankfort have grown rapidly during the past few years, the enrollment in 1912 being 1,424, which is a gain of about 400 in the past five years. The School Board has met this increase in attendance by providing extra teachers and increasing all the educational facilities. The high school has shown the most rapid growth, increasing since 1904, from forty-eight pupils, to one hundred and ninety-three, and the teaching force from three to eight teachers. This is a good indication of the educational progress, for it shows that children are completing their education as far as it can be done in the public school.

Domestic Science and Art, Drawing, Manual Training and Book Binding and the commercial branches have been added to the high school course of study. This course of study has been approved by the Kentucky Southern College Association, and the pupils are admitted to any university in these associations without examination. A free scholarship is granted to all who enter the State University at Lexington.

The school census of colored children in 1900 was 989, and in 1912 was 554, yet the attendance in 1912 was 66 per cent. based upon enrollment, which was the largest per cent of attendance ever recorded by this school. The per cent of attendance in all of the schools is greater than in any past year, the curriculum of study broader, the interest in education greater and the facilities better than they have ever been.

The State Normal School for colored persons, located in the eastern suburb of Frankfort, is well located upon one of the highest hills which surround the city. The grounds are well drained, with healthful, agreeable surroundings and picturesque scenery. The school was opened in 1887, and has been in operation for a quarter of a century. The State owns a large farm which is run in connection with the school. The State has been very liberal in providing buildings and other facilities for the higher education of the colored race. This school is a part of the common school system of Kentucky and its chief object is to train teachers for the colored common schools of the Commonwealth. It has been productive of great good especially to the colored race.

The following named lawyers were members of the Frankfort bar, located at Frankfort in the year 1912; the positions held by each are noted: J. C. W. Beckham, Representative of Nelson County, Speaker of the House, Lieutenant Governor and

Governor of Kentucky. J. W. Blackburn, Jr., Assistant Adjutant General with the rank of Major, present Auditor's Agent for Franklin County. Guy H. Briggs, Auditor's Agent, Judge Advocate Gen. with rank of Col. Eli H. Brown, Representative of Nelson County, Speaker of the House, Prison Commissioner. James T. Buford, County Attorney, Representative of Franklin County. J. Morgan Chinn, Representative of Mercer County. Frank Chinn, Master Commissioner of the Franklin Circuit Court. T. H. Crockett, City Attorney, present City Prosecutor. Frank M. Dailey, County Attorney, present City Attorney. T. L. Edelen. Robert B. Franklin, present Commonwealth's Attorney 14th District. James Garnett, present Attorney General. Paul C. Gaines. Robert L. Green, present Clerk of the Court of Appeals. Elwood Hamilton, present Representative of Franklin County. J. H. Hazelrigg, County Judge of Montgomery County, Chief Justice of Kentucky. Dyke Hazelrigg. W. C. Herndon, City Attorney, present Police Judge of Frankfort. J. Hunt Jackson, Representative of Owen County. W. L. Jett, Supt. of Schools of Franklin County, Police Judge of Frankfort, Master Commissioner of the Franklin Circuit Court, Auditor's Agent, Postoffice Inspector under President Cleveland. J. W. Jeffers, present Master Commissioner of Franklin Circuit Court. L. F. Johnson, County Attorney, Auditor's Agent, Representative of Franklin County. Ira Julian, County Attorney, Representative of Franklin County, Circuit Judge of 14th Judicial District. M. M. Logan, present Assistant Attorney General. J. F. Lockett, Assistant Attorney General. D. W. Lindsey, City Attorney of Frankfort, Col. in Federal Army, Inspector General and Adjutant General of Kentucky. John B. Lindsey. T. N. Lindsey. D. W. Lindsey, Jr., County Judge of Franklin County. W. C. Marshall, present County Attorney of Franklin County. L. W. Morris. Charles H. Morris, present Assistant Attorney General. Dulin Moss. Chas. Mason. H. V. McChesney, Supt. of Livingston Public Schools, Supt. of Public Instruction and Secretary of State. Thomas B. McGregor, Assistant Attorney General. Lewis McQuown, Chairman of the Democratic State Central and State Executive Committee. Lewis A. Nuckols,

Representative of Woodford County, Commissioner of the Woodford Circuit Court. Edward C. O'Rear, County Judge of Montgomery County, Chief Justice of Kentucky. Thomas H. Paynter, Representative in Congress, Chief Justice of Kentucky, present United States Senator. James H. Polsgrove, County Attorney, and County Judge of Franklin County, present Mayor of Frankfort. W. H. Posey, Master Commissioner of Franklin Circuit Court. J. A. Scott, Representative of Franklin County, Master Commissioner of Franklin Circuit Court. Robert L. Stout, present Circuit Judge of 14th Judicial District. Samuel A. Thomas. A. C. Vanwinkle. B. G. Williams, County Attorney and County Judge of Franklin County. Oscar Wolf. Physicians and surgeons located in Frankfort in 1912: C. W. Anderson (colored), Joseph Barr, R. M. Coblin, J. S. Coleman, C. P. Coleman, O. B. Demaree, C. A. Fish, Neville M. Garrett, J. W. Hill, Josephine Hoggins, Harlan Heilman, H. S. Keller, Flora W. Mastin, L. T. Minish, W. L. Montgomery, Thomas R. Moore, Warren Monfort, John Patterson, O. H. Reynolds, E. C. Roemele, John G. South, A. Stewart, E. E. Underwood (colored), C. K. Wallace, J. W. Willson and U. V. Williams.

The State Historical rooms, under the care and supervision of Mrs. Jennie C. Morton, Secretary-Treasurer of the State Historical Society, are located on the first floor and in the southwest corner of the new capitol building. For nearly half a century relics and specimens of historical nature have been collected and preserved. At the present time there are several rooms filled with articles of almost priceless value; if destroyed many of them could not be reproduced. If the collection was properly advertised and sold at public sale, it would likely bring more than one hundred thousand dollars.

The collection contains the portraits of all the Governors of the Commonwealth except three, and efforts are being made to complete the collection. Twenty-nine of these portraits are in oil.

There are two portraits of Daniel Boone, one of them, an oil painting by Chester Harding, copied by Marshall, of Louisville, Ky., and the other is in water color, copied from Thomas Sully, by Miss Chesney.

The portraits of General Harrison and Gen. Lafayette are the most valuable in the collection; they could be sold for $25,000.00. In the list of highly appreciated portraits are those of Col. B. H. Young and Col. R. T. Durrett, of Louisville, and Col. D. Howard Smith and Col. Ambrose Dudley. Some of the oil paintings are those of General John C. Breckinridge, Gen. Zachary Taylor, by Allen, Henry Clay, painted at Paris, France, after the treaty of Ghent. John G. Carlisle, which is valued at one thousand dollars. George Washington, a copy of Peel's portrait of 1778, Richard Collins, the historian, and those of the two greatest poets Kentucky has ever produced, both of whom were citizens of Franklin County, Theodore O'Hara and Henry T. Stanton. The oil paintings of Martin Luther and his wife, which were painted in 1543, are supposed to be the only oil portraits extant of that noted reformer and his wife. The society has a large collection of other oil paintings, such as Simon Kenton making his escape from the Indians, and the five paintings donated by the city of Philadelphia to the State of Kentucky, and which were brought to Frankfort by a committee of prominent citizens appointed by the city of Philadelphia. The paintings are those of Independence Hall, the State House at Philadelphia, the house where Thomas Jefferson wrote the Declaration of Independence, and Carpenters Hall, where the first Continental Congress was held.

The society, also, has a large collection of books, the most of which treat of historical subjects. An especial effort has been made to secure histories of Kentucky and Kentuckians. There are thousands of other things which have been collected and which are of great interest to all who love the history and traditions of the Kentucky pioneers.

The Frankfort or State cemetery is located in an ideal place, the grounds include one hundred acres of table land in the suburbs of the city. The contour of the land is sufficiently undulating to furnish a variety of scenery and at the same time sufficiently level for the purpose for which it has been set aside. The Frankfort Cemetery Company was formed and a part of the land purchased in 1845. The charter which was granted by the Legislature forever restrains the company from dividing any profits. Should any excess of funds arise from the sale of burial lots, or otherwise, beyond the original cost and current expenses of the grounds, it is to be applied to the permanent improvement and embellishment of the grounds.

Mr. Robert Carmichael, the first landscape gardener who laid off the grounds and improved them, was engaged for a term of years to superintend them. He was a gentleman of great taste and accomplishments. He was regularly educated to his profession in Scotland. He died July 17th, 1858, and was buried in the grounds which he had done so much to beautify. He was succeeded by Mr. R. H. Nicol, who held the position until his death, eighteen years later. Mr. William Craik was then appointed (1877) and he retained the position until his death in 1904, since which time his son, Henry Craik, has been in charge. The excellent condition in which the grounds are at the present time is a guarantee of his ability to properly discharge the duties of the position.

In the year 1851 the Legislature of Kentucky passed an act authorizing and directing the Governor of the Commonwealth to purchase from the Frankfort Cemetery Company the lots numbered 131, 132, 143, 144, 154 and 155 "in which to bury the remains of Kentucky's illustrious dead." The price paid for which was six hundred dollars. These lots are located some distance south of the State monument and being the lots in which Governors Greenup, Adair and Madison are buried, and where Hart, Eliott and many other noted Kentuckians are to be found. The lots where the State monument and the Johnson monument are located and where the Mexican soldiers are buried were donated by the cemetery company; they are not a part of those purchased by the State.

The Legislature of Kentucky, by act of 1847-8, directed a military monument to be erected in honor of her illustrious dead on the State mound which is located near the center of the grounds and which is more elevated than any other part of the grounds. Mr. Robert E. Launtiz, of New York, one of the most skilled workmen in America, was employed to do the work, the most of which was done in Italy. The material was shipped to Frankfort by way of the Mississippi river. A barge was sent to New Orleans expressly for the purpose of receiving it directly from the vessel and it was delivered at Frankfort without the slightest injury.

The monument rests on a base twenty feet square, made of Connecticut granite. Many of the blocks of which the monument is made weighs five tons each, the weight of the whole being more than one hundred and fifty tons. The monument is sixty-five feet high and it cost the State $15,000. The Statue of Victory, which crowns the column, was elevated and placed in position in June, 1849. The material of the monument is the purest and richest monumental marble ever brought to America, though it has become discolored in places, caused by the rust of the dowel pins which were used to hold the blocks in place. Some of the blocks are slightly showing the effects of the elements to which they have been exposed for more than half a century, but at the time they were received they were free from all blemishes and were perfectly uniform in color. This material was imported expressly for the purpose from the celebrated quarry of C. Fabricotti, Carrara.

The statue of victory which crowns the work and the four eagles which guard the corners of the die were sculptured in Italy from models prepared by Mr. Launitz.

The Bass or relief figures on the panels and the coat of arms were sculptured, and the rest of the marble work executed in the studio of Mr. Launitz in New York City.

On the upper base facing the west is the following inscription: "The Principal Battles and Campaigns in Which Her Sons Devoted Their Lives to Their Country," are inscribed on the bands and beneath the same are the names of her officers who fell. The names of her soldiers who died for their country are too numerous to be inscribed on any column. On the north side of the upper base is a tablet on which is inscribed "Military monument erected by Kentucky, A. D. 1850." On the east side of same is the inscription "Kentucky has erected this column in gratitude equally to her officers and soldiers." Facing the south is the coat of arms of Kentucky with the motto of the State, "United We Stand Divided We Fall." On the bands are inscribed the names of twenty-two battles, or campaigns, and beneath these bands are the names of eighty-four officers who fell in battle.

There are four cannon located near the monument, two of which were taken from the enemy at the battle of Buena Vista, the other two belonged to the State. On the north side of the State monument is the sarcophagus of Henry Clay, Jr., who was Lieutenant Colonel of 2nd regiment of Kentucky Infantry. He fell at Buena Vista, February 23rd, 1847. Near him, on his left, is that of Cary H. Fry, Major of 2nd Kentucky regiment, and the next one on the left is that of Adjutant G. N. Cardwell, and the last one in that row is that of Col. W. R. McKee, who also fell at Buena Vista.

A short distance northwest of the State monument is a small marker on which is inscribed "Capt. A. G. Bacon, 3rd Kentucky Cavalry, U. S. A., killed at Sacramento, Ky., December 28th, 1861; aged 42 years." The A. G. Bacon post of the Franklin County G. A. R. was so named for Capt. Bacon. About half way between the State monument and the R. M. Johnson monument is the sarcophagus of "Theodore O'Hara, Major and A. D. C., died June 5th, 1867."

In 1851 the Legislature of Kentucky, by commissioners, contracted with Mr. Robert E. Launitz for the erection of a monument to the memory of Col. Richard Mentor Johnson and for which the State paid the sum of nine hundred dollars. At the time this work was completed it was the most beautiful monumental structure in America and though it has been injured by vandals and the ravages of time, it still shows that a master in his art planned and executed the work. It is located at the extreme southern part of the military lot. It is made of Italian marble, the base is of granite on which is a shaft ten feet tall and four feet square. A good likeness of Col. Johnson is carved on the north side, and cannon are on each corner. On the east side is inscribed: Richard Mentor Johnson, born at Bryant's Station, Kentucky, 1781; died in Frankfort, Kentucky, on the 19th day of November, 1850.

On the south side Col. Johnson is represented on horseback

in the act of killing Tecumseh. The Indian is on one knee, falling backwards, with a tomahawk in his hand.

On the west side is the following inscription: "To the memory of Col. Richard M. Johnson, a faithful public servant for nearly a century." As a member of the Kentucky Legislature and Representative and Senator in Congress. Author of the Sunday mail report and of laws abolishing imprisonment for debt in Kentucky and in the United States. Distinguished by his valor as a Colonel of a Kentucky regiment in the battle of the Thames. For four years Vice-President of the United States. Kentucky, his native State, to mark the sense of his eminent services in the cabinet and in the field, has erected this monument, in the resting place of her illustrious dead.

The shaft has a flag of stars and stripes around the top, falling to one side and crowned with a large American eagle which holds a laurel wreath in its beak. The work is most excellent and the whole design beautiful beyond description.

The monument of Daniel Boone and Rebecca, his wife, is located on the brow of the hill overlooking the city and the Kentucky river, the panels of which have recently been replaced, the new panels being an exact reproduction of the old. The whole monument was practically rebuilt and enclosed by an iron fence to prevent vandals in the nature of relic hunters, from again destroying it. The remains of Ellison Williams, a friend and companion of Boone, were removed from Kenton County to Frankfort by resolution of the Kentucky Legislature. He was buried near the tomb of Daniel Boone on May 21st, 1860, with military honors. Gen. D. W. Lindsey was in charge of the military.

Elizabeth Love, one of the greatest women of pioneer days, and Margaretta Brown, widow of United States Senator John Brown, are buried only a short distance south of the Boone monument.

Inscribed on the John Brown monument is the following: "Margaretta Brown, wife of John Brown, and daughter of Rev. John Mason and Catherine Vanwick. Born in the city of New York on the 12th of November, 1772; died in Frankfort, Ky., on the 28th of May, 1838. She was eminent for talents, learning, charity, piety and all the virtues that adorn the female character. It should be recorded on her tomb that she organized the first Sabbath School in the Mississippi valley."

Near the southern portion of the grounds is the last resting place of Joel T. Hart which is marked by a black block of Quincy marble from Quincy, Mass., which is nearly square. The top slopes to the east and on which is inscribed, "Erected to the memory of Joel T. Hart by the State of Kentucky. Born February 11th, 1810; died March 2nd, 1877." "Seek him not here but in the stone where he lives in his own art's immortality."

The monument which was dedicated to the memory of the Confederate dead was placed in position and unveiled in the spring of 1892. It stands in the center of the Confederate lot, encircled by the graves of the Confederate dead. The base of the structure is of solid granite. The figure is a statue of James G. Crockett at parade rest. He was a Franklin County soldier in the Confederate army and lost a leg in the defense of the South. In a short time after his return from the war he was elected County Court Clerk of Franklin County which position he held until his death, about 1883. The monument was made of the finest Italian marble, imported from the Carrara quarries, Italy. The statue is six feet in height. The following are the inscriptions on the face of the base:

"Our Confederate dead 1861-1865."

"They sleep—what need the question now if they
    be right or wrong
They know ere this whose cause was just in God the
    Father's sight,
They wield no warlike weapons now, return no foe-
    man's thrust,
Who but a coward would revile the honored soldier's
    dust."

Reverse Side.

"Greater love hath no man than this that a man lay down his life for his friends."

West Side.

"The marble minstrels voiceful tone
In deathless songs shall tell
When many a vanquished age hath flown
The story, how ye fell;
Nor wreck, nor change, nor winter blight,
Nor time's remorseless doom
Shall dim one ray of holy light
That gilds your glorious tomb."

East Side.

"To every man upon the earth
Death cometh soon or late
And how can man die better
Than facing fearful odds
For the ashes of his fathers
And the temples of his God's."

The Trabue lot is the largest one in the grounds, and it is the only one in which there is a vault.

Col. S. F. J. Trabue was a good lawyer and a good citizen He was several times a candidate for Congress in the Ashland district, and he displayed ability as a debater. He was an optimistic land dealer and railroad promoter. He died in December, 1898, at an advanced age.

The remains of Solomon P. Sharp were buried in the old cemetery on the back part of A. C. Henry's place at Thorn Hill in 1825, but were removed to the new cemetery about 1850. So also were the remains of Governor Madison buried there and afterwards removed by the State to their present resting place, over which a monument was erected, suitably inscribed. Over seven thousand people are buried in the Frankfort cemetery. During the past ten years the average has been one hundred and fifty per year. In the list of noted men buried there, is one Vice President of the United States and eight United States Senators, nine Governors of Kentucky, four ministers to foreign countries, four naval commanders and three United

States District Judges, two poets of national reputation, one sculptor of international note and two historians.

To give a biographical sketch of all who are buried there, who are worthy of being mentioned and who have done their part in making history, would be to re-write a history of Franklin County which would be extended into a history of Kentucky, with many important facts in the history of the nation.

There were statesmen, soldiers and patriots, orators, sculptors and men of letters, in fact they carved for themselves honorable names in nearly every calling and avocation in life.

Women, too, are buried there, who were equally patriotic, who were God fearing, honest and true; who were warm hearted, generous and affectionate and who acted well their part in the formation of character, and in the training of men. Woman's work has too often been that of "Martha," but her service was none the less acceptable and necessary for the development, progress, prosperity and happiness of men. She, too, is entitled to the meeds of valor. The most costly monument should be erected to commemorate her virtues and her worth and her grave should be decorated with flowers and the laurel wreath.

INDEX

	Page
Abbett, Rev. William McD.	261
Acres of Land	112, 173, 177, 232, 265
Adams, Augustene, Hung	11
Alfalfa, Clover, etc.	22
Allen, Gen. R. T. P.	124-188
Allen, Col. R. D.	189
Allen, Joseph W.	102
American Independence Celebrated	18, 42, 71, 97, 103, 104
Anderson County Formed	88
Anderson, Richard C.	148, 174
Ann Street Named	33
Appropriation for Public buildings	238
Arnold, Stephen Pursued by Indians	16
Arnold, Stephen	7, 8, 9, 40, 42, 51
Arnold, James	8, 17, 23, 28, 38, 51, 61, 183
Arnold, John	6, 7, 8, 51, 54, 69
Arnold, Berresford	62
Arnold, Rev. T. N.	257
Arboretum Commenced	267
Armstrong, R. D.	220
Attorneys Prior to 1800	19
Attorneys 1810 and 1835	52, 102
Attorneys	10, 19, 64, 65, 72, 130, 277
Arsenal Built	97, 133
Assessed Valuation	112, 173, 177, 232, 265
Aurora Borealis	108, 176
Bacon, John M.	107, 150
Bacon, Capt. Albert G.	150, 151, 154, 282
Baker Bro's. Distillery	271
Ballard, Capt. Bland	138
Bank Established	67, 68, 76, 272
Bank Association	224
Banquet for Gov. Beckham	236
Baptist Church	177, 247, 249, 259
Baptist, First Colored	262
Baptist Association	183, 246
Barbecue	98, 116, 148
Barnes, Rev. Geo. O.	201
Bartlett, John	45, 66
Bartlett, Harry	45
Barrett, D. C.	225
Barry, Maj. William T.	138
Battle of the Thames	59
Battle, Soldiers, Civilians	238
Beatty, Otho	40
Beauchamp, Jereboam O.	80, 81, 82, 84, 86
Beauchamp's Confession	82, 83
Beckham, J. C. W.	231, 234, 235, 236, 240, 276

INDEX.

	Page
Bedford, H. M.	161
Belle Point	217
Benson Creek	26, 130, 167, 168, 172, 222
Belt, Joseph	134
Benefit of Clergy	10, 11
Bennett, Judge Caswell	217
Berberich, V.	154
Bethel Church	247
Bicycles, used	197
Bird, Chas. M.	8, 9, 19
Bird, Chas. F.	10
Birdseye Limestone	21
Bibb, George M.	69, 160
Bibb, Chas. S.	72, 84
Birdseye View of Frankfort	179
Blackburn, J. W., Jr.	277
Blackburn, Dr. Churchill	113
Blackburn, Gov. Luke P.	113, 212
Blackburn, J. C. S.	103
Blackburn, James	103
Blackwell, Robert	51
Blair, Francis B.	64, 71
Blair, James	10, 15
Bluegrass	27
Blayney, Dr. J. McClusky	251
Board of Magistrate Sent to Jail	118, 120
Boiler Explosion	162, 199
Boat Racing	190
Bohannon, J. W.	219
Bond Issue and Debt	51, 141, 177, 188, 266
Boone, Daniel	120 to 124, 278, 283
Boone, Daniel and Rebecca	28, 120, 121, 240
Boone Monument	240, 241
Bottling in Bond	272
Bragg, Gen., at Frankfort	152
Bradford, Daniel	40
Bradley, William E.	198
Bradley, Gov. W. O.	236
Breathitt, Gov. John	99
Breckinridge, Hon. John C.	113, 149, 194, 279
Breckinridge, John	10
Bridge Company, Incorporated	41
Bridges Across Benson Creek	64, 65, 130, 176, 198
Bridges	51, 53, 65, 71, 75, 89, 104, 130, 168, 170, 203
Bridgeport	130, 143, 196
Bridgeport Robbed	162
Briggs, Guy H.	277
Brown, Scott	19, 45, 71, 73, 93, 115, 116
Brown, Gen. Scott	116, 174, 214, 221
Brown, Judge Reuben	116, 141, 221
Brown, Orlando, Jr.	150, 160, 182
Brown, Mrs. John	76, 283
Brown, John Mason	165, 166, 208
Brown, Capt. Henry	221
Brown's Walk to Lexington	17
Brown, Orlando	103, 108, 160

INDEX.

	Page
Brown, John	48, 49, 69, 76, 104
Brown, John, Appointed Sheriff	89
Brown, Eli H.	277
Brawner, John	73
Buckner, S. B.	210
Buckley, Lee	238, 240
Buck Run Church	246, 247
Buffalo Trace	28
Buford, James T.	174, 233, 266, 277
Bullock, Rev. Joseph J.	107
Burley Tobacco	268
Burr, Aaron	46, 47
Cantrill, Judge James E.	232
Campbell, Rev. Alexander	258
Capital Removal	145, 146
Capital Grounds	146, 208
Capitol Built	76, 180
Capital Hotel	80, 137, 145, 148, 192, 183
Cane-breaks	23
Cardwell, John	19, 58, 180, 193
Cardwell, Margaret Arnold	97
Carlisle, Hon. John G.	279
Carmichael, Robert	280
Carlisle, Benedict	93
Cates, O. G.	162
Catholic Church	177, 252, 253
Cemetery Lots Purchased	280
Cemetery Lots Donated	280
Cemetery at Monroe, Michigan	59
Centennial Celebration	207, 208
Centennial Records Destroyed	208
Cereals of the County	22
Chair Company Fire	218
Chinn, J. Morgan	277
Chinn, Frank	277
Chinn, Morgan B.	100
Chinn, Franklin	148, 187
Chinn, W. J.	166, 182, 203
Church of the Good Shepherd	252
Churches	74, 75, 140, 177
Cholera in Frankfort	97, 134
Charge of the Light Brigade	59
Circuit Court First Held	44
Christian Church	177, 181, 182, 255 to 258
Civil War	150
Clay, Henry	10, 111, 117, 127, 135, 145, 163
Clay, Porter	73, 248
Clay, Col. Henry	127, 282
Clay, Potter's	25
Clay, Fire	26
Clark, Joseph	92, 187
Clark, Daniel, (a negro)	180
Clark, Gov. James	108
Clinton Street	124
Coleman, John M.	154

INDEX.

	Page
Coleman, Edward S.	100
Coleman's Spring	50
Coleman, E. Spillsbee	50, 100, 133
Commissioners	8, 72, 134
Commissioners for Court House	92, 168
Cook, Miss Ann	80, 81, 86
Cook Bros., Killed	14, 15
Colston-Scott Tragedy	229
Cove Spring	45, 97, 106
County Levy	9, 43, 45, 64
County Attorneys	66, 72, 182
Counties Formed	5
Confederates	150, 151, 152, 153, 157
Confederate Infantry	157, 158
Convicts in Frankfort	191
Counterfeit Money	191, 192
County Court Clerk's Office	63, 71, 111
Commentator	79
Constitutional Advocate	79
Corner Stone, New Capitol	235
Corinthian Baptist Church	263
Cowan, Rev. Robert L.	262
Confederate Monument	284
Congressmen Visit Frankfort	116
Cox, Austin P.	102, 115
Cox, Len J.	174, 216
County Jail	8, 12, 64, 67, 72
Court of Appeals	77, 78, 92, 97, 119, 263
Court House	43, 44, 92
County Seal	124
County Officers Elected 135, 138, 146, 149, 163, 175, 182, 191, 201, 207, 214, 220, 225, 233, 234, 238.	
Contested Election	146, 217
Crane, Simeon H.	88
Craik, William	161, 280
Craik, Henry	280
Crockett, John B.	93
Crockett, Col. Anthony	7, 37, 40, 54, 61, 62
Crockett, Dandridge S.	110
Crockett, Samuel	130
Crockett, James G.	205, 284
Crockett, T. H.	277
Crittenden, John J., 76, 77, 78, 79, 87, 89, 93, 98, 99, 101, 103, 108, 110, 116, 117, 137, 148, 159, 160, 250.	
Crittenden, Gen. Geo. B.	103, 197
Crittenden, Gen. Thomas L.	103, 137, 150
Crittenden, Col. Eugene	103
Crittenden, T. T.	103
Crittenden, Lt. John J., Killed	187
Cromwell, William	239
Cramer, Zadoc	35-52
Craddock, Hon. Geo. W.	112, 113, 165, 187
Crutcher, John N.	236
Custom House and Post Office Built	204
Dailey, Frank M.	277

INDEX.

	Page
Damage by Storm	238
Dana, James G.	113
Darby, Patrick H.	72, 79, 80, 81, 82, 84
Darsie, Rev. George	209, 257
Day, Mrs. M. B. R.	172, 214, 215
Deakins, Tes, Killed	225
Davridge, Henry	54, 63
Desha, Gov. Joseph	78, 82
Debt, Imprisonment for	37
Denny, Gen. James W.	84
District Court, Officers of	10
Disorderly Citizens	36
Dire Calamity	54
Distilleries	203, 238, 269, 270
Dollerhide, Thomas	74
Downing, James	89
Dougherty, William	11
Drane, Judge George C.	168, 191, 225
Dryden, John B.	155, 235
Drouth of 1854	137
Duels	17, 67, 141, 142
Dudley, Peter	56, 57, 76, 103, 171, 248
Dudley, Jeptha	63, 92
Dudley, Peter, Volunteers Under	58, 171
Dudley, Ambrose W.	93, 96, 107, 205, 279
Duvall, Ben F.	214
Duvall, Judge Alvin	215
Durrett, Col. R. T.	279
Duncan Trial	237
Earthquake in Frankfort	116
Ear Marks	9
Early Settlements on South Side	28
East Frankfort Ferry Established	41
Eberhardt, Rev. F. W.	246, 249
Evergreen Church	246, 247, 248
Eclipse of the Sun	172
Edelen, T. L.	23, 277
Egbert, Frank	202, 224
Election, First County	135
Elkhorn Creek	26, 68, 75
Elkhorn, Co. to Navigate	68
Elkhorn Bridges	8, 53
Eliott, Judge John M.	192
Elks' Lodge	233
English Prisoners Brought to Frankfort	59
Ewing, Baker	7, 40
Evens, Evans	76
Exciting Incidents	46, 199
Explosion, Foree and Sanders Killed	215
Explosion at Pence's Mill	218
Explosion at Jail	224
Episcopal Church	133, 177, 254, 255, 259
Fall, Rev. P. S.	93, 208, 255, 256
Farmer's Bank Organized	133
Farmer, Ben, Assassinated	175

INDEX.

	Page
F. & C. R. R. Trestle	29, 212
Federals	150, 152, 153
Federal Cavalry Roster	154
Federal Infantry Roster	156
Fellmer, Prof. E. A.	219
Flood, Joseph	108
Ferry	12, 30, 41, 63, 93
Fillmore, Millard	137
Fields, Henry	11, 12, 44, 66
Fires in Frankfort	137, 176, 202, 206, 218, 221, 223
Fire Alarm System	213
Fincel Block Burns	221
Fish Trap Island	35
Fiscal Court	91, 169, 173, 191, 197, 223
Flynn, Rev. J. A.	253
F. M. I. Burns	223
Fowler, Col. C. W.	189, 241
Forepaugh's Circus, Contest Over	199
Foreign Immigration	111
Forests	23
Forts, Name of	14
Formation of Ground N. E. of Frankfort	30
Frankfort High School	276
Frankfort Bank	68
Frankfort, Name Derived From	14
Frankfort Topographical Situation	26
Frankfort Surveyed	28
Frankfort, When Established	30
Frankfort Bridge Co.	13, 41, 42, 117
Frankfort Academy	102
Frankfort, Description of	38
Frankfort Water Co.	45, 106, 267
Frankfort Fire Co.	45
Frankfort & Shelbyville T. P. Road	68, 72
Frankfort Cemetery	59, 74, 103, 132, 138, 184, 185, 194, 279, 283
Frankfort, Manufacturing Center	96
Frankfort, Incorporated	100, 133
Frankfort, Common School System	114
Frankfort, Assessed Valuation	266
Frankfort and Lexington T. P. R. Co.	68, 93
Frankfort Lyceum Organized	99
Frankfort Library Co.	63
Frankfort and Lawrenceburg Road, Inc.	130, 134
Frankfort to Harrodsburg, Distance	135
Frankfort Woolen Mills	136, 173
Frankfort in Politics	144, 145
Frankfort Citizens Ordered to Report	152
Frankfort, Lexington and Versailles T. P. Road	93
Frankfort Seminary	105
Frankfort and Benson T. P. Co.	186
Frankfort, North and South United	196
Frankfort Centennial	207
Frankfort, Georgetown and Paris R. R. Tax Voted	212
Frankfort and Shelbyville T. P. Co.	68, 72
Franklin County, From Other Counties	6

INDEX.

	Page
Franklin County, Established, Boundary	5, 6
Franklin County, Surface of	21
Franklin County, Purchased From	28
Franklin County, Protected From the Indians	14
Franklin Paper Mills	96
Franklin County Fair Association	108, 109, 110
Franklin and Scott Line Settled	115
Franklin and Anderson line	125
Franklin County, Size and Shape	6
Franklin Springs	124
Franklin, Robt. B.	232, 277
Franklin, Massie	92
Franklin, Walter	119, 226
Francis, A Slave Hung	149
Fruits and Trees	22, 267
Freesetown	184
Gallows Erected	8
Gaines, J. W.	200
Gaines, Hugh	215
Gaines, W. A., & Co.	270, 271
Gaines, Paul C.	277
Gaines, Noel	228
Gano, Rev. John	243, 244
Garth, Rodes	146
Garnett, James	277
Gas, Natural	25
Gas, Illuminating	130, 163
Gas Works Sold	201
Gayle, George	133
Gardner, Hezekiah	193
Gainey's Bridge	223
Geological Formation	21
Georgetown & Frankfort T. P. R. Co.	98
George, Edward	89
Glass Factory	52
Glenn's Creek Road	8, 134
Glenn's Creek	63, 269
Goebel, Gov. William	230, 240
Gower, Stanley P.	65, 71
Governor's Mansion	69, 75, 267
Goram, William A., Removed	118
Graham, John R.	161
Graham, David	133
Governor's of 23 States at Frankfort	241
Goebel, Arthur	240
Graft in County Affairs	237
Green, T. M.	48, 49, 141, 143
Greene, Robt. L.	277
Green, John	63, 64
Greenup, Christopher	41, 43, 51, 52, 74, 184, 185, 280
Grangers	183
Giraffe, First in Frankfort	108
Guerrillas	161, 162
Gwin, Geo. W.	198
Hamilton, Elwood	174, 237, 267, 277

INDEX.

	Page
Hall, William	54, 62
Hardin, Martin D.	69
Hardin, Ben	77, 82
Hardin, Gen. William	116
Harney, William Wallace	152
Hardinsville Bridge Rebuilt	65, 89
Hanna, John H.	92, 136, 250, 254
Harvie, John	76, 107, 110
Harvie, Col. Lewis	107, 143, 255
Harlan, James	112, 159
Harlan, Judge John M.	137, 144, 146, 148, 154, 159
Hart, Joel T.	211, 280, 284
Hawkins, Dr. J. Russell	223
Hazelrigg, Judge Jas. H.	277
Hazelrigg, Dyke	277
Harris, Daniel H.	116
Hawkins, E. O.	200
Henry County, Part Taken	88
Heeney, James	12
Hermitage Distillery	203, 271
Hendrick, Rev. John R.	251
Herndon, W. T.	130, 135, 137
Herndon, John C.	100, 102, 135, 141
Henderson, H. A. M.	169
Herndon, W. C.	277
Hickman, Pascal	19, 51, 54, 56, 57, 62, 192
Hickman, Benjamin	62, 64, 261
Hickman's, Pascal, Company	55
Hieatt, R. C.	233, 234, 237, 238
Hickman, Rev. William	243, 244, 247
Hines, Judge T. H.	192, 214, 225
High Water	202, 203
Hiram Lodge No. 4	43, 44
Historical Collection	279
Hodges, Rev. Frank H.	95, 247, 248
Hodges, A. G.	102, 144, 145, 199
Hodges, S. N.	149
Holeman, Jacob H.	67
Holeman, William H.	111
Holton, Capt. John A.	109, 131, 171
Hogs	9, 118, 190
Hoge-Montgomery Co.	273
House Bill No. 69	234
Hoge, Col. Chas. E.	93, 273
Home Guards	154
Hord, Lysander	135, 141, 147, 174, 195
Holman, Rev. William	261
Huett, John M.	117, 147, 173
Hughes, James	10
Hunter, William	89
Hutchinson, Maj. Thos. J.	154
Hutton, Nancy, Contempt	40
Hudson, Rev. C. R.	237, 257
Hungerford, Rev. Frank	248
Ice Machine	197

INDEX.

ix

	Page
Illuminating Gas	130
Imprisonment for Debt	54, 74
Improvements for Frankfort	182, 235
Incomes	168, 177
Indian Depridations	50
Indian Slaughter	56
Indian Gap	17
Indians Killed	16, 17
Inhuman Outrage	66
Indictment of County Court	67
Innis, Harry	37
Innis, Harry B.	161
Inspection of Tobacco	65
Internal Improvements	91
Irish	142, 143
Jail, Public	8, 12, 62, 63, 66, 51, 54, 72, 73, 115, 118, 182
Jett, Peter	115, 146, 261
Jett, W. L.	57, 158, 190, 206, 277
Jersey Cattle	178, 203
Jackson, J. Hunt	277
Jeffers, J. W.	277
Johnson, George W.	238
Johnson, Harrison, Hung	179
Johnson, William T.	71
Johnson, Frank	101, 115
Johnson, L. F.	174, 207, 214, 233, 237, 277
Johnson, Hugh, Burned in Hand	10
Johnson, E. P.	92
Johnson, Gen. P. P.	111
Johnson, Richard M.	58, 59, 128, 134, 282, 283
Johnson, Mrs. Mary E.	63, 193
Johnson, B. F.	124, 136
Johnston, Col. J. Stoddard	168, 171, 190
Julian, John	191
Julian, Judge Ira	191, 204, 277
July 4th Celebration	18, 42, 97, 103, 104
Kavanaugh, Rev. H. H.	215
Kavanaugh, F. K.	215
Kavanaugh, Bishop H. H.	261
Kentucky River Marble	21, 22
Kentucky River	26, 50, 96, 177, 195, 202, 203
Kentucky Historical Society	106, 199, 227
Kentucky Gazette Published	10
Kentucky Military Institute	24, 102, 188, 189, 241
Kentucky River on Fire	171
Kentucky Mineral Paint Co.	186
Kentucky Midland R. R.	199
Kentucky River Mills	204
Kenton, Simon	80
Kendall, Amos	79, 82
Keenon, Buck	154
King, Robt. H.	148, 150, 163, 164
King's Daughters	216
Kelley, Rev. Gilby C.	261
Kissinger, Smelting, etc.	24

INDEX.

	Page
Knight's Bridge Built	75, 161
Knott, J. Proctor	204, 205
Ku-Klux	176
Kirtley, John E.	186
Ladies' Guild	254
Lacy, J.	84
LaFayette, Visited Frankfort	61, 87
LaFayette, Portrait Painted	87
Lawyers in Frankfort in 1912	276
Launitz, Robert E.	280, 281, 282
Lawrenceburg Established	72
Lancaster, Rev. James M.	252, 253
Lee, Willis	9, 17, 19, 44
Lee, Willis A.	7, 73, 63
Lee, Capt. Jerry	179, 202
Lee, Crawford	238
Leestown	17, 28, 29, 30
Leestown Bridge	71, 168
Lead Found	24
Leonard, James Francis	206
Lexington and Frankfort R. Co., Incorporated	88
Lexington, Ohio R. R. Surveyed	93
Lexington Higher than Frankfort	93, 94
Letcher, Robt. P.	111, 149
Legislature, Members of	89, 110, 131
Library Established	73
Lindsey, Gen. D. W., 90, 103, 146, 150, 153, 154, 172, 190, 192, 196, 224, 235, 277	285
Lindsey, John B.	277
Lindsay, Judge William	107, 208, 216, 235, 239
Lindsey, Thos. N.	24, 130, 147, 190
Lindsey, T. N.	277
Lindsey, D. W., Jr.	277
Lights of Frankfort	114
Littell, William	69
L. & N. R. R. Co.	169, 218, 222, 238
Logan, John	44
Logan, M. M.	277
Log houses	23
Locusts Desolate Country	107
Lottery for School and Water	105, 112, 191
Lottery Privileges	74, 105, 191, 112, 250
Lockett, J. F.	277
London, Catherine, Hung	10
Lock Number 4 Built	95, 96, 204
Lock and Dam Kentucky River	50
Love, Mrs. Elizabeth	60, 283
Love, James Y.	60
Luckett, Benjamin	109, 118, 135, 119
Lucas, Jeff	220
Lucas, M. B.	238
Lynn, Oberson	115
Luscher, Sigmund	197
Macklin, A. W.	92, 117, 140
Madison, Gov. George	69, 74, 185, 280
Mardi Gras	183

INDEX. XI

	Page
Magruder, Allen B.	48
Magee, Geo., Hung	220
Magnesia Water	24
Magistrates elected in 1908	238
Magistrates, Ruled	118, 119, 120
Major, Rev. Thomas	253
Major Hall	169
Major, John B.	176
Major, Lewis R.	64, 92, 93
Major, Patrick	89
Major, Judge P. U.	103, 144, 149, 165, 232, 233
Major, Col. S. I. M.	103, 111, 135, 141, 168, 174, 190, 197, 205, 206
Mansion	80, 114
Manufactures	96, 97, 177, 269, 270, 274
Marshall, Humphrey	17, 37, 69, 89, 139, 185
Marshall, John J.	52, 62, 63, 64, 69, 79, 92, 110
Marshall, Thos. F.	101
Marshall, Dr. Lewis	40
Marshall, W. C.	238, 277
Marshall, Ben	238
Mason, Charles E.	277
Medical Association	219
Medals for Lake Erie Soldiers	166, 167
Meek, B. F.	167, 196
Meriweather, David	136
Methodist Conference	121, 147, 169, 217, 259
Mexican Soldiers in Frankfort	195
Mexican Veterans, Roster	125, 126, 195
Mexican Soldiers, Buried	127, 128, 129
Mexican Soldiers, Captured	129
Milam, John	51
Milam, Capt. Ben	125, 127, 129, 167
Milam, John W.	235
Mills, James, Benefit of Clergy Granted	11
Mill at the Penitentiary	124
Milam, James	131
Mineral Waters	24, 124
Mitchell, John A.	51, 62
Mitchell, Rev. Robert	263
Miro, Intendant of La.	34, 49
Mobs and Riots	142, 164, 178, 179, 218, 222, 224, 238
Montgomery Street Named	33
Monroe, T. B.	77, 143, 150
Monroe, James	141
Monroes	147, 150, 154
Monroe, George W.	150
Moore, J. D.	222, 225
Modern Knights	268
Morgan's Command	153, 157
Morton, Mrs. Jennie C.	111, 208, 278
Morehead, Chas. S.	92, 103, 110, 137, 140, 168
Morehead, James T.	103, 104, 107, 110, 140
Morris, John	115
Morris, H. I.	140, 182
Morris, L. W.	277

INDEX.

	Page
Morris, Charles H.	277
Moss, Dulin	277
Montgomery, Jas. F.	273
Mount Pleasant School	93
Muster Roll of Soldiers, 1812	55
Murder Indictments	66, 183
Mt. Pleasant Church	246
Murfreesboro, Charge Made	151
Murray, James	25
McBride, Lapsley	57, 63
McBride, William	54, 57, 63
McBrayer, William	51
McChesney, David	97
McCreary, Gov. Jas. B.	199, 240
H. V. McChesney	235, 277
McClure Building	267
McDonald, John A.	62
McDonald, Pat	182, 186, 216, 232
McGain, Thomas	96
McGee, John D.	96
McGregor, Thomas B.	277
McKee, William R.	127, 282
McKee, Robt. C.	119
McManama, O. D.	192
McQueen, Joshua	136
McIntosh, John	73, 89
McQuown, Lewis	277
Names of State Officers Published	144
National Authorities Refused to Help	50
Natural Gas	25
Nash, L. B.	102
Negroes, Sale of	112
Negroes	97, 112, 180, 242, 275, 276
New Court	78, 79
Newspapers in Frankfort	100
News, How Conveyed	18, 43
Newton, Cal	220
Newman, William	178
Night Riders	223, 236
Nicol, R. H.	280
Noel, Rev. Silas M.	62, 63, 99, 243, 245, 247, 248
Noel, J. C.	213
Nolan, Mrs. Martin	218
Nooe, Rev. Roger T.	257
Norton, Rev. John N.	254, 255
Noted People Buried	285
North Fork Church	247
Nuckols, Lewis A.	277
O'Hara, Col. Theodore	139, 168, 184, 186, 194, 279, 282
O. F. C. Distillery	238, 270, 271
Old Court	78, 79
Old Crow	270
Old State Capitol	21, 76, 180, 267
Old Judge Distillery	271
O'Rear, Judge Edward C.	278

INDEX.

	Page
Owen County Line	73
Old Miss	189
Page, Thos. S.	74, 97, 105, 144
Parker, John	63
Patriot, The	79, 84
Pattie, P. R.	168
Parnell, Chas. Stewart, Visit	195
Parrent, Wm. F.	149
Palladium, Weekly Newspaper	16, 17, 35, 42
Palladium, Items From	17, 18, 36, 37, 40
Payne, William	9, 19, 40
Payne, John W.	218
Paynter, Senator Thomas H.	21, 278
Penitentiary	13, 74, 124, 125, 163, 181, 191, 192, 204, 221
Penitentiary Outbreak	204
Penitentiary Burned	54
Penn, Charles, Assassinated	201
Perry, Lake Erie Medal	167
Physicians in 1912	278
Physicians in 1850	131
Pleasant Hill	130
Polsgrove, James H.	220, 225, 233, 278
Pope, John	84
Population of Frankfort	90, 118, 131
Population of Franklin County	40, 110, 131, 147, 180, 242
Posey, W. H.	278
Powell, Gov.	138
Pigeon Tournament	183, 187
Pioneers of Franklin County	18
Precious Metals in Bridgeport	186
Preachers	65, 73, 147, 148, 169
Prentice, George D.	146
Press Association	217
Presbyterian Church	177, 249 to 252, 259
Prominent Men in South Frankfort	133
Prison Bounds Extended	54
Preface	3
Prominent Men in County Prior to 1800	19
Price, John	45
Pryor, Judge W. S.	192
Public Men	69
Public Roads	68, 135
Public School Building	209, 274
Quarles, William E.	62
Quarles, Ambrose	19
Quarles, William	19
Quinn's Bottom	14, 15
Races	109
Rapid Growth of Frankfort	118
Railroad, Lexington to Frankfort Opened	94, 95, 135, 165
Railroad Accident	94
R. R. Bridge	135, 218
Rebel Soldiers Shot	162
Religious Paper Published	134
Religious Revival in Frankfort	130, 201
Re-Interment, Greenup, Madison, etc.	184

INDEX.

	Page
Relief and Anti-Relief Parties	76, 77, 78
Remains of Dead Removed to Frankfort	59, 60
Rennick, Alexander	73, 135, 149, 180
Report of Grand Jury	10
Representatives	110, 131, 147, 174
Revenue of County	65
Revolutionary Soldiers	71, 72
Revolution in Making Whiskey	198
Reynolds, J. W. Hunt	197
Richardson, Turner	7, 19
Richardson, Samuel Q.	84, 100, 101
Richardson, Nathaniel	9, 19, 38, 63
Riot Call	222
Ripley, Capt. Garnett D.	231
River Raisin	56, 58, 59, 132
Roads, Public	8, 12, 66, 68, 89
Road From Lexington to Frankfort	68
Robards, James, Removed	9, 46
Roberts, H. H.	273
Robertson, Geo. A.	219
Robertson, Judge	77
Robinson, J. F.	160
Roberts, Lt. John J.	153
Roberts, E. A. W.	176
Rodman, Gen. John	147, 209
Rogers, J. C.	224
Rope Walk	12, 41
Russell, James	64
Russell, Capt. John W.	172
Runyan, Mrs. M. Train	124
Sabbath School, First	61, 75, 76
Samuels, William	64
Samuel, Jameson	92, 110
Samuels, Churchill	93
Sanders, Lewis, Jr.	89, 101, 103
Sargent, John D.	170
Sayre, B. B.	102, 103, 111, 182
Schools, Public	13, 105, 114, 168, 220, 274, 275, 276
Scott, T. W.	174, 190
Scott, Gen. Winfield	136
Scott, Gen. Charles	74, 138
Scott, James A.	15, 102, 174, 237, 278
Scott, John L.	149, 207
Settlements on South Side	28
Severe Storm	116
Sharp, S. P.	77, 78, 79, 80, 81, 83, 86, 285
Sharp, Miss Eliza T.	81, 82
Sharp, Dr. Leander	82, 86
Shelby, Gov. Isaac	6, 59, 111, 132
Sheriffs	65, 66, 73
Scott, John M.	54
Scroggans, Thompson	178
Shoe Factory	272, 273, 274
Shannon, James	76, 92, 102, 115
Shannon, Rev. Samuel	244, 249, 250

INDEX.

	Page
Shryock, Gideon	92
Side Walk	35, 114
Slaves, Number of in 1840 and 1850	131
Small Pox	97, 100
Smith, Green Clay	248, 249
Smith, Raccoon John	256, 258
Smith, Napolean B.	205, 207, 214, 220
Smith, John	7, 9, 18, 19, 37
Smith, George and J. D.	220
Sneed, Achilles	45, 65
Sneed, W. H.	148, 149, 207
Sneed, Dr. W. C.	159
Soldiers of 1812	54, 55, 58, 59, 60, 180
South, Samuel	88
South, Martin V.	175
South, Thomas J.	187
South, Col. J. W.	192, 196
South, Mrs. Eudora	208
South, L. C.	183
South Frankfort	12, 261
South Benson Church	247
Southern Presbyterian Church	261, 262
Soil of the County	22, 23, 26
Spanish-American Soldiers	227
Spanish Government	50
Spanish Conspiracy	46
Spirit of Seventy-Six	79
Stage Coach	113
State Capitol dedicated	241
State Election of 1899	230
State Bank Established	51
State Capitol Committee	76
State Normal School (Colored)	276
State Cemetery Described	279, 285
State House Burnt	88, 163
State Librarian	97
State Monument	132, 280, 281
State Historical Society	95, 106, 112, 132, 278
Statistics	173, 174, 177, 178, 182, 265
Stanton, Henry T.	208, 209, 226, 279
St. Clair Street Bridge Fell	100, 170, 202
Steam Cars, of Interest	49, 95
Steamboats	95, 113, 114
E. H. Steadman	25, 205
Steadmantown	25, 205
Steel's Ferry	51
Steadman, E. H. and S.	96
St. John in the Wilderness	169, 255
Stewart, Dr. J. Q. A.	24, 190
Stafford, Hiram	238
Stout, Robert L.	278
Streets, Dangerous	35, 38, 114, 124
Street Cars	217, 240
St. Clair Street Bridge Built	216
Street Fair	226

INDEX.

	Page
Streets, How Named	32
Streets and Sewers	266
St. John's A. M. E. Church	263, 264
Strausner, Chas. F.	273
Suicides	237
Sulphur Springs	24
Sunday Taverns	64
Suter, Dick	219
Swigert, Philip	102, 105, 113, 118, 136, 178, 180
Swigert, Jacob	64, 66, 73, 115, 118, 136, 149, 150, 166
Swingle, Maj. George	113
Sullivan, Nick	238
Talbott, Isham	10, 52, 69
Tate, James W.	146, 209, 210, 211
Tate, James W., Trial of	211
Taylor, Edmond H.	89, 97, 103, 105
Taylor, Col. E. H. Jr.,	174, 179, 182, 190, 199, 200, 206, 208, 209, 215, 216, 233, 270
Taylor, Gen. Zachary	130, 279
Taylor, Richard	64
Taylor, Benjamin	89
Taylor, Gov. W. S.	230, 231
Taylor, Rev. John	243, 244, 245, 247
Taylor, Rev. W. C.	249
Taylor, E. H., Jr. & Sons, Incorporated	270
Tavern Keepers	62
Telephone Exchange	197
Telegraph Line Completed	130
The Capitol Question	234, 237
The Old Thames Cannon	111
The United American Insurance	267
The State Journal	268
The Commonwealth	94, 138, 152
Theobald, Samuel A.	59
Thornton, Harry J.	72
Thomas, Landon A.	102, 129, 131, 181, 182, 208
Thomas, Western B.	65
Thomas, Samuel A.	278
Thompson, R. A.	182, 191, 200, 214
Thompson, Ed Porter	214, 224
Tithes Assessed	65, 66, 72, 73, 88, 265
Transportation Difficult	50
Travel, Method of Prior to 1851	43, 113
Triplett, Lee	217
Trimble, South	174, 233
Toulmin, Harry	69
Throckmorton, Richard	45
Tobacco Raised	195, 268
Todd, Hon. Thomas	10, 19, 69, 87
Todd, Chas. S.	69, 70
Todd, John H.	89
Todd, Samuel	111
Todd, James M.	133, 180
Todd, Harry I.	146, 148
Todd, Lieut. Lewis Franklin	152
Trabue, Col. S. F. J.	191, 285
Troops Ordered Out	200

INDEX.

	Page
Trigg, Fleming	44, 62, 63
Trigg, William	9, 19, 53, 62
Tracy, Jeremiah	181
Trustees of City School	115
Trustees of Frankfort	102, 115, 127
Trustees, Mount Pleasant School	93
Tubman, Mrs. Emily	117, 181
Turner, Rev. H. G.	260, 261
Utterback, Ben	196
Vanwinkle, A. C.	278
Vest, George	189
Vest, Senator George	103, 189
Vest, J. J.	102, 105, 133
Violett, J. A.	174, 221
Virginia Legislature	5
Waldner, James	238
Waits, David	99
Walnut Logs	23
Wapping Street Named	33
War of Rebellion	150
Waring, Francis	67, 142
Waring, John U.	80, 81, 100, 101
Warehouses Established	9, 32, 65, 271, 272
Washington Street Named	33
Water Street, Act to Open	68
Waterway Through Cumberland Gap	50
Warren, Roger, Hung	240
Webster, Daniel, Visited Frankfort	103
Weiseger, Samuel P.	93
Weiseger, Daniel	17, 36, 19, 42, 43, 44, 45, 53, 76, 90
Western World	47, 48
Whiskey Warehouses	272
Whig Barbecue	98
Whigs and Democrats	142
Whipping Post	44
Wiley, R. L.	238
Williams, Elias	283
Williams, B. G.	214, 220, 221, 232, 278
Williams, M. H. P.	182, 193
Williams, Bros.	197
Williams, Dr. U. V.	196, 278
Williams, Minus	220, 221
Williamson, Jerry, Killed	214
Wilkinson Street Named	32
Wilkinson, James	30, 31, 49
Wickliffe, Robert	77
Wingate, Henry	92
Winter of 1838	107
Wind and Rain Storm	116
Wolfe, Oscar	278
Wolves	8
Woods, John D.	100
Woods, Col. John	103
Woman's Club Organized	221
Women, Buried	286

	Page
Woodson, R. K., Jr.	151
Workhouse Established	187
Yeager, James	221
Young, Rev. Lambert	165, 166, 253
Young, Col. B. W.	279
Young Men's Christian Association	262, 267
Youtsey, Henry	251
Zeigler, Dr. Jesse R.	232

www.ingramcontent.com/pod-product-compliance
Lightning Source LLC
Chambersburg PA
CBHW071958220426
43662CB00009B/1189